FAMOUS & INFAMOUS
LONDONERS

Peter de Loriol

SUTTON PUBLISHING

First published in the United Kingdom in 2004 by
Sutton Publishing Limited · Phoenix Mill
Thrupp · Stroud · Gloucestershire · GL5 2BU

British Library Cataloguing in Publication Data
A catalogue record for this book is available from the British Library.

ISBN 0-7509-3822-6

Typeset in 10.5/13.5 pt ACaslon Regular.
Typesetting and origination by
Sutton Publishing Limited.
Printed and bound in England by
J.H. Haynes & Co. Ltd, Sparkford.

Contents

Foreword

People – you love them, you hate them, you understand them or you don't. People are the lifeblood of one's life and heritage. They make you tick, they make you scream, laugh, cry: their presence and their absence make the individual. Their lives form a rich tapestry through which you live yours. People are the masters – they dictate, they form and they emulate each other. People create the environment, be it village, town or city.

London was created by people, and it is the Londoners, whether native or passing through, who give the visitor their impressions of this great city. D.H. Lawrence, in his unfortunate stay in Hampstead, was to say of London that it was 'geographically remote and personally very near – of the horrors of the middle distance, war, winter, the town, I would not speak'. Voltaire, the French philosopher, came to London on a sunlit and balmy day. His first impression was to liken the city to the Elysian Fields. He was later to revise his opinion when the winds blew, particularly when 'the wind was in the East, everyone was very morose and there was murder abroad'. Astonished, he asked the reasons for such extremes of behaviour, and was told that in November and March he would see people hang themselves by the dozen – 'Everyone', he wrote, 'looks stern and crossed and indisposed to form a desperate resolution.' After all, he was informed, 'it was in an east wind that Charles I was beheaded and James II dethroned'! Another was to describe the city and its people with venom, saying that 'if you do not want to dwell with evil-doers, do not live in London'.

London and the people that live within it: the two are inextricably linked. London would be nothing without people and it is for this reason that I have selected just a over hundred different people, their lives, their loves, their passions, to tell the story of this great city from the twelfth to the twentieth century. Some led blameless normal lives, and some achieved greatness and recognition through their skills or selfless devotion to others, such as Sir Astley Paston Cooper, Bart, and Noel Coward. Some were misguided and committed atrocious crimes, such as James Greenacre and Ronald True. Others were reviled for their apparent difference, like Mother Red Cap. But they all lived in the mass that we today call London.

London's mass would start in the City, and spread both east and west. The great developments of the seventeenth century following the Great Fire were followed by further development in the eighteenth century, turning the villages of Paddington, Camden and Kilburn into villa developments for the affluent. The arrival of the railways in the nineteenth century was to completely alter the face of London, creating huge areas of building around the newly created railway stations and engulfing whole villages and communities like Canonbury, Hampstead, Highgate, Kensal Green, Kensington, Chelsea, Fulham, Ealing, Brentford, Wimbledon, Wandsworth, Norwood, Norbury, Deptford and Greenwich into the new monster that is present-day London. Beneath our modern London stood, for instance, the mansion and park of the 3rd Earl of Peterborough, wit, raconteur and politician, in Parson's Green. By Tooting Broadway stood Dr Drouet's children's 'farm' that was forcibly closed thanks to the writings of the journalist Charles Dickens. Chalk Farm, Camden and Kentish Town, now built up, were the pastoral scenes of duels and murder. Belsize Park, the gateway to Hampstead, was a mansion set in acres of countryside known for its riotous living. Norwood boasted tribes of gypsies in its huge woods, and large mansions of the rich and famous of the day. Southwark, long considered the sin-bin of London where 'all manners of vice' were perpetrated, is now an industrious and busy addition to the City.

People have streamed into London for different reasons. Some have fled from the provinces and from the continent, for real crimes or spurious 'crimes against the state', such as differences of religious or political opinions. Some came to find employment and fortune. Some stayed, some were murdered, others moved on, only to return. Their lives created London as it is, a vibrant, exciting and sometimes merciless city that continues to enthral and capture the minds of visitors and its people alike.

I would like to thank and acknowledge the following for their assistance and support:

Highbury Local Publications, Bromley Local Archives, the Camden Society, the Clapham Society, the Dulwich Museum, the Dulwich Society, the Ealing Historical Society, the Horniman Museum, the LB Camden Local Studies, the LB Ealing Local Studies, the LB Hammersmith and Fulham Local Studies Centre, the LB Lambeth Minet Archives, the LB Southwark Local Studies, the LB Wandsworth Local Studies for the use of the photograph of Mr Saklatvala and for their continued support, the LB Westminster Archives, the Nightingale Museum, the Norwood Society and the Wandsworth Museum.

I would also like to thank Mike Ashley, author of *Starman*, for the use of material and the photograph of Algernon Blackwood, and Sarah Hodgson, editorial director of Highbury Local Publications and valued friend, who took the bold step of asking me to write for her magazines many years ago and gave me the idea for this book. Lastly, but most importantly, I would like to thank my sub-editor-in-chief and selfless wife Janey, for her immeasurable and constant devotion, her positivity in times of stress and the time she has taken to correct my errant punctuation and my European capital letters!

I have made every reasonable effort to contact all copyright holders. Any errors that may have occurred are inadvertent and anyone who for any reason has not been contacted is invited to write to the publishers so that a full acknowledgement may be made in subsequent editions of this work.

Peter de Loriol
2004

Bloody Kilburn

STEPHEN DE MORTON AND A TWELFTH-CENTURY FRATRICIDE

It is difficult to imagine that the large urban mass consisting mainly of Victorian development that is Kilburn was once a hamlet in the rural parish of Hampstead through which the little bourne or brook, the Kele, meandered. The Kele rose on the southern slopes of Hampstead, ran to Bayswater and fed the Serpentine. The 'burn' now forms part of the London sewerage system.

Kilburn remained a rural area well into the nineteenth century. One resident, an impecunious and fervent pedestrian John Pocock, left a diary of the years 1826–30: '11 August 1828 from Kilburn to Paddington before breakfast, with my father as far as Soho, on to Limehouse . . . came back to my uncle's, had tea and came home very tired, having walked nearly 20 miles today'! The road to Kilburn was such that anyone walking even a mile northwards from Oxford Street found himself among fields and farmhouses.

Westminster Abbey was the original landlord. By the Reformation all church establishments including the Nunnery and Priory at Kilburn were secularised. The Priory, established in 1130, was situated in what is now known as St George's Terrace. It was owned by a succession of families: the Warwicks, the Devonshires, the Howards and finally

Kilburn Priory.

1

the Uptons. Ironically 300 years after the dissolution of the monasteries a new Catholic church was built in 1866 in Quex Road. In the twelfth century one Godwin, hermit at Kilburn, gave his hermitage to three nuns, 'the Holy Virgins of St John the Baptist'. This was not the only medieval association with the area. One darker legend, a 'crime passionel' of the Middle Ages, occurred in Kilburn.

Stephen de Morton, a twelfth-century Kilburn gent, was infatuated with the wife of his brother, Sir Gervaise de Morton. The good lady did not reciprocate and even threatened to tell her husband. Undeterred, Stephen tried again, but the faithful wife would have none of it. He resolved to rid himself of his unwanted sibling and engineered a meeting in a quiet lane. There he stabbed him to death. Sir Gervaise fell on a nearby rock, his lifeblood seeping into it, dyeing it red, and uttering with his dying breath, 'This stone shall be thy death bed'.

Stephen rushed back to Kilburn with the news that he had found his dead brother's body. He went so far as to organise a manhunt. Thinking that his brother's death would make his sister-in-law see sense, he hurried back to his dead brother's house to woo her, only to be refused yet again. Furious, Stephen had the grieving widow imprisoned in a fetid dungeon and later placed in the local nunnery. He then embarked on a hedonistic lifestyle.

But time did not erase the memory of the dreadful deed. Stephen ordered that his brother's body be removed to Kilburn and interred in a mausoleum expressly built for it. The mausoleum was made with the stone from the quarry near where he had murdered his brother, one of the stones being the one he had died on.

The moment Stephen set eyes on the finished mausoleum the stone began to seep blood. Horrified, the murderer confessed to the Bishop of London, donated his lands to the Priory at Kilburn and died soon afterwards.

Will the Real Falstaff Come Forward?

SIR JOHN FASTOLFF OF SOUTHWARK

Shakespeare's Sir John Falstaff was a rotund, cowardly knight, a comical figure in four of his plays. He had originally intended the unworthy knight to be called Sir John Oldcastle, after a martyred leader of the Lollards. Sir John's descendants, prominent courtiers, protested, however, so he changed the name to Falstaff, possibly based on the knight, Sir John Fastolff, of Southwark.

Sir John Fastolff (*c.* 1378–1459) was a completely different person to the comical and hapless knight in Shakespeare's plays. He was a career soldier from Norfolk who rose to be a governor of Harfleur and the Bastille, Master of the Household of the Duke of Bedford, Regent of France, Lieutenant Governor of Normandy and Governor of Anjou and Maine. He was made a Knight of the Garter in 1426 and defeated the French at the 'battle of the Herrings' near Orleans in 1429. He was groundlessly accused of cowardice for retreating at the battle of Patay in 1429, which in fact was the fault of Lord Talbot's mishandling of the situation. Fastolff demanded an enquiry and was acquitted. The news of his 'cowardice' reached England before his acquittal, and the English continued to consider the successful war leader and administrator as a coward. In the end, the only thing the original Fastolff may have had in common with Shakespeare's burlesque character was his military service.

Despite these accusations, Fastolff continued to serve his king in many important posts; governor of Caen, ambassador and Privy Councillor. Once returned to England in 1440 he divided his time between his castle of Caister in Norfolk and his house at Southwark.

His Southwark house was on the river bank in Stoney Lane (now leading from Tooley Street to Pickleherring Street). It was probably one of the last great houses on the east side of London Bridge. It was large, with its own quay where a small private fleet of boats sailed to and from Caister, Yarmouth and London. He had powerful neighbours, the Abbot of St Augustine's, Canterbury, and the Abbot of Battle's mansion with gardens on what is now the other side of Tooley Street.

In 1450 the Commons of Kent, under the leadership of Jack Cade, were reported to be approaching London. Sir John, who had already sent a servant, John Pain, to spy on the rebels, fortified his mansion and filled it with soldiers. John Pain was unmasked by the rebels and instead of being summarily executed he was asked to take a message to the worthy knight, for help and support against the king, and then return to fight for them. Naturally Pain gave a very detailed and succinct account of the size and strength of Jack Cade's army to his lord. Fastolff then made him return, as part of his promise to Cade, to the rebel army while he and his retinue retreated across the river to the Tower of London.

Site of Sir John Fastolff's house on Tooley Street.

Jack Cade and his thousands entered London, murdered Lord Saye and Sir James Cromer, the Sheriff of Kent, but stopped short of pillaging. The battle of London Bridge on the night of 5 July 1450 was long and bloody. In turn, the rebels were repulsed to Southwark, then the Londoners were beaten back to the bridge. By the morning both sides agreed to stop fighting until the next day on condition that no Londoner should set foot in Southwark and no Kentish man set foot in London. The rebellion was quickly suppressed.

Fastolff's servant, Pain, fought on the bridge for the rebels and was one of the lucky ones to be captured and imprisoned. He was tortured and his jailers tried to force him to admit that his master had tried to fight against the king – but he would not admit to anything.

Fastolff, disgusted at his enemies' antics, repaired to his Castle of Caister, rarely setting foot in Southwark again. It was his misfortune that he had been the scapegoat of his senior officer's ineptitude while in France – something he was never to live down.

Putney's Two Devils

THOMAS CROMWELL OF PUTNEY AND OLIVER CROMWELL

It's ironic that two men who shaped modern Britain had two things in common: Putney, and the fact that they were related. Were it not for one, the other would have never been. One was a lawyer whose logical mind and incisive reasoning made his King the Head of State in both temporal and spiritual matters. The other was a progressive politician whose 'vision' of England was shared by many and whose leadership led to a regicide, the formation of an almost 'republican' Britain and the basis of the world's most proficient army.

Cromwell is a name we associate with the execution of Charles I, one of the most austere periods in British history and with the 'Puritans', Yet Oliver Cromwell (1599–1658) owed his original position, as a scion of one of Huntingdonshire's leading gentry to the munificence of his great-great-great-granduncle Thomas Cromwell (*c.* 1485–1540).

Thomas Cromwell was the son of a Putney brewer, reputedly born on Bowling Green Hill. His rise from the articulate, intelligent son of an inebriated local businessman to Henry VIII's supremely proficient administrator and legal adviser and the instrument of his monarch's secession from the Church of Rome to secure a divorce from Katherine of Aragon, thereby securing for his king complete control of the Kingdom without interference from the Vatican theocracy, was nothing short of brilliant.

Thomas Cromwell, the 'Hammer of the Monks', became hugely wealthy on the caprice of a king. This son of Putney became Lord Great Chamberlain, Lord of the Manor of Wimbledon (which included Putney) and was created Earl of Essex by a grateful king for arranging his marriage to Anne of Cleves. Unfortunately a swift ascent in the king's service made him many enemies and Henry's fury at being presented with such an ugly wife gave them a weapon. He was imprisoned in the Tower of London and executed on the whim of his monarch – a whim the despondent monarch later bitterly regretted.

Thomas Cromwell's niece, Katherine, married Morgan Williams of Putney, bringing him a substantial dowry provided mostly by her uncle. The Williams, in the second generation, dropped their patronymic for Cromwell and settled as substantial country gentry in Huntingdonshire, also acquiring lands in Fulham, notably a property called Passors.

Morgan Williams' great-great-grandson, Oliver Cromwell (pictured), the future 'Lord Protector', was the son of a younger son. He was to become a tenant farmer before using family connections to become an MP. He converted to an extreme form of Protestantism in his early years, and this totally changed his life. His religious beliefs would motivate the rest of his life and colour his judgement, particularly when he became Lord Protector. In one instance he tried to have tennis abolished as it was associated with the excesses of the Court. He also tried to clamp down on Christmas celebrations, Saints' Days and Holy

Days as these were marked with sexual excesses. Yet he himself was known for a few pertinent incidents with some of his junior officers.

He joined the Army in 1640 at the beginning of the Civil War and was on active service in 1642, becoming Lieutenant General in 1643. He believed that he and his troops had been chosen by God to perform his will. By 1647 King Charles was under guard at Hampton Court and relations between Parliament and the army had become very strained. Cromwell decided to place his army between them and he chose Putney for a council of war. It met at St Mary's Church in September 1647 and thrashed out some remarkably democratic doctrines such as 'the poorest in England hath a life to live as the greatest' and 'a man is not bound to a system of government which he hath not had any hand in setting over him'. These 'Putney debates' were to last until 11 November under Cromwell's chairmanship. It was also in Putney that the politically conscious Cromwell and his officers thrashed out their template for the future of the constitution – a republic or a monarchy. It was in 1649 when Charles' head fell off the execution block, a 'cruel necessity' as Cromwell saw it, that England chose a republic.

The Strand Cobbler

HENRY VIII'S FRIENDSHIP WITH HIS LOCAL COBBLER

Henry VIII (1491–1547), when not attending to his wives or to affairs of state, would surreptitiously disguise himself and walk the streets of London at dead of night. Ostensibly, he would do this to check to see if the City constables were doing their job, but it was also freedom from his duties – a boon! He noticed a jolly, whistling cobbler who set up his stall early in the mornings on the Strand. Very early one morning, bored and needing someone to chat with, Henry deftly broke one of his heels and approached the cobbler's stall.

The king asked the cobbler if he could re-heel his shoe. Very obligingly the cobbler told him he would do it in a trice – would the gentleman care to take a seat? This Henry duly did and, thirsty, asked if there were a local inn where he could find himself something to drink. Yes, indeed, there was one very near, open to all the carriers. The king borrowed a pair of shoes from the cobbler, asking him to bring the repaired shoe to him at the inn.

On his arrival at the inn with the mended shoe the cobbler affirmed that the shoe was well and truly mended and, when asked the price, twopence, the king gave him sixpence for his service and honesty and asked him to join him in a drink or two. The cobbler was happy to do so.

They both became merry, sang songs, told jokes and had a good time. The king told the cobbler his name, Harry Tudor, said he was well known at his place of work, the king's Court, and he would be very happy to see him if he cared to visit. All he needed to do was ask for him and someone would bring him to him. The cobbler, completely unaware of his king's name let alone his new friend's identity, was very touched by this token of friendship and, doffing his hat, told Henry that he was one of the most honest men he had met and he would definitely visit him – would he care to return to his humble abode to share some

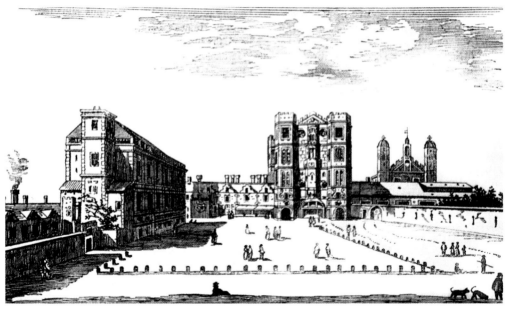

Westminster Palace.

strong but tasty home brew? This he did until the cobbler's wife, Joan, told the cobbler he must do some work. The king left slightly the worse for wear and reiterated his offer.

The cobbler took the king up on this suggestion, and dressed in his best clothes arrived at Court to ask the Yeomen of the Guard if they knew one Harry Tudor. Yes, they did. He asked if he could see his friend, and one led him through the sumptuous apartments. The cobbler thought that the yeoman had misheard. His drinking companion couldn't possibly be living here. He stopped the yeoman and told him that he must have made a mistake – his friend was a plain, honest, merry fellow with whom he had had a few jars recently; his name was Harry Tudor and he might be a lord's servant. The yeoman replied that he knew Harry Tudor very well and the cobbler should follow him. So he was led to the room where the king was with his courtiers. He announced that 'one enquires for Harry Tudor'. The poor cobbler took fright and scuttled away, only to be caught and brought before the king.

He recounted his story. The king then asked him if anyone in the room looked like his drinking companion – well, the king looked vaguely like him but it couldn't be him. Would he recognise his friend if he saw him? Oh yes. Then why didn't he look for him in his cellar? The cobbler was conducted to the cellars.

The king put on his disguise and went to meet his friend. The cobbler recognised him immediately and told him the trouble he had in finding him. Harry Tudor then asked for a glass and wine and they both toasted the cobbler and the king. They quaffed more and the cobbler started singing and making Henry laugh. Some nobles came to see what the din was. The king was in the cellar, plainly clothed, drunk as a lord and laughing with a servant! They asked if there were a problem. It was only then that the cobbler realised who Harry Tudor was and begged forgiveness, to which the king replied that there was nothing to forgive!

Hobson's Choice

THOMAS HOBSON OF CAMBRIDGE WHO FREQUENTED THE BLACK BULL IN BISHOPSGATE

Slowly old phrases are being replaced by hip new ones. The English language reinvents itself and evolves as the generations pass. Some of the choice phrases of yesteryear are tucked away in some book of phrase and fable and referred to when a particularly hard crossword is being puzzled over or when one wants to confound others by new-found erudition or to impress.

Such sayings or phrases as 'How now, brown cow?' or 'Hobson's Choice' have all but gone through the proverbial window of obsolete language. Yet there is always a story behind these sayings, and such is the case with 'Hobson's Choice'. . .

The story begins, strangely enough, in the Black Bull Inn at Bishopsgate, where up to 1810 people might have noticed a strange fresco. The fresco was of an old, bearded, honest and earnest-looking man in Puritan garb, wearing a large felt hat, a long cloak and a ruff around his neck. A hundred-pound bag, on which is written 'the fruitful mother of a hundred more' hangs from his arm – showing that he was an astute businessman. The gentleman in question was Thomas Hobson (1544–1630), official carrier (a postman before the post office was invented) to the University of Cambridge. He had inherited this post from his father, together with his cart and eight horses. He carried everything from letters to humans from Cambridge to London.

Thomas Hobson.

The Black Bull Inn was the recognised hostelry for Cambridge carriers and one most frequently used by patrons of the stage in Elizabethan and Stuart times. Here plays and musical performances were staged and the inn's patrons could view them comfortably from the building's many galleries.

Hobson became rich through astute reasoning – he purchased about forty horses and then rented them out, and became the first person to be recorded as such. 'Observing that the scholars rid hard, his manner was to keep a large stable of horses, with boots, bridles and whips to furnish the gentlemen at once without going from college to college to borrow', said Steele of the *Spectator*. He also stabled his horses at the Black Bull Inn.

So as not to tire one horse out, or seem to favour one particular mount, Hobson insisted that the horses should be taken in strict rotation – 'the horse nearest the door should start the first in course, this or none'. This would be his stock saying so that 'Hobson's Choice' became a byword where the choice is apparent rather than real, since there is no alternative.

Judging by the frequent allusions to this worthy gentleman, he must have been one of the celebrities of the day. He had several portraits painted, one of which showed one of his horses, and his saddle and bridle were preserved in Cambridge Town Hall all through the nineteenth century. He became a friend to the great and the good. One such luminary was the poet John Milton, who penned two epitaphs to his old friend, one of which reads:

> Rest that gives all men life, gave him his death,
> And too much breathing, put him out of breath.

Milton, an otherwise sober individual, indulged in a whole series of puns on Hobson and his trade. He wrote 'his wain was his increase' and 'If I mayn't carry, sure I'll ne'er be fetched'. His last word was that 'He died for heaviness that his cart was light' – but then he had no choice!

From Grace to Majesty
PRINCESS ELIZABETH'S INCARCERATION IN HIGHGATE

The Old Hall, off South Grove in Highgate, consists of two distinct but adjoining parts, one Tudor and the other seventeenth-century. It is the most historically important house in the area. It was originally called Arundel House. Named after its seventeenth-century owners, the Earls of Arundel, it had previously belonged to the Cornwallis family. 'Cornwalleis Esquire, hath a very faire house from which he may beholde with greite delight the staitlie citie of London, Westminter, Greenwych, the famous river Thamesyse and the country towards the south very farr', said John Norden in 1593.

Princess Elizabeth.

It was in this house that the young Princess Elizabeth, the future Queen Bess, was briefly imprisoned before her eventual incarceration in the Tower. Henry VIII, in his libidinous and material ambitions, had created a Protestant state and had fathered seven children by three of his six unfortunate wives. Only three of these children survived him, of whom Elizabeth was one.

The sickly infant and only son King Edward VI, 'God's Imp', succeeded him. Edward became very much the puppet of the ruling faction and a fanatical Protestant, whose Protestant legacy relied on his having children, but he died childless in 1553 leaving the succession open to his half-sister Mary, a fanatical Roman Catholic.

Mary's re-establishment of Catholicism and her betrothal to Philip of Spain produced an immediate backlash from the Protestant faction. The Earl of Devonshire and Sir Thomas Wyatt joined forces and led a failed insurrection to prevent the marriage.

Meanwhile the young Elizabeth was having a hard childhood. She had never known her mother's love, for her mother, Anne Boleyn, had been beheaded, and Elizabeth had carried the stigma of bastardy, had faced terror and suspicion during her brother's reign and the ignominy of continued suspicion by her sister. Popular and Protestant, Elizabeth was implicated, whether rightly or not, in Wyatt's rebellion. Thus Sir Thomas Cornwallis, Treasurer of Calais and Comptroller of Queen Mary's Household, was ordered with two other knights to arrest the 21-year-old princess and bring her to London. Cornwallis and a retinue of 250 arrived at Ashridge House in Hertfordshire the day after Wyatt's arrest. It was late at night. Despite the princess's pleas to wait until daybreak because she was unwell, the emissaries 'came rushing into her Grace's chamber unbidden'. Their orders were to bring her back 'quick or dead'. Elizabeth protested that she was not well enough to travel but they would tolerate no opposition, informing her that she was to be ready at 9 the next morning. They had brought the queen's litter to carry her.

She was carried 'faint and feeble' from Ashridge to Redbourn. They reached St Albans the next day and by the third day they had travelled as far as Mimms. By the fourth day the party had reached Sir Thomas Cornwallis's house in Highgate, but by now the princess's condition had deteriorated so much that they had to stay there that night and the following day.

When they eventually reached Whitehall, Mary refused to see her. Elizabeth was sent to the Tower in terror by the embittered and angry queen. She bravely told her warders that she was no traitor, 'but as true a woman to the Queen's Majesty as any'. Mary suspected much and didn't believe Elizabeth when she swore that while Sir Thomas Wyatt may have written to her, she had never received anything from him.

There was no evidence, thus no justification for a trial and no warrant for incarceration. After a terrifying eight weeks in the Tower she was moved to Woodstock in Oxfordshire where she remained until 1555.

Three years later, a completely different woman returned to Highgate. The new Queen Elizabeth rode in her carriage from Hatfield House to London for her coronation. She was met at Highgate by the Lord Mayor, Aldermen and Sheriffs, 'who conducted her Majesty in great pomp to the City; where she was received with great acclamation both from Protestants and Papists, who seemed to vie with each other in their demonstrations of joy'!

Keeper of the King's Beasts

THE ACTOR-MANAGER EDWARD ALLEYN'S SURPRISING SIDELINE

Edward Alleyn (1566–1626), the Elizabethan actor-manager and future founder of Dulwich College, was by the 1590s a widely respected actor and head of his company. The critics of the day said, 'not Roscius nor Aesop, those tragedians admyred before Christ was borne, could ever perform more in action than famous Ned Allen'.

In 1594 he and his father-in-law, Philip Henslowe, became joint lessees of the Paris Bear Garden (an open theatre used for bear baiting) on Bankside, alongside the Globe, the Rose, the Fortune and the Swan theatres. This part of Southwark was the West End of its day, where the theatres flourished alongside other places of entertainment such as the semi-official whorehouses that straddled the South Bank and the Vauxhall Pleasure Gardens. Bankside and all that it seemed to represent was regarded by the more puritanical as 'Pleasure that was sin'. Sometimes, however, sin's a pleasure – and indeed it was for Ned Allen and his partner. It was a goldmine!

The European traveller, Paul Hentzner, alluded to this pleasuredome of delights in 1597 where:

> without the city are some theatres, where actors do represent almost everyday some tragedy or comedy . . . these are concluded with excellent music, a variety of dances amid the excessive applause of those that are present. There is also another place, built in the form of a theatre, which serves for the baiting of bulls and of bears; they are fastened behind, and then worried by great English Bull-dogs, but not without great risk to the dogs from the horns of the one, and the teeth of the other; and it sometimes happens they are killed on the spot: fresh ones are immediately supplied in the places of those that are wounded or tired. To this entertainment there often follows that of whipping a blinded bear, which is performed by five or six men, standing circularly with whips . . . and at these spectacles the English are constantly smoking tobacco.

The Bear Garden.

Flags were flown all around the Bear Garden before the performances and the bears' keeper and a musician marched the bears through the streets. One of Alleyn's own advertisements for the show is preserved in Dulwich.

Royalty patronised the gardens. Queen Elizabeth and the French ambassador witnessed bull and bear baiting in 1599, as did James I later. It was also the scene of an accident which did much to create Sunday as the 'Sabbath'. A packed scaffolding structure collapsed, killing many of its occupants. The Lord Mayor, a Puritan, sent a formal notice to Lord Burleigh, as 'a judgement of heaven for the violation of the Sabbath', confusing the seventh day of the week with the first.

Despite his Puritan education James I legalised many of these amusements and published the *Book of Sport*. His was a benign reign for the upwardly mobile Alleyn, as Alleyn and Henslowe, anxious to make even more money out of their garden, cultivated the monarch. They provided him with dogs for his favourite sport, lion baiting. Alleyn became the 'Keeper of the King's wild beasts, or Master of the Royal Bear Garden', and enjoyed further this lucrative post and the business it brought him. Some say that his yearly revenue from the Bear Garden alone was £500 (about £50,000 nowadays) and this was only the takings at the entrance! It didn't account for the food and drink supplied by the clever Alleyn.

But the business did not prove as profitable as the King's Master considered it should. Alleyn and Henslowe asked for larger and larger fees and privileges. In 1605 he was already purchasing tracts of land in Dulwich and in 1606 Alleyn engaged the carpenter Peter Streete (who had built the Globe Theatre in 1593 and the Fortune in 1599) to rebuild the Paris Garden in June 1606. It was to be completed by September but was only finished the following January.

Alleyn was to retain this sideline until shortly before his death when he sold his share to his father-in-law. By then its profits and those of his theatre had been heavily invested in his memorial, Dulwich College!

Madame Sin

ELIZABETH HOLLAND, QUEEN OF VICE IN SOUTHWARK

Southwark, confusingly called Borough, has been part of London's history for the last 2,000 years. It has contributed in the field of transport, industry and all forms of entertainment.

Southwark High Street was, throughout the Roman occupation, the principal road in the country. All the way from the coast the route was lined with inns and, as the number of travellers increased, so did the inns; and with the inns, one or more prostitutes laid on by mine host or an equally astute businessman. Some of the ladies were independent and were known by such quaint names as 'noctiluces' (night-moths). Others, the twopenny whores, were known as 'diabolares', diabolical in the extreme. Southwark was the Trastevere (red light) quarter of London, where the ships would disgorge their panting seamen. It continued to be so for another seventeen centuries, at least!

There had been vain attempts to contain or even eradicate prostitution in London for many centuries. London's ban on this game within its walls was effective, it seems, as by far the largest number of prostitutes was clustered in St Katherine's, Bishopsgate, Cock Lane and around Holborn and Fleet Street in the fourteenth century. In 1339 London officially sanctioned prostitution in two districts; Cock Lane and Bankside. This area of Southwark was already notorious for its string of licensed brothels known as the Stews. The Southwark poll tax returns of 1381 identified seven men as being Stewmongers. These were the proprietors of the Bankside Stewhouses in the diocese of Winchester. By 1506 the Stewhouses had increased to eighteen. The Bishops of Winchester tacitly sanctioned their existence and regulated them through their officers. One record shows that the bishops tried to uphold the civil liberties of the whores because 'olde customes that hath been usyd' were being disregarded 'to the gret displeasure of God . . . and utter undoing to all his pouere tenantis . . . and also to the gret multiplicacion of orrible synne upon the single

Bankhouses in Southwark.

women which ought to have thyre free goyng and commyng ate theire owne libertees'.

Many regulations were enforced upon the prostitutes: the Stewholders had to be married men; they were forbidden to sell anything other than their whores' services; the prostitutes were forbidden to eat in their Stews' houses; the Stewholders and their wives were forbidden to hinder a prostitute's comings and goings, and finally a prostitute was required to 'ly still with' a man until morning and was taxed like everybody else.

One gentlewoman, Elizabeth Holland, was the most successful madam London has ever seen. She was born into county affluence in Elizabeth I's reign. She was a beautiful and over-indulged child who became an imperious nymphomaniac. She married but her extramarital liaisons weren't tolerated. She then became the mistress of an Italian and opened a de luxe brothel in the City, but was charged with 'depravities and debaucheries' in 1597.

Rich and powerful friends enabled her to open the Hollands Leaguer, the most exclusive, expensive and luxurious 'Howse of Obscenities' ever in Britain. Her slogan was 'chastity is clene oute-of-date, a mere obsolete thynge'. Her bawdy house was a great mansion set in extensive grounds and only accessible over a drawbridge, right next to Bankside. Here she made a fortune and lived in splendour for thirty years, entertaining all creeds and races. A contemporary ballad jested:

> I am a profest courtesan
> What live by people's sinne.
> With half a dozen Punckes I keep,
> I have grete coming in.

By the seventeenth century London was a bawdy city basking in the golden sunset of the Stuart monarchy. Thomas Nashe, the poet and playwright, performed so unsuccessfully that his inamorata was compelled to use an imported French device, a dildo. He also mentioned that there were 'sixpenny whorehouses next dore to the Magistrate' which couldn't have carried on 'if brybory did nott bestir the magistrates . . . Dishoneste Strumpettes . . . and everie one of them claimed to be a Gentlewoman'.

Rapunzel's Tower
MISS SPENCER'S ELOPEMENT FROM CANONBURY TOWER

Highbury and Islington tube station is the gate to one of the most remarkable areas of London. Dilapidated eighteenth-century terraced houses survive side by side with modern blocks, and hidden elderly gems wink at me from around the corners. But I'm not looking for these! Cross over to Canonbury Place and the hubbub of the traffic on the main road disappears, leaving the visitor breathless with the knowledge that here time stands still. Here stand exquisite seventeenth- and eighteenth-century houses around an impeccably manicured fenced garden. It was here that I asked a young lady if she knew of Canonbury Tower – my goal. The answer was a polite 'No', but maybe the tower in the far corner might resolve my unwelcome intrusion? Aha! A huge tower with massive oak doors! Its

Canonbury Tower.

neighbour, Canonbury House, a handsome eighteenth-century mansion, has a tablet on its garden wall. This told me all. The story of Eliza Spencer's elopement in the late seventeenth century unfolded.

The square red-brick sixteenth-century tower stands empty and defiant. It is, so tradition dictates, the remnant of the country retreat that Prior Bolton built in the early sixteenth century. The original house covered what is now Canonbury Place. Yet what remains seems to date from the tenure of Sir John Spencer, 1570–1609, who was a cloth worker from Suffolk. He became an alderman and eventually a Lord Mayor of the City of London – his wealth was legendary. His City residence was Crosby Hall, now transported to Chelsea Embankment. He was to make many alterations to his new country retreat, especially when Queen Elizabeth visited in 1581.

Sir John had an only daughter, Eliza or Elizabeth. Eliza, as the daughter of a rich man, was a perfect fruit to be plucked by a cash-strapped gent. The young man in question was a near neighbour, Lord Compton, profligate but a charmer. Spencer had other ideas and forbade his daughter to see him. She refused so he held her a virtual prisoner in her own home. Spencer attempted to show that she had been contracted in marriage to a son of Sir Arthur Henningham. He then tried to beat her into submission. The authorities had her placed in safekeeping while lawyers tried to settle the matter. One document put it that 'if the obstinate and self-willed fellow shold persist in his doggedness and geve her nothing, the poore Lord should have a warme catch'. He held her prisoner in Canonbury Tower in 1599 as a last resort.

Lord Compton disguised himself as a baker's boy, complete with a large basket, and set about rescuing his girl. Spencer was said to have met the baker's boy in the tower and was so impressed with his industry so early in the morning that he tipped him! Compton carried his bride-to-be off in the basket and they were married within the month at St Catherine Colman, Fenchurch Street. This story is confirmed by a painting of the period preserved at Castle Ashby, a stronghold of the Compton family. Spencer refused to see the young couple and is said to have disinherited his daughter. Queen Elizabeth's interference in the matter effected a reconciliation. She asked that Spencer stood sponsor to the first child of a young unnamed discarded couple. He was honoured by this strange request, especially as the queen dictated that his own surname be used as the Christian name of the child.

Once the ceremony was over Sir John declared that as he had disinherited his 'undutiful' daughter he would adopt the boy as his son and make him his heir. Queen Elizabeth then told him the truth – he had adopted his own grandson who was to succeed his 'father in honour and his grandfather in wealth'. The reconciliation was complete when a granddaughter was born at Canonbury House.

On Sir John's death the house was occupied by Sir Francis Bacon, the Lord Keeper of the Great Seal.

Beware the Old Mother Red Cap!

MURDER AND WITCHCRAFT IN OLD CAMDEN

Camden Town was yet another part of the frenetic building programme that so marked London in the late eighteenth century – a builder's speculation on open fields begun only in 1791. Previously the only buildings were a few cottages and the Old Mother Red Cap public house, the first port of call up the hill to Hampstead and Highgate.

The Old Mother Red Cap pub stood on what is now the northern or uppermost end of Camden High Street in the mid-eighteenth century. It was one of the many resorts for the Londoners who wanted fresh air and the quiet of the country. The pub was named after Mother Red Cap, also known as the 'Mother Damnable of Kentish Town', and it was here at her cottage 'of no small terror to travellers' that the notorious 'Moll Cut Purse', the highwaywoman of Cromwell's days, frequently stayed.

But who was Mother Red Cap, whose name instilled such fear and loathing? Born in the early seventeenth century to Jacob Bingham, a brickmaker of Kentish Town, and his Scots wife, Jinny was their only child. Her apparently blighted life started with the birth of a child when she was fifteen, by her boyfriend, Coulter, better known as Gypsy George. Her father built them a cottage. Unfortunately this relative peace was shattered when Gypsy George was tried, convicted and hanged for sheep stealing.

Jinny's next boyfriend, Darby, drank too much and brutalised her. She had to ask her mother for help. Darby mysteriously disappeared after only a few months, but the

The Old Mother Redcap.

catalogue of personal disasters continued – her parents were accused of killing a woman with witchcraft and were hanged at Tyburn.

Lonely Jinny found herself a new man called Pitcher who moved in with her. Pitcher's charred remains were then discovered in her oven. She was tried but acquitted of murder, because one of her neighbours proved that Pitcher would often hide in the oven to escape Jinny's vitriolic temper, and his death could have been accidental.

A social outcast, she was rarely seen outside her cottage. It was only at night that she would emerge, scrabbling for food under the hedgerows. Jinny's fortunes changed during Cromwell's Protectorate. A political fugitive begged her for one night's shelter, offering her large sums of money. He stayed for many years despite continuous quarrels. At his death an inquest was held, and although there were rumours of poisoning and the Black Arts nothing was proved and Jinny was left alone with plenty of money.

She continued her lonely existence in her ramshackle cottage, screaming profanities at everyone and in turn being baited and taunted by passers-by. Any local mishaps were blamed on her and the mob would come and bay at her outside the cottage. She was reputed to be a witch, told fortunes and healed diseases.

Mother Red Cap, as she came to be known, certainly looked the part: she would sometimes lean out of the stable door with a grotesque red cap on her head. She had a huge wide nose, heavy shaggy eyebrows, sunken eyes, leathery cheeks, a wrinkled forehead and a wide toothless mouth. Around her shoulders hung a grey striped shawl with black patches, which at a distance looked like flying bats, and her huge black cat rarely left her side.

Such was her reputation that her death was recorded in an old pamphlet. Hundreds of people, it seemed, watched the Devil enter her house and never reappear. She died alone, at night, and was found dead in the morning, sitting in front of the fireplace with a teapot full of herbs, drugs and liquid. Some of this brew was fed to the cat and it died soon afterwards. The undertaker had to break Jinny's stiffened limbs to fit in her coffin.

The cottage then became a tavern and was owned by another old woman also nicknamed Mother Red Cap. A much friendlier person, she had been a camp follower in the Duke of Marlborough's armies. The pub became a favourite watering hole for all her old army cronies, not the least because her home-brewed beer was excellent. The sign hanging outside showed the figure of Mother Red Cap with a tall conical hat!

The area remained grim and was even suggested as the location for a second Tyburn, or so the *Morning Post* reported in 1776.

The Gilded Cage

THE TRAGIC TALE OF ARABELLA STUART

Lauderdale House, on the west side of Highgate Hill, was built on the site of an Elizabethan mansion. Alderman Sir William Bond and his family lived there in the early part of the seventeenth century. It was here that the tragic Arabella Stuart was lodged as a state prisoner from March 1611 for a couple of months. Arabella Stuart (1575–1615) was

The Tower of London.

born cursed. The daughter of Charles Stuart, Earl of Lennox (the younger brother of Lord Darnley) and the granddaughter of Bess of Hardwick, this semi-royal gentlewoman had the 'cursed blood' of the Stuarts and a termagant for a grandmother. She was the great-granddaughter of Margaret, sister of Henry VIII and therefore next in line of succession to the throne, after her cousin James I.

Her life was delicately balanced between the Elizabethan and Stuart political factions. Born in England and a ward of the irascible but astute Bess of Hardwick, Arabella passed a miserable childhood with no one to play with, or people to talk to, save the servants and her tutor. Her formidable grandmother was determined to use Arabella to further her dynastic ambitions. Queen Elizabeth had even intimated that the young girl might be 'a woman to rule, and mistress here even as I am; I recognise much of myself in her.'

Aged twelve, Arabella was sent to Court. The attention lavished on her went to her head and through a series of rash tantrums the young girl was banished! She was totally oblivious to the political machinations behind the scenes for and against her.

Her grandmother became the object of a profound hatred. Arabella studied Greek and Hebrew while plotting how she could gain her freedom . . . and aged twenty-two she was reinstated at Court. This small-boned, attractive, blue-eyed blonde discovered men and promptly fell out of favour.

The death of Elizabeth in 1603 and the accession of James I enabled Arabella to move away from Hardwick to relations and thence to the Court once again. This time the monarch was a close cousin, but he had retained Elizabeth's advisers. Two treasonable plots (possibly engineered by William Cecil, the most powerful politician of his time) were discovered and many prominent figures were implicated, among them Arabella. But Arabella's name had only been inserted by Cecil to foment opinions.

In December 1609, Arabella truly fell in love. William Seymour was a good-looking 22-year-old. He shared her love of books and academic pursuits. He too had royal blood. The news reached the king's ears and he had both arrested, forbidding them to marry.

Six months later the couple made what they fondly hoped was a secret marriage. But they were both arrested. Seymour went to the Tower and Arabella was to be sent north. The first stop on her journey to Durham was to have been Barnet, but Arabella became ill as they approached Highgate – 'she was assuredly very weak, her pulse dull, melancholy, and very irregular and her countenance very heavy, pale and wan'. A message was quickly sent to Sir William Bond, whose house was the most important in the vicinity.

There she wrote a heart-rending letter to her cousin, Lady Jane Drummond, begging her to plead with the king.

> Good cousin, I pray you to do me the kindness to present this letter of mine in all humility to hir Matie and wh all my most humble and dutifull thanckes for the gratuitous commiseration it pleased hir Maty to have of me, as I hear to my great comfort.
>
> And I do earnestly intreate you to moue hir Mate to vouchsafe the continuance of hir so gracious a beginning on my behalfe, and to perswade hir Majty to weigh my cause aright . . . and will ever endeavour to deserve of him and his whilest I have breath . . .

The king was intractable. She managed to escape dressed in men's clothing but was caught and spent the rest of her life in the Tower. Cecil and King James fretted needlessly over her. Her personality was such that it would never have inspired. She had neither the magic of Mary Stuart nor the determination of Elizabeth Tudor.

Haute Cuisine

AN ATTEMPT ON THE LIFE OF SIR THOMAS FAIRFAX, PARLIAMENTARIAN GENERAL

Crabtree House or Great House once stood in the extreme corner of Fulham parish. It was built by Sir Nicolas Crispe or Cripps, a staunch follower of Charles I. Nicholas Crispe is first mentioned in the parish in about 1626. His family had long resided at North End. Crispe was a City of London merchant. He secured a patent, along with other merchants, to trade exclusively with Guinea in redwood, and was also a Captain of the City. By 1640 his wealth was such that he was knighted. By 1642 he had increased his landholdings in Fulham by about 100 acres. His estate stretched from Bridge Road in the north to Crabtree Lane in the south. The river formed its western boundary and the eastern borders extended across Fulham Fields.

When the Civil War broke out Crispe threw in his lot with the king, lending him large amounts of money. The king commissioned him to raise a regiment in 1643 but before he even had a chance to test it in the field the whole regiment was captured by the Earl of Essex, barring Crispe – he was absent! His estate was plundered several times and about £30,000 of his money was sequestered by Parliament, including his house in Bread Street. This did not deter Crispe from equipping fifteen ships of war to harry Parliamentary troops. His share in the booty was one-tenth. He was also appointed auditor and receiver of the sequestered estates and goods of Parliamentarians.

By 1647 Crispe was in France in his capacity as king's factor, selling tin and wool and buying gunpowder with the proceeds. The same year General Sir Thomas Fairfax (pictured), Parliamentary General, had made his headquarters in Fulham. He and Cromwell needed to have a base between London and Richmond, a Royalist stronghold. Parliament owed the army large amounts of back pay and was trying to curtail the power of its generals.

Fairfax had commandeered Sir Nicholas Crispe's house according to one broadsheet. We do know that he lived there from at least 5 August 1647, as it was from there that he penned a letter to the City declaring the pacific intentions of his army. Another pamphlet printed in the same year states that Sir Thomas and Lady Fairfax were staying in Turnham Green. This latter pamphlet, entitled *The General's Dinner at the Lady Crispe's with his Lady and Officers of the Armie, the Manner of the Diner, their great danger of being poisoned, and remedies used to preserve them, and the Cooke, who was the Chiefe Actor*, recounted a curious story.

A French cook employed by Lady Crispe asked to be allowed to cook a dinner for Sir Thomas, Lady Fairfax and his officers. He purchased 16 shillings worth of meat for the dinner and made it up into twenty dishes called 'French Quickshas' or 'Quelquechose', now passed into the English culinary language as kickshaws. The cook was, according to another source, 'known to be a shifter, and one that lives by shirking, he had about a fortnight since, used the Lady Crispe's name to His Excellency the General, to invite him and his Lady to dinner, and used Sir Nicholas his name to his Lady for the house and made about 20 messes it is said. The engagement was by some of France, but such audacious fellows deserve to be made examples; he pretended to show his skill with small cost, a poore excuse for so great a contempt. This youth is one of Melancholicus, the mad Priest's Desciples.'

It seems that either the meat was infected or poison was deliberately placed in the twenty dishes prepared by the unfortunate cook. The hapless and perhaps wicked cook was discovered and committed to the Marshalsea prison where he no doubt died. The sick general and his officers were 'well physicked'. None of them seem to have suffered too much, and it seems that the absent Sir Nicholas Crispe was never accused of this novel way of getting rid of one of the senior Parliamentarian generals and his staff, nor does history relate whether Fairfax stuck to good olde English cooking thenceforth.

The Courtier, Conspirator, Wit & Rake of Parsons Green

A LOOK AT THE LIFE OF CHARLES, EARL OF PETERBOROUGH

From 1660 a sizeable estate at Parsons Green (about 100 acres) became the property, by right of his wife, of John Lord Mordaunt. Lord Mordaunt was to live at Peterborough House for a total of about twenty years, creating some quite splendid gardens.

His eldest son Charles, later 3rd Earl of Peterborough (1658–1735), first went to Eton then Oxford. Oxford was tedious for the fearless young lad who craved excitement. He gave up his studies in 1674 to join the navy as a volunteer. He inherited the estate of Parsons Green in 1675 on the death of his father and in the same year went to Africa where he distinguished himself at the Battle of Tangier. He returned to England and settled on his estate and plunged into an active political life as a zealous Whig and an unswerving opponent of the Duke of York. His politics, however, were too extreme and he fled to Holland where he offered his services to William, Prince of Orange.

He returned triumphant with his new king, William, in 1688. Honours galore were showered on him. He fought in the campaign for Flanders in 1692 and was later implicated in Sir John Fenwick's plot to murder William III in 1696. He was briefly sent to the Tower and, stung by this, and realising that he needed to tread carefully, he retired from active politics until Queen Anne's accession. One consolation in this period of forced retirement was that he inherited the title of Earl of Peterborough.

During the War of the Spanish Succession he was made commander-in-chief of the British forces in Spain. He fought at Valencia and took Barcelona – one of his greatest coups. His conduct in Spain was contentious. He continually argued with his peers and was always hankering for more action – a fault that would land him in constant hot water. In fact his whole life was a search for diversity and excitement. He was autocratic, immeasurably vain and loved practical jokes. On his return home, although a Whig, he allied himself with the Tories to spite his great rival the Duke of Marlborough. Once he was mistaken for the great duke, to which he replied, 'Gentlemen I shall convince you by two good and sufficient reasons that I am not the duke. First I have five guineas in my pocket and secondly they are at your service' – referring to Marlborough's great failings, greed and penny-pinching and his own poverty. One contemporary said that 'he affects popularity and loves to preach in coffee house and open places, is an open enemy to revealed religion; brave in person; hath a good estate . . . yet always in debt and very poor'.

Peterborough House, the earl's house at Parsons Green, was a haven for the literati and wits of the day. Addison, Swift, Pope, Locke, Bolingbroke and Voltaire (an atheist like his host) were among its guests. Jonathan Swift wrote:

> Mordanto fills the trump of fame,
> The Christian world his deeds proclaim,
> And prints are crowded with his name.

Peterborough House.

Swift also said that his 'activity of body and mind was incessantly hurrying him into suspicious designs and perils of a thousand kinds'. Peterborough was hyperactive. He travelled through all the European capitals and principalities. Crown ministers said that they wrote *at* him rather than *to* him. In 1722 the earl, now a widower, secretly married a very pretty singer, Anastasia Robinson, some thirty-seven years his junior. The marriage, however, was kept secret for a few years – whether at her insistence or his cannot be established. The earl even arranged for a house (reputedly Vine Cottage) near Parsons Green to be made available for her, her mother and her two sisters. There the new countess established a musical society where musicians of the day such as Bononcini, Martini, Greene and Tosi performed.

It was only in 1735 that he publicly acknowledged her as his countess. He was to die in the same year. Peterborough House was to languish until the early twentieth century when it was pulled down.

Primrose Hill's Beauty

THE MURDER OF SIR EDMUND BERRY GODFREY

The seventeenth century, particularly the latter half, was highlighted by suspicion, terror and doubt, engendered by religious intolerance. The murder of Sir Edmund Berry Godfrey, knight and magistrate, whose body was found on Primrose Hill, bears witness to this.

On 17 October 1678 the landlord of the White House Inn at Chalk Farm accompanied two of his patrons to the south side of Primrose Hill where, they had told him, they had seen a sword, belt, stick and gloves lying by a hedge. There, in a ditch, lay a body skewered by a sword! Once the body was back at the inn the authorities were informed. A jury was empanelled and two surgeons gave evidence: 'His sword was thrust through him but no blood was on his clothes or about him; his shoes were clean, money in his pocket . . . and a mark, an inch thick, was around his neck, shewing he had been strangled. His chest was bruised and his neck broken. He had been strangled then carried to that place where his sword was run through his dead body.'

The only missing item was his magistrate's notebook. There were some curious spots of wax scattered over his clothes. Sir Edmund never used white wax, but Roman Catholics used it in church! The stage was set! The perpetrators were Catholics! It was a Popish plot! The public was up in arms!

So, who was Sir Edmund Berry Godfrey? He was a successful wood merchant who lived in Green's Lane in the Strand, near Hungerford Market where he had his business. He had

The murder of Sir Edmund Berry Godfrey in Somerset House.

been knighted for services in the Great Fire and was a magistrate for Westminster, reputedly the best JP in England and a zealous Protestant.

Five weeks beforehand political activists Titus Oates and Israel Tonge had affirmed before Godfrey that Charles II was to be killed and the country administered by Jesuits. Three weeks later Oates was summoned before the Privy Council to repeat his allegations. Godfrey was blamed for meddling in such matters and for not disclosing his interview with Oates. Oates was rewarded with £40 per month.

A fortnight later, on Saturday 12 October, Godfrey was missing from home. He had been seen near St Clement's Church in the Strand at Marylebone and was last seen talking to one of the churchwardens of St Martin-in-the-Fields.

On the strength of Oates' evidence, warrants were issued for twenty-six people who were imprisoned in the Tower, and perfectly innocent men were hanged. It seemed that the magistrate had been lured to Somerset House on the pretext of stopping a quarrel. There he was strangled with a twisted kerchief and conveyed to Primrose Hill where a Jesuit ran him through with his sword. The most probable theory, however, is that Oates had Godfrey murdered to give credence to his lies and to excite the public fervour.

Godfrey's body was carried by eight knights, all JPs, and was followed by all the City aldermen and seventy-two clergymen to St Martin's Church to be buried. A tablet to his memory was erected in the east cloister of Westminster Abbey.

A £500 reward was offered for any information and, on the strength of the statement of a Catholic goldsmith, Miles Prance, and an ex-serviceman, William Bledloe, three clerks at Somerset House – Green, Berry and Hill – were arrested, tried and executed despite their protestations of innocence.

Ironically, the older name for Primrose Hill had been Greenberry Hill – and it was re-christened Greenberry for a short period to mark the death of the hero of this tale.

The Sound of Music

THOMAS BRITTON, THE COAL-MERCHANT OF CLERKENWELL

Jerusalem Passage, near St John's Gate, was bathed in the sounds of music in the late seventeenth century. Bewigged gentlemen of all persuasions would congregate in this mean area. Just what was it that attracted some of the leading lights of the musical world to this dank extremity of the City?

The reason was a curious character, Thomas Britton by name, a Northamptonshire man who had come to London to seek his fortune. He apprenticed himself to a small-coal man (itinerant coal vendor) in John Street, Clerkenwell, and on finishing his apprenticeship he rented a stable in Jerusalem Passage, near St John's Square, with living accommodation above.

Thomas Britton was not just a small-coal man. He had caught the learning bug. His neighbour Dr Garencières taught him the basics of chemistry, and he was a second-hand book dealer with a nose for a good book. The visiting gentry and nobility, avid for bargains to replenish or increase their libraries, would repair to the City on Saturdays to look for books. Some would go to Moorfields, others to Little Britain, and many would finally end up at Christopher Bateman's shop on the corner of Ave Maria Lane in Paternoster Row. They would be joined by Mr Britton, who having finished his rounds and put on his best clothes, would sell his books and manuscripts. The company would then adjourn to the Mourning Bush Inn at Aldersgate for lunch.

Mr Britton was also a musician. He played the viol da gamba. He hit on the idea of having select concerts in his stable loft on Thursdays. Here Handel played the organ or the harpsichord and other musicians of repute, Pepusch, Banister and Whichello joined in. They were initially free, but in later years Britton set an annual subscription of 10 shillings, and sold cups of coffee at a penny each.

Ned Ward penned the verse to the little man of Clerkenwell:

> Upon Thursdays repair to my Palace, and there
> Hobble up stair by stair; But I pray ye take care
> That you break not your shins by a stumble;
> And without e'er a souse, Paid to me or my spouse,
> Sit as still as a mouse At the top of the house,
> And there you shall hear how we fumble.

Ned Ward described this tiny concert hall as a 'hut wherein he dwells, which has long been honoured with such good company, looks without side as if some of his ancestors had happened to be executors to old snorling Diogenes, and that they had carefully transplanted the Athenian tub into Clerkenwell; for his house is not much higher than a Canary pipe, and the Window of his state room but very little bigger than the bunghole of a Cask.'

This peaceful man, described as 'the small-coal man, who is a lover of learning, a performer of music and a companion for gentlemen', died rather suddenly in 1714. A fellow musician introduced him to a ventriloquist, a certain Mr Honeyman, who tried out his talent on the unsuspecting Thomas by throwing his voice from nowhere, announcing that the fervently religious Mr Britton would die within a few hours unless he fell on his knees and said the Lord's Prayer. Poor old Thomas died a few days later and was buried in St James's churchyard in Clerkenwell. His epitaph was:

Thomas Britton.

Tho doomed to small coal yet to arts allied:
Rich without wealth, and famous without pride.

The Kat's Whiskers

THE STORY OF THE KIT-KAT CLUB IN HAMPSTEAD

The mid-seventeenth century saw the emergence of the London clubs. Their headquarters were at first in City taverns or in the newly established coffee houses. Some were social, others political, and one of the most famous was the Kit-Kat Club, a Whig club founded in about 1700.

Its origins are obscure, but it could have started as a weekly dinner party given by Jacob Tonson, the famous publisher, for his equally distinguished authors. The venue was the Cat and Fiddle in Shoe Lane, the shop of Christopher Kat, a pastrycook, whose mutton pies were dubbed Kit-Kats. The club had an initial thirty-nine members – authors, wits, noblemen and other men of substance – all bound by a common concern, to secure the Protestant Hanoverian succession and put an end to the last hopes of the Stuarts.

In the summer months the club met weekly at the Upper Flask Tavern, 124 Heath Street, Hampstead, now Queen Mary's Maternity Home. Samuel Richardson in his novel *Clarissa* celebrated this pub. Its walls, still standing, must have listened to some choice bits of gossip. Under the mulberry tree in the garden, this brilliantly gifted group, sometimes a rather too aristocratic crowd for gatherings of such republican equality, would talk, drink, argue, debate and eat well. Such illuminati as Sir Richard Steele, wit, moralist,

Jacob Tonson.

accomplished writer and politician, the dukes of Marlborough, Kingston and four other dukes, Sir Robert Walpole, William Congreve the dramatist, Sir Samuel Garth the poet physician, Sir John Vanbrugh the dramatist and architect, and the Earl of Dorset, would grace the grounds of the tavern. They were a constructive pressure group with a far-reaching influence – despite the opinion of a Tory lampooner who declared that they taught the youth of Queen Anne's day to 'sleep away the day and drink away the night'.

One member of this august assembly was the portrait painter, Sir Godfrey Kneller, whose talent was put to use – he painted all the members at three-quarters length to suit the walls of Tonson's villa at Barn Elms.

Stories about this club abound. One night the amiable Dr Garth was in his cups at the tavern when Steele reproved him for attending too much to food and wine and not enough to his patients. Garth pulled out a list of fifteen patients from his pocket and said, 'It's not great matter after all, for nine of them have such bad constitution that not all the physicians in the world could save them; and the other six have such good constitutions that all the physicians in the world could not kill them.'

Every year the club members would elect a reigning beauty as a toast. The gallant members would then write epigrams to this 'queen of the year'. The verses would be etched with a diamond on the club glasses. The most famous of these toasts were the four daughters of the Duke of Marlborough – Lady Godolphin, Lady Sunderland, Lady Bridgewater and Lady Monthermer. Others were one of Sir Isaac Newton's nieces and Dean Swift's friend, Mrs Long. Lord Halifax penned one such verse:

> All nature's charms in Sunderland appear,
> Bright as her eyes and as her reason clear;
> Yet still their force, to man not safely known,
> Seems undiscovered to herself alone.

The Hanoverian succession of George I in 1714 eliminated the main reason for the club's existence and the weekly meetings at Hampstead stopped. Instead the Kit-Kats met at Tonson's villa at Barn Elms. The early years of the 1720s saw new members who were not of quite the same calibre as the original members. One such member was Lord Mohun, 'a disreputable debauchee and duellist', who killed the Duke of Hamilton in a duel in Hyde Park and broke a gilded emblem off a club chair in a drunken rage. This final act of vandalism made the old Jacob Tonson predict the downfall of the society, saying with a sigh 'the man who would do that would cut a man's throat'. The club did indeed fade away before 1727.

A Battersea Tale

THE LIFE AND LOVE OF HENRY ST JOHN, LORD BOLINGBROKE

Bolingbroke Road, St John's Hill and St John's Road recall a very flamboyant family that dominated the life of Battersea and the politics of the age for about two centuries – the St John family, Lords Grandison, Viscounts Bolingbroke, to list but two of their titles. In the late sixteenth century Battersea was a straggling village perched on the wooded banks of the Thames, an insalubrious spot where one's throat could easily be sliced at the throw of a dice and where the locals would hold their annual libidinous fairs. The hills that meandered down to the Clapham plateau were profuse with lavender fields . . . all in all a far cry from the Clapham of today.

Lord Henry Bolingbroke.

It was here, at the manor of Battersea purchased by Oliver St John in the seventeenth century, that Henry St John, 1st Viscount Bolingbroke was born in 1678. The St Johns' new manor house stood on the site of Price's candle factory. He was educated at a 'dissenting academy' and Oxford. He married and became an MP in 1701. He was a handsome man with exquisite manners, a sharp wit and an even sharper intellect. He was hot-tempered and a supreme orator.

It was this oratory and support for partisan Tory measures that got him noticed. His attacks on Protestant dissenters were a perfect tool for his climb up the precarious pole of politics. Once the Tories regained power in 1710 he was made Secretary for War and created Viscount Bolingbroke in 1712. His 'attachment' to Queen Anne's favourite enabled him to become the leading figure in the government.

Unfortunately his fall was due to his temperament. He was a poor manager, supremely arrogant and unscrupulously ambitious. His hugely unpopular treaty with France after the War of the Spanish Succession proved almost fatal. His tragi-comic effort at leading a Tory rebellion against the First Minister, Lord Oxford, combined with the death of his patron Queen Anne in 1714 led to his downfall. Furthermore it was discovered that he was plotting with the exiled Stuarts in France and he actively worked on the abortive 1715 rebellion. He fled to France, without his wife, once attainted.

Bolingbroke had many affairs while married – but it was during negotiations in Paris in 1711 that he met the sensuous, stunning, rich, young Marie-Claire des Champs de Marcilly, the Marquise de Villette. On her side there was certainly passion. On his there was a mixture of passion of French Court politics, and the wealth and the beauty of the young marquise – in that order! He became secretary of state for the Old Pretender, immersed himself in European politics and in the glittering Paris literary salons.

His wife's death in 1718 ostensibly removed all obstacles to a marriage to his French mistress but for the fact that their marriage would enable the British government to seize all her assets. Marie-Claire's repeated attempts to have the Act of Attainder repealed finally got results. They married and returned to England although Bolingbroke remained an outcast in the world of politics. It was only after his father's death in 1742 that the Bolingbroke estates were restored to him.

He was to settle in his old manor house in sleepy Battersea where he continued on his second career, that of philosopher and political theorist. Here his young wife became depressed in the 'old and decayed habitation' as 'amusement is as necessary to her as food . . . nay more than food', Bolingbroke wrote. It was a quiet life as 'Battersea is much further from London than it ever was before. We have four feet of snow; the wind howls round the house and no-one ever comes near us.' Marie-Claire wrote to a friend that 'my hermit and I go to bed before six o'clock. He gives himself up entirely to looking after me. I cannot tell you how touched I am by his love and care.'

When she died in 1750 Bolingbroke wrote that he was the most 'miserable of all men . . . my heart is broken, my spirit is crushed and my body crippled'. He died shortly afterwards, in 1752 and they are buried alongside each other in Battersea Church.

A Man of Distinction

THEODORE JANSSEN, BANKRUPT OF WIMBLEDON

Britain's liberalism and relatively fluid social structure has always attracted the daring, the impoverished and political and religious refugees to its shores. The Jews were the first to find haven in England in medieval times, closely followed by Dutch settlers on the Kent coast and, from the sixteenth century onwards, the greatest migration of a religious group ever, the French Calvinists better known as Huguenots. France and the rest of Europe were Catholic, retained a feudal system, and had a set of legal estates which defined the social 'castes', the nobility, the bourgeoisie and the Third Estate – these remain clearly defined to date. The combined social, religious and political restrictions led some states to become Protestant, but for many individuals their only salvation lay in uprooting and emigrating.

Britain's gain was France's drain. The Huguenots who arrived on our shores were men of substance – artisans who brought their particular skills to the burgeoning British Empire, military officers, rich 'bourgeois' whose capital, savoir-faire and skills made the British Empire. France's economy never recovered from the 'forced' drain of the backbone of its economy.

One such fortunate immigrant was Theodore Janssen (*c.* 1658–1748), a patrician who arrived, with his brothers, in England in about 1683 with a reputed £20,000. He was of French-Walloon descent and had been educated in Holland. He was well connected and clever. His, however, was not a case of forced immigration, it was a canny move.

The late seventeenth and early eighteenth centuries were very turbulent times for Europe and for Britain. This was the time of the Glorious Revolution and England was fighting a more powerful enemy, France. It needed to find ready loans. Theodore took full advantage of the situation, dabbling in all forms of merchandise: marble, lead, tin and paper, in every major European city, Livorno, Venice, Genoa, Paris and Amsterdam – business, unlike patriotism, had no boundaries. Paper, a family concern, naturally brought him into conflict with English paper manufacturers.

He was a founder member of the Bank of England and of the New East India Company. His biggest profits, however, came from lending money to the government to pay the British Army.

He was rewarded for his financial services with a baronetcy in 1715 and began looking for a suitable country estate for a man of substance. He, like every City merchant, lived

with his wife and family in the City, in the parish of St Stephen Walbrook. He had already acquired lands in Dorset, but needed somewhere near the capital.

He chose the sleepy rural village of Wimbledon. He purchased the manor in 1717, living at first in a house situated on what is now the corner of the High Street and Church Road. The Elizabethan manor of Wimbledon (left) was set in a huge 370-acre park. It had exquisite gardens to which Sir Theodore added. He pulled down the old manor and had his new Palladian-style house built facing the south-east over the valley towards the North Downs. He was now the Lord of the Manor of Wimbledon. He installed his family and his exceptionally large library – he loved his books and had very catholic tastes, purchasing books on architecture, history, diverse cultures, poetry, science and mathematics. His house, park and gardens changed

Wimbledon, attracting many to live there. The Janssens made it their home, several being buried in the local churchyard.

Alas, his nemesis was the South Sea Company, of which he was a founding director in 1711. By 1721 he held about £130,000 worth of stock. Greed played a huge part in the huge speculation in South Sea Company shares.

In autumn 1720 the bubble burst, prices dropped from £290 to £155 within two months. Nearly 30,000 investors lost money. Janssen and the other directors were disqualified from parliament and from holding public office. His estates were sequestered in 1721, although he was allowed to keep Wimbledon and £50,000 – the largest amount any director of the company was allowed.

After his wife's death in 1731 Janssen stayed at Wimbledon and the family retained it until 1766.

A Belsize Affair
MR HOWELL OF BELSIZE HOUSE

The first morality campaign to make frequenters of Hampstead Heath behave the way their social and spiritual betters thought they ought started in the eighteenth century. As more and more Londoners were visiting the delights of the Heath and its surrounds, the demand created more illicit pleasures. Part of the Manor of Hampstead, Bellasys, Belsys, later Belsize, was also called South Hampstead; its history was sometimes as colourful as its neighbour up the hill, and for a while more so!

Belsize House.

At the Dissolution of the Monasteries the Manor of Bellasys was leased to an intrepid explorer, Sir Armigaal Waad. His descendants in the female line held the manor and lands for three centuries. The estate was sub-let to Charles Povey in about 1700. He was a retired 'sea-coal' merchant, a bigoted anti-Papist with an almost equal hatred for paying taxes. His tenancy of the property ran just short of disaster. Pursued by the owner's (Lord Chesterfield's) agents for failing to maintain payments and negligence in the property's upkeep, Povey tried sub-letting. The French ambassador offered £1,000 a year, but was refused lest he desecrated the chapel with Popery! This was a somewhat ill-timed move by Povey as anti-Catholicism had abated, and he received a severe reprimand from the Privy Council.

In desperation Povey eventually sub-let to a Welshman, Mr Howell, who planned to turn the house and grounds into a pleasure resort to rival and even outdo Hampstead Wells. In this Howell was supremely successful, and from 1720 the estate was a centre for amusement for twenty years. The gossips of the time regarded Belsize House as a second-rate house of refreshments and gambling. Announcements of the opening of the house appeared in *Mist's Journal* of 16 April 1720: 'Whereas that the ancient and noble house near Hampstead, commonly called Bellasys House, is now taken and fitted up for the entertainment of gentlemen and ladies during the whole summer season, the same will be opened with an uncommon solemnity of music and dancing.'

A year after its opening the denizens of Hampstead complained about the multitude of coaches that ruined their solitude. Indeed the *St James's Journal* of 7 June 1722 reported that the 'appearance of the nobility and gentry at Bellsize was so great that they reckoned between 300–400 coaches'. Howell also introduced deer to this square mile estate and hunting became immensely popular. Horse racing and foot racing were also introduced, with huge bets on the outcome. High society frequented this new 'Pleasure Dome': 'last Saturday their Royal Highnesses the Prince and Princess of Wales dined at Belsize House, attended by several persons of quality, where they were entertained with the diversion of hunting and such other as the place afforded', ran an item in *Read's Journal* of 15 July 1721.

But the fashion waned and Howell made the fatal mistake of announcing that part of the house would be for the use of the 'meaner sort'. The *St James's Journal* of 24 May 1722 reported that the 'Court of Justices have ordered the High Constable of Holborn division to issue his precepts to the petty constables and headboroughs of the parish of Hampstead, to prevent all unlawful gaming, riots, etc. at Belsize House'.

The 'Welsh ambassador' Mr Howell visited the New Prison with several gamesters. How long he was held we don't know but it prompted a satirical verse about him:

> But since he hath obtained his liberty
> By Habeas, the wicked merry be;
> Whom he by advertisement invites
> To visit him among his false delights.

People continued to flock there and a satire entitled *Belsize House* exposed the 'fops and Beaux who daily frequent that academy; the women who make this an exchange for assignations; the buffoonery of the Welsh Ambassador and the humour of his customers'. The satire exposed Belsize as an academy for dissipation and lewdness. An anonymous satirist was somewhat blunter about Belsize:

> the scandalous lewd house that's call'd Belsize
> Where sharpers lurk, yet Vice in Publick lies,
> Is publicly become a Rendezvous
> Of strumpets, common as in common Stews,
> . . . convenient this defiled house is made
> To bring the Welsh Ambassador a trade.

It stayed open until 1745 when Ranelagh Gardens opened, and it reverted to private ownership at Mr Howell's death. It was pulled down in 1852. All that remains of this house is Belsize Avenue – which used to be its driveway.

The French Philosopher

VOLTAIRE IN WANDSWORTH

It was Whit Monday 1726. François-Marie Arouet de Voltaire (1694–1778), the French philosopher and poet, set foot on English soil at Greenwich. This voluntary exile, the fair climate and the air of liberty was to make him wax lyrical: 'I fancied that I was transported to the Olympian Games; but the beauty of the Thames, the crowd of vessels and the vast size of the City of London soon made me blush to have likened Elis to England. . . . A courier from Denmark believed that the entire nation was always gay that all the women were sprightly and beautiful and that the sky of England was always pure and serene.'

Voltaire welcomed this change. He'd had a rough time in France. He had spent some time in the Bastille and then quarrelled with an aristocrat and was sent back to the Bastille for a second time. He finally agreed that he would spend some time away from Paris – and this was the perfect place! Although he gave his postal address as Lord Bolingbroke's house in Pall Mall, he took up the long-standing invitation of an English merchant, Everard Falkener, to stay at his house, Sword House, where Wandsworth police station now stands, on Wandsworth High Street.

Everard Falkener was a City merchant whose family specialised in trade with the Levant. Everard had spent nine years in the Levant learning his trade and taken a leisurely trip back through Europe on his way home, and in Paris he met Voltaire. The two thirty-year-olds had hit it off and the affluent Falkener had given Voltaire an open invitation to England, where Voltaire met Jonathan Swift, the Earl of Peterborough, William Congreve and many other celebrities of the day. At his friend's house he concentrated on learning English and practising fencing for the day he returned to France, so he could confront the aristocrat who had sent him to the Bastille.

He was to revise his first statement about London. He declared that London was not the equal of Paris in material things. Paris, he said, 'had five hundred times more silver plate in the house of a bourgeois than in those of London'. A Paris draper, notary or solicitor was better lodged than a magistrate in London. 'In the affairs of the mind', however, he 'respected the freedom and sincerity of England', and preferred England before all other countries, in Robert Hooke's words, because 'the first was liberty, the second was liberty, and the third was liberty'.

Voltaire's appreciation of England and the English increased when he attended Sir Isaac Newton's funeral. The pall-bearers numbered two scientific dukes, three learned earls and the Lord Chancellor. What completely threw him was the fact that a professor of mathematics, a great one at that, was buried in a chapel where the ashes of monarchs and great nobles reposed, and that 'the highest subjects in the kingdom felt it an honour to assist in bearing thither his body'.

He was presented at Court and, forever the businessman, he wrote a dedication in English to Queen Caroline for the London edition of his book *La Henriade*, in 1727, for which he was given a gift of 2,000 crowns by King George II. But Voltaire preferred his unknown retreat in Wandsworth, at least for the first six months of his stay. The reason behind this was possibly that his sister had died, he had reached a low point in his life when everything seemed to be a peregrination and he needed to learn the tongue of his host country.

Voltaire did return to France, in 1728, after a stay of just over two years. He had arrived as a famous poet and left as a famous philosopher. His visit to England, France's traditional enemy, had left an indelible mark on him, and concreted his 'modernist' thoughts that were to help change France for the better.

The Big Swiss Cheese

AN ELABORATE TRICK PLAYED ON BARN ELMS RESIDENT HEIDEGGER

The austerity of Oliver Cromwell's regime was followed by the excesses of the Glorious Revolution! The country was rich and wanted to indulge. Libidinous venues such as the Ranelagh Club and Vauxhall Gardens came into their own. Enterprising Europeans flocked to Albion to taste commercial success – among these, Georg Friedrich Händel and Johann-Jakob Heidegger, the lessee of Barn Elms, from about 1728 to 1734. Heidegger (1666–1749) was the son of a Zurich pastor. He was ugly, he was big and he had commercial flair. He moved to London in about 1708 to pursue a career as an opera impresario, although he is more famous for having introduced masquerades from Italy.

Masquerades were the dominant form of entertainment in the capital and were initiated by such men as Heidegger. He turned a vestige of the ancient and powerful world of the Carnival into a very stylised and commercial enterprise worthy of the emerging new capitalist world of public entertainment. The dominant apparel of the masquerade was the 'domino costume' – a loose cloak and a mask, the cloak invariably made of black and white diamond-shaped pieces of cloth. The domino costume represented intrigue, adventure, conspiracy and mystery, four elements that were a distinctive part of the masquerade atmosphere.

A stroke of good fortune enabled our enterprising adventurer to manage the Haymarket theatre almost continuously from 1713 to 1734, combining his business acumen with the musical talents of another immigrant, G.F. Händel. The almost simultaneous lighting of 3,000 candles marked the coronation feast of George II in 1727, 'by an invention of Mr Heidegger's'. George II

Johann-Jakob Heidegger.

was so impressed that he made the 'Swiss count', so derided by the *Tatler*, Master of his Revels. This did not particularly impress a Middlesex grand jury, which labelled Heidegger as the 'principal promoter of vice and immorality' in 1729.

Heidegger seems to have first settled in Richmond near the royal palace. He then moved to Barn Elms (now Barnes), where King George invited himself for supper one evening. The king arrived by boat from Richmond and was perturbed to find that the house and grounds were in darkness. Heidegger repeated his coronation trick and in an instant the whole place was ablaze with light. The Duke of Montague played an elaborate hoax on our hero. He invited some hard drinkers, including Heidegger, to a boozy evening. Once dead drunk, a mould was taken of his face. The stage was set!

At the next masquerade Heidegger ordered the band to play 'God Save the King', but once his back was turned his 'double' appeared, complete with face-mask and identical clothes, and ordered the band to play a nationalist Scottish tune. The whole assembly hushed, waiting to see the king's reaction. Heidegger rushed to the music gallery in a rage and ordered them to play the proper song – which they did. On leaving the gallery the false Heidegger returned shouting and ranting, in true Heidegger style, that he had ordered them to play the Scottish tune! Everyone knew that the Swiss had a mercurial temperament. They waited and the real Heidegger screamed the house down while the king and all his court wept with laughter. Heidegger, on Montague's instructions, apologised to the king, at which point he was confronted by the false Heidegger!

The 'Swiss count' was eventually to retire to Richmond, but it was at his Barn Elms dinner table that he paid his warmest tribute to the English nation, saying 'I was born a Swiss where twenty pounds a year would have been the utmost that art or industry could have procured me. With an empty purse and almost two shirts, I arrived in England and by the munificence of a generous Prince and the liberality of a wealthy nation, am now at the head of a table covered with delicacies; I have an income of £5,000 a year [about £375,000 in today's money]. Today I am honoured with the company of the first characters of the age. Now I defy any Englishman however much he may be gifted to go to Switzerland and raise or even spend such a sum there!'

Strong Man

THOMAS TOPHAM, STRONG MAN OF ISLINGTON

The Duke's Head pub once stood in St Alban's Place in Islington. Its owner in the eighteenth century was one Thomas Topham, known as the 'Strong Man of Islington'.

Topham (1710–49), was a successful carpenter who, aged twenty-four, purchased a pub, the Red Lion, near St Luke's Hospital in Finsbury. Finsbury was known for its prize fighting, wrestling, boxing and similar pursuits – and Thomas excelled as a pugilist. His business went bust because he preferred the great outdoors. Undaunted, he purchased another inn, the Duke's Head, in the more fashionable Islington. His above average height and his strength suited a publican's life, and it was during this tenancy that he achieved national fame.

Topham's main biographer was Dr John Desaguliers, an Islington resident, who praised Topham's feats of strength. Some of his exploits nearly landed him in trouble! Sitting at the first floor window of a pub, he spied a butcher carrying a freshly slaughtered ox on his back. He gently lifted the ox off his back without the butcher seeing who did it – he thought it was the devil! Another time he removed part of a builder's scaffold from a building, only to have the wall it was supporting fall on him. One of the poles nearly broke his ribs. At a race meeting in Hackney a man with a horse and cart persisted in following the contestants, to everyone's fury. Topham seized the back of the cart and despite the man goading his horse, Topham pulled the cart backwards.

He toured the country. In Derby he performed such feats as rolling up heavy 7lb pewter dishes like paper, holding a pewter quart at arm's length and crushing it like an eggshell, lifting a two hundred weight with his little finger and a solid six-foot table with his teeth. He also lifted a 27-stone clergyman with one hand, and bent a 1-inch thick piece of iron round his arm.

Mr Topham (left) also considered himself an accomplished singer and once sang 'Mad Tom', a popular song of the day, so loudly it frightened most of Derby! Sometimes his voice wasn't appreciated and an ostler of an inn he was staying at told him he sang flat. Topham grabbed a kitchen spit and bent it round the ostler's neck like a cravat.

He got up to more pranks in London. He found a night-watchman fast asleep in his box near the Barbican, so he lifted watchman and box up, carried them to Bunhill Fields Cemetery and carefully dropped them over the wall into the graveyard. Topham's most famous feat of strength was to commemorate Admiral Vernon's taking of Portobello. In front of massed crowds and the admiral himself, on 28 May 1741 in Bath Street, Colbath Fields, three hogsheads of water weighing 11,831lb were placed on a strong timber frame. Topham stood on a platform directly above them with a strap over his shoulders, fastened to a thick rope binding the three hogsheads. He then effortlessly raised them at least 3 inches.

He left Islington and took another pub in Hog Lane, Shoreditch, where he killed his wife in a jealous rage and then committed suicide on 10 August 1749. The *Daily Advertiser* reported the facts the following day: 'Yesterday died Thomas Topham, known by the name of Strong Man, master of a public house in Hog Lane, Shoreditch, occasioned by several wounds he gave himself Tuesday last.'

But imagination, hero-worship and superstition wouldn't let go of the memory of the great 'Strong Man of Islington', so much so that the *Daily Advertiser* reported his final bow with the Grim Reaper himself, on 16 August 1749: 'For these few days past there has been a great commotion in Shoreditch parish – an apprehension that a resurrection had begun it, and several witnesses have been examined by the magistrates in relation thereto. Yesterday it was said that Topham, the Strong Man had, the night before, with the assistance of some surgeons, got the better of his grave, though some eight feet of earth had been laid on him.'

The Monk's Carpet Factory

PETER PARISOT, FULHAM CARPET MANUFACTURER

Towards the end of the seventeenth century, Walloons and Flemish makers of Turkey pile carpets had settled and set up works in different parts of England. King William III granted a protective charter, for instance, to weavers in Axminster and Wilton in 1701. The renown of the pile carpet industry at Wilton was due mainly to Henry, Earl of Pembroke and Montgomery, who in the course of his travels in Europe collected French and Walloon carpet-makers to work for him in Wiltshire. These carpet-makers were supervised by two Frenchmen, Antoine Dufossy and Pierre Jemale. Another Frenchman and his carpet factory were to eclipse others in England, albeit for a short time. This was Peter Parisot (1697–1769) one-time priest, adventurer and a man with a penchant for the good things in life.

The site of the carpet factory, Fulham.

Pierre Parisot was born in Bar le Duc, France, trained at the Bar le Duc Jesuit College and entered the novitiate with the Capuchins as 'Père Norbert'. He was to become a secretary to the General Chapter in Rome and a roving ambassador for the Capuchin foreign missions. His 'experiences' with the Jesuits in India made him become virulently anti-Jesuit to the point where he openly accused them of infringing on Capuchin territory and waging a propaganda war against the Capuchins, lies on the number of supposed conversions and a host of other real or supposed wrongs. These contentions were published once he returned to Rome in 1744 to the delight of the followers of the Enlightenment and the ire of the Roman Catholic establishment. He wrote several other books for which he has been castigated by the Catholic Church ever since and which determined his future. He travelled all over the continent, eventually ending up in London where as Pierre or Peter Parisot, a defrocked priest, he set up carpet weaving in Paddington with two Savonnerie (Gobelin) weavers under the liberal patronage of the Duke of Cumberland in 1750.

He moved his business to what is now 49–55 Fulham High Street in 1752, next to the Golden Lion pub where he grandly established 'a manufacture of carpets and tapestries where both the work of the Gobelins, and the art of dyeing scarlet and black, as then practised at Chaillot and Sedan, were carried on . . . where he had conveniences for a great number of artists of both sexes and for such young persons as might be sent to learn the arts of drawing, weaving, dyeing . . .'. But it seems that this little exercise in salesmanship was merely an excuse to get cheap labour. One Fulham worthy went to visit this 'Manufacture of Tapestry from France, now set up at Fulham by the Duke of Cumberland. The work, both of the Gobelins and of Chaillot, called Savonnerie, is very fine but very dear.'

His personality was amusingly described by Giuseppe Baretti, Dr Johnson's friend: 'As to the Gobelin tapestry, the art of making it in its complete perfection was brought to England by a distinguished anti-Jesuit, the renowned Father Norbert, a French Capuchin whom Benedict XIV, himself an anti-Jesuit, permitted to live in England on condition that he went as a missionary converting the good souls who tasted his doctrines. For him seeking to fulfil this duty, this honest monk has taken the liberty of secularising himself and has appeared under the name of Parisot. He has made himself the director of a manufactory for this kind of tapestry. He has, by means of a voluntary subscription among the gentry and the well-to-do, succeeded in obtaining help to the extent of £10,000 sterling. Of this I was assured at the time. This gentleman, shortly after his arrival in London, found means to pocket this sum. I have several times gone from this capital to Fulham to see his looms which might have procured an honest livelihood had he exercised the least economy, but he was a spendthrift and possessed some eminent qualities – especially those two cardinal virtues known by the name of incontinence and vanity – so that he did not take long to run into debt; he became a bankrupt and took to his heels.' Indeed M. Parisot sold up to cover his losses in 1755 and moved to Exeter. From there, after another loss-making venture, he returned to the continent.

A Captain by Any Other Name

LAMBETH'S CAPTAIN BLIGH

The fourteenth-century church of St Mary's at Lambeth, adjacent to Lambeth Palace, was for 900 years the parish church of Lambeth. It was deconsecrated in 1972 and became largely derelict. In 1976 an exciting discovery was made in the overgrown graveyard. The tomb of the two greatest English gardeners, the Tradescants, was discovered under the mass

St Mary's, Lambeth.

of dense undergrowth. Another tomb, that of Vice-Admiral Bligh (1754–1817), his wife and children also lay largely forgotten in the same graveyard.

Everyone knows the story of the mutiny on the *Bounty*. Some of us even remember the leering face of Charles Laughton as the obnoxious Bligh, or the coldly imperious Trevor Howard, with the handsome Marlon Brando as Fletcher Christian. But do we really know anything about the truth? Has history as we know it given Captain Bligh a fair hearing?

William Bligh was born in Cornwall in 1754. He went to sea at an early age and at twenty-one he served as master on one of the ships on Captain Cook's third and final voyage to discover the North-west Passage. He was dubbed 'Breadfruit Bligh' through discovering this plant in Tahiti.

Bligh was appointed captain in command of HMS *Bounty* in 1787. The ship left England too late to arrive at Tahiti at the right time for obtaining breadfruit. The late departure was owing to the unexpected extra work that had to be done on the ship to make it seaworthy. The *Bounty* was too small to take marines. Many have said that the mutiny would not have taken place had there been marines on board. True, Bligh had a temper, but it was one that cooled very quickly. He was by nature a kindly man who thought nothing of giving up part of his cabin for some of his crew when they were ill, and even had hot meals prepared for the invalids.

Bligh was personally highly disciplined and expected complete obedience from his subordinates, not so much to him but to the holder of His Majesty's Commission. He did not keelhaul a sailor, nor did he return to capture the mutineers. He didn't appear at the mutineers' courts-martial either. Hollywood just did not want the facts to get in the way of a good story!

One of Bligh's main faults lay in his giving his crew too much freedom in Tahiti. When they were eventually ordered to knuckle down, they wouldn't. His epic voyage back to Britain in the longboat was a tribute to his skill as a navigator and his capacity for leadership. The Admiralty had faith in him despite his being in the middle of another dispute in 1797, when he was embroiled in a mutiny in port over better pay and conditions. He just happened to be in the wrong place at the wrong time. But he did agree, in principle, to the mutineers' gripes. Ironically, after this mutiny Bligh's crew elected to have him as their commander!

His undoubted abilities enabled him to take part in the Battle of Copenhagen in 1801. His efforts almost destroyed the Danish Navy. For his singular efforts he received Nelson's public and personal thanks. The two became great friends.

Later, William Bligh was appointed Governor of New South Wales. This was an appointment given to him in part because of his reputation. He lived up to it, ruthlessly stamping out sedition and halting the monopolies of already rich settlers, distributing communal wealth and food to the needy, much to the rage of the oligarchy. Effectively, Bligh restored discipline to the region, which had been sadly neglected by the two previous governors. Eventually, he returned to England, settled briefly at 100 Lambeth Road, and was appointed Rear-Admiral then Vice-Admiral. He was considered a hard man to do business with. He was a mixture of a mild, good-natured, compassionate man and an equally arrogant and overbearing one.

William Bligh and his spouse now rest in one of the prettiest gardens in London. The graveyard is a tribute to the Tradescants, and Bligh's tomb stands as its centrepiece.

The Norwood Nightingale
THE EIGHTEENTH-CENTURY SINGER ANN CATLEY OF KNIGHT'S HILL

Most of the land between Knight's Hill and the Leigham Court Ridge, on the fringes of today's Streatham and Norwood, bordered on an expansive common in the latter part of the eighteenth century. It was here, close to St Luke's Church, that the Horns pub stood. Here travellers would stop for refreshment and water their horses before making the steep climb up the hill. The undistinguished father of Ann Catley (1745–89), the celebrated singer, was its landlord.

The eighteenth century saw a variety of gifted comediennes and singers, among them Ann. She was a free spirit whose remarkable singing voice was a joy for all the travellers to her father's pub. Aged fifteen she was apprenticed to a musician and composer, Mr Bates. There is, however, considerable evidence to show that her mother, in an effort to leave her husband, sold her to Mr Bates and came along for the ride!

Ann Catley started singing in public in 1762, joining the troupe of singers of the Pleasure Gardens at Vauxhall. Her voice was her fortune and before the end of that year she was one of the leading lights of the Gardens. Her father, realising that he had lost out on a possible goldmine, tried in vain to regain custody of her before her eighteenth birthday.

Charles Macklin, the actor and stage-manager, realised her potential, brought her to Covent Garden and introduced her to the Dublin stage where she was a resounding success. He introduced her to Henry Mossop, a Dublin theatre owner, who engaged her at great expense and lodged her and her mother in Drumcondra Lane. She enslaved Dublin, so much so that even her hairstyle was copied. Her hair was cut straight across the forehead, in a style that the Victorians would call a Piccadilly fringe.

It was in Dublin that the dramatist John O'Keefe met her. Her personality as well as her beauty besotted him. He said that 'she wore her hair plain over her forehead in an even line almost to her eyebrows, and the word was with all the ladies to have their hair *Catleyfied*. Miss Catley and her oddities were well known to all. She was one of the most beautiful women I ever saw, the expression of her eyes, and the smiles and dimples that played around her lips and cheeks, enchanting. She was eccentric but had an excellent heart.'

Eccentric she was! She was noted for her repartee with the audience when she would step out of character in the part she was playing on the stage to sharpen her wits on someone in the pit, and then, without pausing, return to the part she was playing. In one such instance she eyed a former lover, a Mr Leoni, with a lady leaning on his arm. 'How do you do, Leoni?' she called out. 'I hear you're married; is that your wife? Bid her stand up till I see her.' The lady stood up graciously. Miss Catley eyed her up and down. 'Ha! Very well indeed, I like your choice.'

In another instance she had heard that O'Keefe had produced an opera called *The Banditti*, which had been panned by the critics and hissed off the stage. Both O'Keefe and Miss Catley were later in the audience at a theatre one evening. She accosted him and shouted out, 'So, O'Keefe, you had a piece damned the other night. I'm glad of it; the devil mend you for writing an opera without bringing me into it.'

She returned to London in 1770 to act and sing at Covent Garden in a play called *Elfrida*. Horace Walpole, a man not noted for his insouciance, commented that she had 'impudence'. It has been mooted that she and Charles Macklin had had an affair – it wouldn't be the first time that a lady had slept her way to the top. Indeed, Miss Catley made no bones about her busy social life, and like all those with an eye for the main chance she landed herself a well-connected husband, General Lascelles, at whose house, near Brentford, she died on 14 October 1789.

The Brewer, his Wife & the Lexicographer

THE INTRIGUING FRIENDSHIP BETWEEN DR JOHNSON, HENRY THRALE OF STREATHAM AND HIS WIFE HESTER

In 1765 Henry Thrale, a very affluent Southwark brewer and MP, secured an introduction to the new 'lion' of literary society, Samuel Johnson (1709–84), man of letters, author, critic, moralist and lexicographer. The 41-year-old Henry Thrale (*c.* 1724–81) had a

Streatham Place.

dainty wife, Hester Salusbury, and a 100-acre estate in Streatham, Streatham Place. He was a 'new' man whose wealth enabled him to find a wife from an impoverished but very well-connected gentry family – in fact 'the only pretty girl who would consent to live in Southwark'. Once married, he proceeded to enjoy himself with ladies of somewhat doubtful reputations.

Hester Thrale (1741–1821), was twenty-four, 'a lady of lively talents improved by education – she was short, plump and brisk'. She was a consummate gossip, an incessant chatterer, precious, a snob and educated – something not generally encouraged in the women of those days. Her command of languages and agile mind were to make her one of the most accomplished hostesses of the time.

Samuel Johnson was a 51-year-old widower whose literary talents, razor-sharp wit and congeniality far outweighed his lack of physical charms. His first dinner in October 1765, at the townhouse of the 'eminent and haughty brewer' of Southwark, cemented a deep and lasting friendship between the two men and secured a devoted patroness and feminine admirer in Hester (left). Johnson, who didn't think much of women, said that her 'colloquial wit was a fountain of perpetual flow': was this a reference to her constant chatter?

Johnson would come to his new friends at least once a week and eventually had an apartment in the town house in Deadman's Alley, Southwark, and one at Streatham Place. Georgian Streatham was a genteel country village a few miles from the centre of London. Streatham Place had been purchased by Ralph Thrale, Henry's father, in 1830, from the Duke of Bedford. It overlooked the wilds of Tooting Common and extended as far as the parish church. Here Ralph Thrale built his white-painted mansion where later his son's friend, Dr Johnson, would live from 1766 to 1781.

It was to Streatham Place that the lonely Hester Thrale invited some of the greats of the day, such as Sir Joshua Reynolds, Fanny Burney and Edmund Burke, and where the resident guest, Samuel Johnson, spent many happy years pontificating and carousing. Yet Johnson was at his happiest playing with his patron's three daughters, laughing, chasing and being chased. He could also drink any man under the table except perhaps his best friend, Dr Taylor of Ashbourne, an enormously rich squire-parson whose facility to make money was legendary.

While history remembers Johnson and Mrs Thrale, Henry Thrale seems to be largely forgotten – yet Johnson had a high regard for him and said that it was 'a great mistake to think that Mrs Thrale is above him in literary attainment. She is more flippant but he has ten times more learning . . . he is a regular scholar, but her learning is that of a schoolboy in one of the lower forms.'

It is tempting to see Henry as the absent ambitious husband, hence Hester's salons and her association with Johnson. But Johnson observed that he knew 'of no man who is more master of his wife and family than Thrale – if he but holds up a finger he is obeyed'.

Henry Thrale's death, furthermore, severed Hester's and Johnson's friendship. This may have been because of loyalty but it could also have been because he expected her to continue to look after him. She had other plans. She was to become Mrs Piozzi! In 1782 Johnson wrote that on 'Sunday, went to church at Streatham. I bade farewell to the church with a kiss.' He never returned, and Streatham Place was sold and eventually pulled down to make way for the Streatham Park Estate.

The Dragoon in Drag
THE CHEVALIER D'EON DE BEAUMONT

The Chevalier d'Eon.

'Is he a he, or is he a she?' was the question on many Londoners' lips in the latter half of the eighteenth century and the beginning of the nineteenth. Huge bets were laid on the sex of this particular individual in coffee houses and on the Stock Exchange. It was rumoured that £200,000 had been wagered. The bets became international, stretching from America to Europe. The person in question was Charles Geneviève Louis Auguste André Thimothée d'Eon de Beaumont (1728–1810), Captain of the Dragoon Guards and a Chevalier de St Louis. Or was it Charlotte? He had arrived in London in 1762 as secretary of the French Embassy. His reputation had preceded him, it seems. A young lawyer at the High Court of Justice, this blond, slight-figured, dapper young man had seduced the Paris salons and shown his mettle as one of the finest swordsmen in France. His donning a lady friend's dress and passing himself off as a woman at Court seduced the king into using him for a delicate mission to Russia, as a woman – but he also distinguished himself on the battlefield.

The Chevalier had settled in a large house at 38 Brewer Street, charming London society, while doing some spying on behalf of his king. He engineered (and took the credit) that the Comte de Guerchy, his ambassador, be disgraced and recalled to France. He was then appointed ambassador and enjoyed life to the full in male and female attire, spending profligately. There was a story that he was caught in Queen Charlotte's apartments by the king and the only way out was for her attendant Cockrell to tell the king that d'Eon was a woman. London, however, was already placing bets on his sex by 1767. Londoners had assumed that this fey man who refused any female company was a female.

By 1775 the impecunious d'Eon had brokered a deal with the King of France's emissary, Caron de Beaumarchais. The king would pay all his debts and give him an allowance as long as he returned vital secret documents he had held as surety to the Secret Service, and he returned to France.

In 1777 Lord Mansfield and a King's Bench Jury, on conclusive evidence, solemnly adjudged M. d'Eon to be a woman, furthermore on 21 October 1777 (ironically, in Britain this was the feast of St Ursula, the patron saint of 11,000 virgins!) the King of France ordered that he should wear only women's clothes and call himself Charlotte – he would be legally a woman! He was thenceforward known as the 'Chevalière' d'Eon.

She was allowed to return to Brewer Street in 1785. She was no longer the slim woman, a rather stout one instead – a lusty dame dressed in black silk. She earned her living by her writings and as a mature female fencer. She even fenced with the renowned Chevalier de St Georges at Angelo's Academy at Carlton House in 1787 and beat him despite being almost twenty years older.

The French Revolution depleted the Chevalière's purse even more and in 1791 she was forced to sell her precious library of 2,000 books. Her pecuniary troubles were magnified when she was badly wounded in a sword fight and had to give up fencing. She moved to Lambeth, near Astley's Theatre, for a while but returned north of the river at the insistence of a friend, Mrs Cole, of St Pancras, only to be flung into a debtors' prison for five months in 1804. Her old friend Queen Charlotte granted her a pension of £50 per annum but this wasn't enough to keep her in frocks!

She died in May 1810 and the post-mortem findings were published on 25 May – she was a he! The Chevalier d'Eon de Beaumont was buried in St Pancras Churchyard on 28 May. He had written his own epitaph some years before:

Nu du ciel je suis descendu	I came naked from the sky
Et nu je suis sous cette pierre . . .	And naked I lie beneath this stone . . .
Donc, pour avoir vécu sur terre,	Therefore, I have neither lost nor gained anything
Je n'ai ni gagné ni perdu . . .	Whilst living on this earth . . .

My Lord's Folly

THE UNHAPPY TIMES OF THE LORD CHANCELLOR THURLOW IN KNIGHT'S HILL

As the Lord Chancellor, Edward Lord Thurlow (1731–1806), was leaving King George's wife's drawing room, a naïve and rather silly woman stopped to ask him when he would be moving into his new house. 'Madam,' said the irascible Lord Chancellor, 'the Queen has just asked me that impudent question; and as I would not tell her, I will not tell you!' Such was the effect his newly finished stately home had on him!

Lord Thurlow was huge in every respect. He was tall, loud-voiced, pompous, filled with gravitas, an excessive drinker, womaniser, had a massive ego and was street-wise. He revelled in his notoriety and basked in the spurious glory the papers afforded him. He was also rude, crude and obstreperous. Lord Byron was to relate a particularly crude story about the man when an acquaintance told Thurlow that he had seen graffiti on the park wall saying 'Death to the King'. Thurlow (right) asked him if he had ever seen the word 'cunt' written on the same wall. The hapless man said he had, to which Thurlow answered, 'and so have I for the last thirty years and yet it never made my prick stand'!

His rise to power was not due to hard work (he could never be accused of this), but more to venality. The young barrister got his first big break at Nando's coffee house in Fleet Street where his swaggering and loud political conversation got him his first well-paid defence. It was here that he also met Polly Humphrys, daughter of the coffee house owner. They were to continue an affair for the next thirty years, and she was to bear him two daughters.

He was Lord Chancellor almost continuously from 1778 till 1792. His reputation was such that he was almost always associated with the Devil. The Lampoonists had a field day. His rise to power was also matched by his hunger for an estate in the surrounds of London.

The district known as Knight's Hill started, as far as the 1746 maps show, from what is now Herne Hill spreading to Streatham Common. Lord Thurlow first rented Knight's Hill Farm and then purchased it in 1772. It stood near the present Thurlow Park Road, just off Elmcourt Road. And it was to Knight's Hill Farm that Lord Thurlow brought his pretty mistress, Miss Humphrys, for her confinements. The farm could still be seen in maps in the early nineteenth century. It was here that M'Lud started purchasing vast tracts of land. He bought Brockwell Green Farm in 1785, the Manor of Leigham Court in 1789 and various other parcels of land, the whole lot amounting to at least 1,000 acres.

The avaricious Lord Chancellor decided that he needed a house befitting his station, but he imposed a £6,000 ceiling on its construction. The location was the top of Knight's Hill and the architect for a short time was Henry Holland, who had built Carlton House and

Drury Lane Theatre. But Henry Holland proved inept and even less trustworthy than his employer! Horace Twiss, author of *The Life of Lord Eldon*, added that 'Lord Thurlow was first cheated by his architect, and then he cheated himself; for the house cost more than he expected, so he never would go into it.' Another architect, Samuel Wyatt, was employed to finish the job. The house and its magnificent park were finished in about 1787. His political opponents nicknamed him 'the King of the Gypsies', alluding to his swarthy complexion and the fact that he lived in an area known for its large gypsy community.

The ill-fated Knight's Hill House became a hugely expensive white elephant, costing at least £18,000, some say £60,000. The ageing Lord Thurlow never got over it, preferring instead to reside in Knight's Hill Farm with yet another mistress. He was to live in Norwood until his death. His grand house was pulled down shortly afterwards to make way for the development of the area. His huge personality, like his palatial residence, is long forgotten, with only a couple of roads named after him.

The Epicurean Curate
THE SORRY TALE OF DR DODD, VICAR OF EALING

He was smooth, he was refined, he was cultured and he was passionate. He was Dr William Dodd, a silken tongued, periwigged aesthete born to a scholarly Norfolk clergyman in 1729. William Dodd was undoubtedly intelligent, graduating from Clare Hall, Cambridge, with a BA in 1750. His eloquence gained him a curacy in East Ham and his success with society congregations and his cultivation of these acquired him a royal chaplaincy in 1764. His eye was on the main chance . . . and it wasn't chance that made him build a chapel in Palace Street called the Pimlico chapel, right opposite Buckingham Palace. The world came to him, Queen Charlotte and Horace Walpole among them, and the world belonged briefly to this 'Macaroni Parson'.

Dodd's eloquent and passionate sermons were published and promptly became best-sellers, and the pews occupied by his increasingly large flock were expensive. He was also a frequenter of Vauxhall and Ranelagh Gardens and openly declared himself a fan of 'the God of dancing'. He never repudiated a press accusation of an affair with a married woman of twenty-three. But the cultivation of the glitterati necessitated a more than handsome income. His was depleted by expensive venues and suppers in the 'in' places of the capital. He found himself financially embarrassed and his attempt at a slight financial legerdemain was so inept it was disastrous. Dr Dodd's mistake was to offer the Lord Chancellor's wife a 'thumping bribe', in Horace Walpole's own words. She was to secure him the rich living of St George's, Hanover Square. Unfortunately the lady told her husband who immediately informed the king, who was so incensed that he promptly deprived him of his royal chaplaincy!

Dodd thought it wise to go to France for a protracted holiday until the scandal died down. His return was no more fruitful. He sold his chapel and purchased the Manor House at Ealing in 1776 and converted it into a boarding school for boys. With powerful backers such as Lord Chesterfield he couldn't go wrong. But he had had a taste of the high life and his lifestyle was still beyond his income. It was then that he made his fatal mistake. He forged the Earl of Chesterfield's signature on a £4,200 bond, hoping to cash it in the City. Mr Manley, the recipient of the bond, became suspicious and discovered that Lord Chesterfield hadn't signed it. Manley travelled to Ealing Manor House to confront the Reverend Doctor. Dodd caved in and admitted that 'only the most urgent necessity had driven him to such a desperate expedient'.

In the debtors' prison he came to within £400 of making restitution. Despite powerful friends, Dodd was put on trial for forgery. Dr Johnson wrote him a mitigating speech which he read in court: 'my name and my crime fill the ballads – the sport of the thoughtless and the triumph of the wicked'. It was an impassioned appeal, but he was found guilty. The jury, however, recommended he receive the royal mercy. Petitions were presented to the king by the sheriffs and by Lord Percy, signed by 23,000 people, to no avail.

On 27 June 1776 the former royal chaplain was taken from Newgate Prison to Tyburn. An eye-witness recounts his last journey: 'the doctor was rendered perfectly stupid from despair. His hat was pulled over his eyes which were never raised except now and then in the course of his prayers. He came in a coach, and a very heavy shower of rain fell just upon entering the cart, and another just upon putting his nightcap. During the showers an umbrella was held over his head, which Gilly Williams, who was present, thought was inappropriate as the doctor was going to a place where he might be dried. The wind blew off his hat. Two clergymen attended him. The executioner took both hat and wig off. Why he put the wig on again I don't know, but he did and tied on a nightcap which did not fit him. I stayed until he was cut down, and put into the hearse.'

And Now for Something Completely Different

THE MAYORS OF WANDSWORTH

On the road between Wandsworth and Tooting, today's Garratt Lane, there stood early in the eighteenth century a single house called The Garrett. When Lysons wrote his *Environs of London* in 1792 this area had a cluster of about fifty houses beside a small common. It was to this hamlet that huge crowds, sometimes as many as 100,000, would converge once a year from about 1747. This phenomenon was due to a mock ceremony or election of a 'Mayor of Garratt' held at each General Election. Enclosures and their threat seem to have been one of the excuses for this election, but a more likely reason would have been a wish

The Garratt Elections.

to relieve the tedium of everyday life and create a special day for the local community. This ceremony would achieve much more impetus when such radicals as John Wilkes, Foote and Garrick would write some of the candidates' speeches.

The publicans of Wandsworth, Tooting, Battersea, Vauxhall and Clapham seized the opportunity to give this event pomp and circumstance by donating a 'purse' or sum of money to finance the new incumbent. The rules were that any 'old and disreputable street character, provided he was a favourite and something of a scandal' should wear the mayoral chains of office. In fact the candidates were chosen from people with a drink problem and with some physical deformity. The candidates would walk or ride in procession from Southwark to Garratt Lane with their retinue comprising a clerk, a recorder and a master of horse and diverse other 'officials'. There they would swear an oath at this 'insignificant dirt village in the parish of Wandsworth; a place that has had the honour of giving the title of Mayor to the most deformed and stupid of John Bull's children', on a specially erected platform – this was handed down from 'the Grand Volgee, by order of the Great Chin Kow Chipo, first Emperor of the Moon'.

The first known 'Mayor of Garratt' was 'Sir' John Harper in 1777 (every mayor was knighted by the throng as a matter of course). He was a 'man of the greatest abilities and integrity, and his estate lies wherever he goes; his wants are supplied by the oil of his tongue, and is of the strictest honour: he made an oath against work when in his youth, and was never known to break it'. An armoured knight rode in the mayoral procession of a motley crowd of bodyguards and officials. Sir John's knight or champion was Jem

Anderson, a Wandsworth breechmaker and a 'wonderful humourist'. Harper held his seat for two elections, by reason of his ready wit. On one occasion a dead cat was thrown at him and a bystander exclaimed the cat stank worse than a fox. Sir John retorted, 'That's no wonder, for you see it's a *poll*-cat!'

The most famous 'mayor' was 'Sir' Jeffrey Dunstan, a purveyor of old wigs. He was returned for three Parliaments. He usually carried his wig bag over his shoulder and to avoid being classed as a vagrant he would occasionally call out 'old wigs'. His ready humour and cheery face made him enough money not to have to beg and maintain his exalted position! He used his sometimes virulent wit to attack corruption and shady dealings in the government, which in Pitt's regime caused him to be prosecuted for using seditious expressions. He was tried, convicted and imprisoned in 1793.

The mayoralty passed to 'Sir' Harry Dimsdale on 'Sir' Jeffrey's demise, despite strong opposition from two other candidates: 'Squire' Jobson, the billsticker, and 'Lord' Goring, the barber. 'Sir' Harry was elected four times. The most glorious was when his manifesto was dated 'from my attic chamber, the dirty end of Monmouth Street'. This elaborate and increasingly expensive burlesque suffered from its own popularity. It became almost too expensive to hold as the ceremony and costumes increased in ostentation. The last known mock election was in 1826, but it seems to some that its spirit lives on in national politics!

An American at the Court of King George

CIVIL WAR GENERAL BENEDICT ARNOLD'S DUEL AT KILBURN WELLS

On 22 January 1782 the London *Daily Advertiser* reported the arrival in London, on a typically rainy, windy and cold winter's day, of Brigadier General and Mrs Arnold. Britain, it seemed, was charmed by this American couple who had settled in Portland Square. Some wags even said of the much younger Mrs Arnold that 'she is an amiable woman, and was her husband dead, would be much noticed'. But the general was very much alive and much noticed in government circles. The Secretary of State Germain received him well, as did Lord Amherst at the War Office. Both regarded him as a very sensible man, familiar with American affairs. But the Arnolds' warmest reception was at the Court of King George III. Reporters covering the Court soon noticed Benedict Arnold leaning on the arm of Sir Guy Carleton, the king and the Prince of Wales strolling in St James's Park, deep in conversation. The king, a somewhat naïve and stubborn man, requested that General Arnold draw up a paper (which was published in 1782) on his 'Thoughts on the American War', a shrewd and politically astute document on how there might be a reconciliation between the Crown and its erstwhile American colonies.

Meanwhile, in Paris, where American negotiators were concluding peace talks with the British, Benjamin Franklin wrote nervously, 'we hear much of audiences given to Arnold and his being present at Councils'.

But who was this Arnold of whom Benjamin Franklin was so frightened? Benedict Arnold (1741–1801) was a fourth-generation Connecticut American, who by the age of thirty-four was by far the richest man in the Connecticut capital, an aggressive ship's captain, successful smuggler and an accomplished dandy with a wife and two sons.

The outbreak of hostilities against the British taxes imposed on the population that led to the American War of Independence saw Captain, later Colonel Arnold as a fierce and inspired advocate of the Revolution. He adopted the military mantle with ease, and proved a natural tactician, a perfect commander and a brilliant innovator. He was above all a war-machine that used everything to his advantage. He devised a light infantry regiment, created America's first fleet – it successfully thwarted the British fleet in Valcourt Bay – and he won some morale-boosting and important battles such as the siege of Fort Ticonderaga, St John's and Crown Point. He was feared by the British who said that he was 'the most enterprising and dangerous' and respected by his peers, George Washington and Philip Schuyler. His total belief in himself, quite right as it transpired, created enemies. Congress saw him as a drain on their financial resources and reneged on many payments, but the people and the military saw him as a hero.

General Benedict Arnold.

Disheartened by the early death of his first wife and sickened by meddling politicians, the lack of any adequate remuneration from Congress and of being passed over for promotion once too often, Arnold, accompanied by his second wife and new son, defected to the British in 1780. Once the Whigs got into power public opinion changed. Arnold was lampooned and reviled by the press and he was publicly snubbed at theatres. The average Englishman thought little of deserting one's country, let alone a traitor. Arnold turned to his old occupation of trading – in which he was only moderately successful.

In 1792 a radical Whig peer, Lord Lauderdale, made an apparently unprovoked attack on Arnold in a heated Lords debate. The affronted Arnold saw his chance to try to win back his reputation and challenged the peer to a duel at Kilburn Wells (now just off Kilburn High Street). The two antagonists accompanied by their seconds, Lord Hawke was Arnold's, Charles James Fox Lauderdale's, met at 8 a.m. on Sunday 7 July 1792. Arnold fired and missed but Lauderdale refused, eventually apologising for casting aspersion on the general's character.

No country, however, likes a traitor, whatever the reason. No Briton could ever forsake his country. The rest of Arnold's tumultuous life was one of oblivion and mediocrity – one created, it seems, by his ego. Had he stuck it out he might have died a hero's death, lauded by friend and foe alike. He lies buried along with his wife at St Mary's parish church, Battersea.

The Man Who Weighed the World

HENRY CAVENDISH OF CLAPHAM, INVENTOR EXTRAORDINAIRE

The Victorian terraced houses on the junction of Cavendish Road and Clapham Common Southside were built on the site of Cavendish House, a large sprawling mansion with equally impressive grounds. The house was named after its most famous occupant, Henry Cavendish, who purchased it from the failed banker Henton Brown in 1782 and lived there until his death in 1810. This scion of one of England's most famous families is credited with being the first man to have worked out the density of the earth.

Henry Cavendish (pictured below), 'the modern Newton', was a grandson of the 2nd Duke of Devonshire. Born in 1731, he was educated privately in Hackney and then Cambridge. There he was a shy retiring student. He left without a degree but devoted the rest of his life to chemistry and science. His purchase of the solitary mansion in Clapham meant that he could bury his science and wealth in splendid isolation. He certainly wasn't adept at social intercourse and didn't even try to be civil. Dr Wollaston, a friend, said, 'the way to approach him is never to look at him, but to talk, as it were, into vacancy, and then it is not unlikely you may set him going'. Another noted, 'if men were a trouble to him, women were his abhorrence' – except, it seemed, his beautiful cousin the Duchess of Devonshire! He communicated with his housekeeper by notes on the hall table and if an unlucky maid showed herself, 'she was instantly dismissed. . . . Two ladies led a gentleman on his track, in order that he might obtain a sight of the philosopher. As he was getting over a stile, he saw to his horror that he was being watched and he never appeared in the path again.' His fashion habits never changed from the day he left university, so the locals thought him a wizard!

Cavendish had two houses, one on Clapham Common and one on the corner of Gower Street and Montagu Place. His need for privacy was so acute that he rented yet another house in Dean Street to accommodate his library. He paid a librarian to look after his books, and when he needed to refer to one he would take it and leave a receipt.

He arranged the house in Clapham as a vast laboratory, starting in the drawing room and stretching to the upper floor; the ante-room served as a forge. He even had a second staircase built so that he could avoid people. The few people who were admitted to his house were always fed a leg of mutton. Social etiquette was of virtually no importance and, in fact, all the scientist lived for was his experiments. He was described as 'a well-arranged intellectual machine, a thing without enthusiasm sympathy or happiness'. His biographer, Dr George Wilson, said 'there was nothing earnest, heroic or chivalrous in the nature of Cavendish, and as little as there was anything mean, grovelling or ignoble. He was almost passionless . . . and anything that required an emotional response was distasteful to him.' His shyness was almost a disease.

Cavendish may have shrunk from people but his written work was prolific. It was he who converted oxygen and hydrogen into water, proving that water consists of these gases; it was he who first stated the difference between animal and common electricity. His was a world where money never really mattered, especially when an uncle died in 1773 leaving him an enormous fortune. His needs were relatively simple and he left his income to accumulate.

Henry Cavendish's bank balance reached £80,000 and, eager to put this money to good use, the bank sent a senior clerk down to his house to consult him about it. The great man found this intrusion rather painful and trivial. He threatened to take the money elsewhere if they continued to pester him. The senior clerk suggested that the bank invest half the capital. His reply was 'Do so, do so! And don't come here to trouble me, or I'll remove it.'

He never allowed his portrait to be painted. His only memorial is a hasty sketch drawn by William Alexander at the Royal Society Club, which Cavendish regularly attended. This extraordinary man left £1,750,000. His heir, Lord George Cavendish, was allowed to see him once a year, for half an hour! Cavendish House later became the Clapham residence of Thomas Cubitt, the developer. It was pulled down in 1905.

At Death's Door

MR DEATH'S DRINKING ESTABLISHMENT IN BATTERSEA

Battersea pubs have come and gone; some, like the White Hart in Lombard Road, date back to 1600. Here Charles II was a frequent visitor. The Old Swan by the parish church was immortalised in song by Charles Dibdin in one of his operettas. It was also one of the most popular inns on the waterfront. The Old House in Plough Lane, long gone, was famous for its home-brewed ales, and the Raven in the High Street was also popular. The Star and Garter, an original coaching inn, also had an enviable reputation and, past what is now Battersea Park, stood the Nine Elms Tavern. Another was Ye Olde Plough Inn on St John's Hill, built in 1701 and demolished in 1874, where Dick Turpin supposedly holed up. It could well have been one of Jemmy Abershaw's hiding places, as he, rather than Turpin, was connected with the area. The present Plough was then erected on this site. Here stood an old oak under which travellers sat and drank. The Old House at Home stood near Battersea Fields not far from the Red House. A small thatched building, part pub, part farmhouse, with a reputation for its excellent egg flip, a concoction of newly laid eggs beaten into a hot ale or stout with plenty of sugar. This was a favourite Sunday morning drink for those going sporting at the Red House.

One public house, though, became famous for another reason. The Falcon at Clapham Junction claims to be the biggest pub in South London. Its namesake, the Falcon brook, runs beneath its cellars and reputedly used to keep its beers cool. Nearly 400 years ago Falcon Road was Falcon Lane, edged by hawthorn bushes on each side, enclosing meadows, orchards and gardens. The Falcon, named after the 'Falcon rising' crest of the landlords of Battersea, the St John family, ran from Streatham down Falcon Lane to the Thames right past the front door of the pub.

. . . at Death's Door.

At this time, Battersea was a small village outside London. The Falcon serviced the locals and travellers using the London Road (now Wandsworth Road). Despite its history, little is known about the landlords of the pub until 1760 when Ann Smith ran it. But the pub achieved immortal fame under the aegis of Robert Death who ran it from 1786 to 1806. Death, despite his name, was a jovial, portly gent who kept a good house and regaled his patrons with funny anecdotes.

Local undertakers would often quench their thirst at the pub after a burial – there was even a room set aside for wakes; some of these and their friends would often drink too much, and it wasn't uncommon to see a funeral party dancing on the green in front of Mr Death's tavern. The artist, John Nixon, was so amused by this scene that he painted a picture of it entitled *Drinking at Death's door*. The undertaker's director, Mr Sable, was attributed the following rhyme:

> I've kissed and I've prattled with fifty fair maids,
> Dukes, Lords, have I buried, and squires of fame,
> And people of every degree;
> But of all fine jobs that e'er came my way,
> A funeral like this for me.
> This, this is the job
> That fills the fob;
> Oh! The burying of a Nabob for me!
> Unfeather the hearse, put the Pall in the bag,
> Give the horses some oats and some hay;
> Drink our next merry meeting and quackery's increase,
> With three times three and hurra!

Another cantata for the picture was also published at the same time:

> Oh stop not here, ye sottish wights
> For Purl, nor ale, nor gin,
> For if you stop, whoe'er alights,
> By Death is taken in.
>
> When having eat and drank your fill,
> Should ye, O hapless case,
> Neglect to pay your Landlord's bill –
> Death stares you in the face.
>
> With Grief sincere, I pity those
> Who've drawn themselves this scrape in,
> Since from this dreadful grip, Heaven knows,
> Alas! There's no escaping.
>
> This one advice my friend pursue,
> Whilst you have life and breath,
> Ne'er pledge your host for if you do,
> You'll surely drink to Death.

The premises were demolished and rebuilt in 1883 and renamed the Falcon. Death has passed on but the jollity remains!

An Academy of Substance
BYRON'S STAY AT DR GLENNIE'S ACADEMY IN DULWICH

Georgian Camberwell and Dulwich, apart from their regular schools, were also host to select smaller academies run by widowed ladies or by clergymen. One such was Dr Thomas Ready's Peckham Collegiate School, one of whose boarders was the poet Robert Browning (1812–89). Another was the Wanostrocht Academy founded by a Belgian, Dr Nicholas Wanostrocht (1745–1812), who was also a successful author of school textbooks. Miss Pace's School in Camberwell Grove could count as one of its alumni the future statesman Joseph Chamberlain.

On the edge of Dulwich Park, at the junction of Lordship Lane and Dulwich Common, stands the Grove Tavern. A pub has stood on this site for at least three centuries, although it has suffered some changes of use! In 1704 it was the Green Man and by the end of the eighteenth century it ceased to be a pub and became a private residence called Dulwich Grove. One of its more celebrated residents was Lord Thurlow, the Lord Chancellor, who lived there from about 1780 while he was having a much grander residence built on Knight's Hill.

On completion of the much grander house, Dulwich Grove became the Grove House Academy run by Dr Glennie. Glennie, a member of the Dulwich Club, a literary gathering of such illuminati as Dr Babington, Charles Dickens, Thomas Campbell and William Thackeray, held benevolent and liberal sway over his select pupils, some of whom were the future General Le Marchant, the colonial administrator, Sir Donald McLeod, Lieutenant Governor of the Punjab, Captain Barclay, the celebrated pedestrian who walked 1,000 miles in a thousand hours, and Lord Byron.

His neurotic mother had brought the young Lord Byron (1788–1824) to London. She had decided that he should go to Dr Glennie's Academy. He was to stay there from 1789 for two years. He was not a natural academic, but enjoyed his stay there, particularly because it took him away from his mother's incessant tantrums. In one instance she screamed the place down in front of Dr Glennie and the other students. One turned to Byron and said, 'Byron, your mother's a fool', to which the reply was, 'I know'.

Once a week the pupils would congregate in the spacious entrance hall of the academy to listen to the poet Thomas Campbell or to another member of the Dulwich Club, and on Saturday evenings the academicians would, along with other Dulwich residents and visitors, listen to the Dulwich concerts.

Dr Glennie spoke to Tom Moore of Byron's ambition to excel in athletics, despite having a club-foot. 'An ambition', wrote Glennie, 'which I have found to prevail in general in young persons labouring under similar defects of nature.' Byron and his fellow students would abscond to Dulwich Woods and pretend to be brigands, shouting to unsuspecting passers-by 'Stand and deliver'!

Dr Glennie's Academy, Dulwich.

A friend gave Dr Glennie a pamphlet describing the shipwreck of the *Juno* off the coast of Arracan in 1795. The pamphlet was of particular interest because it recounted the touching and tragic story of two fathers on board the ship parting with their dying sons. All the boys read it and Byron re-told it in *Don Juan*, Canto II;

> There were two fathers in this ghastly crew,
> And with then their two sons, of whom the one
> Was more robust and hardy to the view,
> But he died early; and when he was gone,
> His nearest messmate told his sire, who threw
> One glance on him and said, 'Heaven's will be done;
> I can do nothing!' and he saw him thrown
> Into the deep without a tear or groan.

Life for the aspiring poet was idyllic in Dulwich, the narrow lanes, hedgerows and little dells watered by streams, undulating hills and parks, shady walks where he was 'safe from all intrusion but that of the Muses' where:

> Spring green lanes,
> With all the dazzling field-flowers in their prime,
> And gardens haunted by the nightingale's
> Long trills and gushing ecstasies of song.

This carefree life ceased when his mother decided that he needed more discipline. In 1801 he said goodbye to leafy Dulwich and started his life at Harrow.

When All the Saints
WHEN THE CLAPHAM SAINTS ABOLISHED SLAVERY

George Trevelyan, the historian, wrote in his life of Lord Macaulay: 'at Clapham, as elsewhere, the old order is changing. What was once the home of Zachary stands almost within the swing of the bells of a stately and elegant Roman Catholic chapel; and the pleasant mansion of Lord Teignmouth, the cradle of the Bible Society, is now turned into a convent of monks.'

Clapham has indeed changed dramatically from the country atmosphere of the late ceighteenth century. St Mary's was built in the grounds of Lord Teignmouth's mansion, where members of a deeply evangelical community of rich City merchants congregated to change the religiously moribund and capitalistic views of a rich England. Here Henry Thornton, William Wilberforce, Zachary Macaulay, James Stephen, Charles Grant, John Shore and the local rector John Venn saw it as their mission to save souls through faith and good works. From their opulent mansions, now disappeared, these politically powerful individuals chose to awaken society to a sense of the great importance of personal religion. John Venn, the rector for twenty-one years, preached the gospel with zeal and fervour in the new church, the Holy Trinity, on Clapham Common, built with funds from these great merchants.

Indeed Clapham had been a hotbed of Nonconformity for two hundred years. The sinners who attended this church became known as the Clapham Saints or the Clapham Sect. One of the most famous of these was William Wilberforce (1759–1833), who from a particularly wild youth turned into one of the most vociferous voices of the sect. It was largely through his tireless efforts that the Bill for the abolition of slavery was passed one month after his death in 1833.

Holy Trinity Church, Clapham Common.

Yet these affluent do-gooders had their detractors. Tom Ingoldsby spoke sneeringly of Clapham as that 'sanctified ville' and William Cobbett, the radical campaigner and an idealist with no time for Christianity, loathed Wilberforce. At the climax of the campaign against the abolition of slavery Cobbett declared, 'so often as they agitate this question, with all its cant, the relief of 500,000 blacks; so often will I remind them of the one million two hundred thousand white paupers in England and Wales.' He was even more vitriolic fifteen years later when he talked about the labourer's bill of fayre in the glorious times of high prices: 'A gallon loaf and three pence a week for each person in a labourer's family! – That is to say about 18 ounces of bread a day, no meat and nothing and else for food and THREE PENCE to find a drink, clothing, washing, fire, light and lodging for the week! Gracious God! And this is England! And was this what was allowed by English magistrates to English labourers in husbandry? And at this very moment was Mr Wilberforce receiving the incessant plaudits for his human exertions in favour of the black slaves in the colonies? And did he never utter one word on behalf of the poor creatures, the wretched human beings of Wiltshire?'

A less excitable and more balanced critic was William Hazlitt. He accused Wilberforce of acting from mixed motives, of serving two masters, God and Mammon – in short he accused Wilberforce of seeking to be all things to all men, anxious to have everyone's praise. He added: 'Mr Wilberforce is far from being a hypocrite; but he is, we think, as fine a specimen of moral equivocation as can well be conceived.' Henry Thornton, the banker, had a high regard for Wilberforce: 'Some good may come out of our Clapham system. Wilberforce is a candle that should not be hid under a bushel.'

Yes, these saints abolished slavery, created the Bible Society and changed colonial laws. They tempered their idealism with practical awareness, very much as do some of the politicians of today.

Portrait of a Painter

GEORGE ROMNEY, ONE-TIME RESIDENT OF HAMPSTEAD

It is not difficult to ascertain the importance of British pre-Victorian artists in the Pantheon of international painters. George Stubbs, the painter of horses *par excellence* and author of the monumental book on *The Anatomy of a Horse*, John Constable, the landscape painter, Angelica Kauffman, the painter of classical mythology and portraits, are but three of a select band of artists whose works are held in high repute. There are others, too many to mention, who also rank among the great of British art, among whom Thomas Gainsborough, the founder of the true English School of painting, Sir Joshua Reynolds, portrait painter and President of the Royal Academy and George Romney (1734–1802), who at one time rivalled Reynolds. Romney was to live at Holly Bush Hill, Hampstead, from 1796 to 1799.

George Romney (right) was the son of a cabinetmaker. Born near Dalton-in-Furness in Lancashire, he entered his father's business when he was about ten. In 1755 he was apprenticed to a journeyman painter, Christopher Steele, who specialised in portrait and genre painting. Together they toured the northern towns, York, Lancaster and Kendal. It was at Kendal that he caught a fever and was nursed by a local girl. In his gratitude he married her in 1756. Despite the birth of two children the marriage was not a success – probably because the young artist had been too impetuous in his gratitude and was too ambitious to stay in one place. He also realised that his provincial wife would not be an asset. He left his family for London.

His first London success was a picture entitled *Death of General Wolfe* in 1762, for which he was awarded £25 in a Royal Society of Arts competition. He would have won second prize had not Joshua Reynolds quashed this. The prize was given to Reynolds' friend John Hamilton Mortimer. Romney never forgave Reynolds. He settled in Long Acre where he established himself as a popular portrait painter. He also produced historical compositions that were less well received. By the 1770s he was making more than £1,000 (£56,000 nowadays) a year as a portrait painter. His travels to Italy in this decade strongly influenced his style.

Back from Italy in 1775, Romney resided at Cavendish Square where his reputation soon equalled that of Reynolds. His style was flattering; he avoided any suggestion of the character or the sensibilities of the sitter. It was this dispassionate flattery, his supreme ability at grinding and mixing colours and the influence of the flowing rhythms and easy poses of Roman classical sculpture that made him so popular. The most productive and possibly the period in which he was at his best in his craft was about 1780–1, when he met his inspiration, the young and stunningly beautiful Emma Hart, later Nelson's paramour Emma Hamilton. She exercised a morbid fascination over him. 'Divine Emma' appeared in more than fifty paintings, almost all of them painted from memory.

Romney's sensitive and introspective temperament found Central London too much. He tried to find some inspiration in Kilburn but in 1796 he turned to Hampstead. He purchased the large house, stables and two plots of land at the top of Holly Bush Hill, opposite Bolton House. He planned many additions to the house as well as a Studio for himself on the land he had bought. One innovation was a hatch between the kitchen and dining room so that he and his friends could be served piping hot steaks. Once finished, the house was let out and he lived at The Mount above Heath Street, until his studio was finished. But he moved in too soon.

He was his own architect. It was a disaster. His friend Haley said that 'the painting room and gallery had been nobly planned, but all domestic conveniences overlooked'. The place was still damp from the decorators' work and he 'never enjoyed a day of good health afterwards'. In 1799 the ailing Romney left for Kendal to be nursed by the wife he had not seen for years. He was never to return to London.

Lady Be Good

THE TUMBLING TIMES OF NORWOOD'S MRS MARY NESBITT

The *Morning Chronicle* of 25 September 1797 had an article on a lady whose involvement with matters of British diplomacy, concerning French royalists after the Revolution and the French Directory, were of national importance – its premise was an unusual one because, contrary to public mores, it advocated and encouraged the breadth of vision and the intelligence of a *woman*. 'This celebrated woman is likely to suffer a great deal of impertinent slander on account of the allusion to her name. It certainly is no discredit to

Mrs Nesbitt.

the sex that an accomplished woman is capable of playing the part so conspicuous and interesting to the state of the Nations, as that which Mrs Nesbitt has lately performed.'

The eighteenth century saw much change in European politics. England was no exception. The people, as today, were moderate Republicans. The monarchy was under sufferance and no Briton would tolerate the slur that he was a subject – he was a citizen. Women, whose financial power hadn't yet been destroyed by the Industrial Revolution, were perhaps not quite as enfranchised but held power that no man could do without.

The luscious twentyish-year-old fine-legged filly that was Poll Davis made good use of her attributes in the City and the West End in the 1760s. Her sharp wit, cool head and more obvious feminine attributes made her a wealthy woman. She also worked as an artist's model. Sir Joshua Reynolds painted her several times. She eventually hooked herself into matrimony with a besotted and naïve young merchant banker Alexander Nesbitt, of Norwood, whom she bled dry. Divested of his wealth, land and self-respect Mr Nesbitt sank into oblivion and disappeared.

Young Mrs Mary Nesbitt emerged with a fine house and an income to boot! Her next goal was to inveigle and possibly marry further up the social ladder. The Hon. Augustus Hervey (1724–79), captain in the Royal Navy, was married to the infamous Elizabeth Chudleigh and had an impressive list of amorous conquests as well as battle honours. He was also a Norwood neighbour – and theirs was a perfect partnership. He was tall, athletic and a perfect foible to her wiles. His house, Park House, 'was in a woody recess, divided by a space of cleared land enclosed form Norwood Common', to which he could retire from the artificiality of Georgian life into the arms of his amour. They lived together in Norwood and at his town house from 1771 until his death.

Bristol's early death (Hervey had become the Earl of Bristol in 1775) made Mrs Mary Nesbitt a very wealthy woman in her own right. She cultivated politics and moved behind the scenes of power, involving herself in foreign policy, and was also a secret agent for the Crown. Her house, although not the venue for great salons, became a more important venue for international politics. King George himself held Privy Council meetings with his ministers in her ballroom. Other minor but no less important members of the government became close to the merry widow: these included George Rose, an 'éminence grise' of Pitt's, and Lord Mulgrave. Even her deceased husband's cousins, close neighbours, the Champion de Crespignys of Camberwell, visited her many times socially, as did the daughters of the bachelor Lord Thurlow.

Mrs Nesbitt introduced many hungry young politicos to Pitt's government including her dead lover's natural son's best friend, John Stanley (later Lord Stanley), whose family has long been associated with South London.

She was to remain chatelaine of Park House until her death in 1825. Her movements in the two last decades of the eighteenth century remain mysterious. What is known, however, is that she spent some time on the continent cultivating new friends such as Josephine de Beauharnais, Napoleon's future empress, Mme Tussaud and Madame de Staël. She travelled to Holland, Switzerland, Italy and various German states. There is no tangible proof that she was an agent for the Crown but there are several instances in foreign despatches where she is accused of assisting royalists.

Park House eventually became a convent school, the Virgo Fidelis School, a suitable epitaph for this remarkable Grande Dame.

Fall from Eden

THE MURDER OF SAMUEL MATTHEWS, THE DULWICH HERMIT

Dulwich has long been regarded as a quiet rural backwater, especially pre-twentieth century. But when a crime is committed in an apparently quiet and well-ordered environment, its very existence shatters the veneer of respectability of the area, showing it to be no different from others. Dulwich's rural idyll was described as 'pleasantly retired having no high road passing through it . . . formerly the resort of much company on account of a medicinal spring'. A more lavish praise was 'Oh ecstasy of thought! Gentle hills, dark valleys, far spreading groves, luxuriant cornfields, magnificent prospect, then sparkled before us.' Dulwich Wood, now no longer, was immense, intersected with devious paths. Here Byron, the student, made the wood one of his favourite haunts and gypsies moved about freely. Here also Charles I's Court had hunted deer.

On a darker note, however, it was here that Samuel Matthews, the Dulwich hermit, was brutally murdered by persons unknown in 1802. The wood had been gradually disappearing

since Edward Alleyn had purchased the manor in 1604 and issued an edict that 'twenty acres of wood be felled and sold yearly'. But there was still enough there for Samuel Matthews. A Salopian by birth, Matthews (left) had originally lived in Cheapside. At the time of his arrival in Dulwich towards the end of the eighteenth century he was reputedly a man of means – he owned two watches!

His wife's death, it seems, was the reason for his turning into a recluse. He set up home in College Wood despite fierce opposition from the locals: he was chased away on several occasions. Finally he was given permission to dig a cave and build a hut over it. The walls were of mud and clay and the roof was covered by ferns and furze.

Matthews was determined to live a natural life, using nature's resources to the full: kindling an open-air fire, making an oven with stones and clay, using local streams for washing, bathing and drinking water, as well as making a tree his larder. He rarely spoke to anyone except to say 'Hello neighbour'. His simple manners and kindliness soon won over the hardest of local hearts. Neighbours started visiting and the word got around. Travellers began to drop in, locals pointing out a clump of birches behind which his cave was situated.

Crowds would see him on Sundays. His fame spread and his popularity increased: people donated clothes, food and drink, especially at Christmas, and sometimes he would sell his home-made bread and beer to passers-by. Matthews refused to leave his beloved cave for too long. Even in a particularly hard winter, a local resident who had taken a shine to him begged him to use the hayloft at the back of the house – but he refused. Apart from a cat – a companion for a little while – he led a happy life as a recluse, pacing the ground and talking to himself. Only once, it seemed, was he frightened in his solitude. Night was falling and he hurried back home. Just about to enter the cave, his instincts warned him that it was already occupied. Stick in hand, Matthews cautiously crept in only to find another homeless soul sleeping on his bed of ferns. He let the stranger sleep the night and gave him a hearty breakfast.

On Tuesday morning, 28 December 1802, a youth, a regular visitor, discovered the Dulwich hermit's body at the entrance to his cave. The seventy-year-old's jaw was broken in two places and under his arm was a 7-foot oak branch hooked at the end. It seemed that the murderers had used this branch to hook the old man out of his cave. The branch had been cut off a nearby tree and its twigs had been stripped off with a knife. These were shown at the inquest held at the French Horn pub in Dulwich. Matthews had been in the pub on Monday evening, purchased some beer and had some change in his pocket. But his pockets had been turned out. A verdict of 'wilful murder' was returned and the local gypsies were hunted as scapegoats. Samuel Matthews was buried in the Dulwich Chapel cemetery, a huge crowd following the Dulwich hermit to his grave.

Pitt's Last Embrace

THE LAST DAYS OF WILLIAM PITT THE YOUNGER IN PUTNEY

In 1803 the MP for the rotten borough of Appleby leased Bowling Green House. The house once stood on the borders of Putney Heath by the Telegraph pub. William Pitt the Younger (1759–1806), once MP for Appleby and then Cambridge University, had been, at twenty-four, the youngest serving prime minister. This brilliant son of an equally brilliant father, who had also been PM, was to live and breathe politics for the whole of his short life.

William Pitt had crossed the river many times during his life, being a frequent visitor to his friend William Wilberforce. He had designed Henry Thornton's library in Clapham. He'd duelled rather badly with George Tierney, MP for Southwark, on Wimbledon Common and been a frequent visitor to Cannizaro House, home of Henry Dundas, later Lord Melville. It was in Cannizaro House that Dundas encouraged him to drink to epic proportions.

By the time Pitt (pictured) leased Bowling Green House the ravages of alcohol had taken their toll. The French Revolution, initially viewed as a domestic issue and thus of no concern to Britain, had suddenly assumed a menacing mantle as parliamentary reform groups appeared to be in contact with French Revolutionaries. Napoleon was casting a shadow over the whole of Europe.

Pitt's second term as prime minister started in 1804 amid the tumult of the Napoleonic Wars. The French defeat at the battle of Trafalgar was to make Pitt the 'saviour of Europe'. But Napoleon's crushing defeat of the Russians and Austrians at the Battle of Austerlitz in December 1805 made Pitt hurry home from recuperation in Bath on 9 January 1806. He had only two weeks to live. He was emaciated, weak, feeble and low and had only recently got over a severe bout of gout. He couldn't eat and only drank madeira and water. In fact alcohol had been his mainstay for some years. Any solid food brought on spasms of vomiting and he complained of continual stomach pains. On arrival at the house, his devoted niece, Lady Hester Stanhope, recalled that 'the first thing I heard was a voice so changed, that I said to myself, It is all over with him. He was supported by the arms of two people and had a stick, or two sticks, in his hands, and, as he came up, panting for breath . . . I retreated, little by little, not to put him to the pain of making a bow to me, or of speaking.'

Two of the country's leading physicians, Dr Matthew Baillie and Dr Henry Reynolds, were summoned. Both confirmed that there seemed to be no organic damage. Dr Farquhar, Pitt's personal physician, was still unsure. He had made Pitt promise that he would rest and do no work but was shocked to find members of his cabinet at the house. He prescribed him opiates in a vain attempt to cure him. Lord Wellesley, recently returned from India, went to see Pitt and couldn't understand how no-one realised that 'notwithstanding Mr Pitt's kindness and cheerfulness, I saw that the hand of death was fixed on him'.

By the 15th he was very weak. He seemed to rally on the 16th, but in the ensuing days he got progressively weaker. He could take no food, only liquids, and these alcoholic. On the 22nd Pitt's friend Tomline had the task of telling Pitt he was dying. Tomline's later letter to his wife is painful: 'I went to see him this morning about eight – he knew me, though he had been very rambling and confused in the night. I proposed to pray with him, but he objected from an opinion of the inefficacy of prayer in the last moment.'

Pitt died quietly on 23 January of renal failure and cirrhosis of the liver. He died, like his father, almost broke. His will showed a markedly large bequest to Tom Steele, a young man he had long been associated with. He had achieved much. He had devised a system for British rule in India. He carried the Union with Ireland, with lamentable consequences, and invented the income tax, a blessing continued to this day!

Mrs Siddons's Paddington Idyll
THE PADDINGTON TRAGEDIENNE SARAH SIDDONS

The eighteenth century spawned a new breed of actors and a refreshingly modern attitude to the theatrical stage. Edmund Keane and David Garrick were the monarchs of the stage. Garrick, the supreme actor-manager of his time, was to set a precedent. He single-handedly modernised the theatre scene by setting out new guidelines for the cost of seats and insisting that all the paying public remain seated in the auditorium. He also created the modern concept of drama. He was an icon whose swan-song was to try to make the immature young mother, Sarah Siddons, future denizen of Paddington, a star. She was David Garrick's new protégée at Drury Lane in 1775 whose personality, extraordinary stage presence and beauty dominated the English stage for the next fifty years. He saw her potential, but she wasn't then ready and her London debut in the 1775–6 season was almost disastrous.

Sarah Siddons, née Kemble (1755–1831), was arguably the greatest English tragic actress. She was the contemporary of Napoleon, Nelson, James Watt, George Stephenson and Wellington. The Kembles were a provincial acting family, conscious of their superiority, with marked good looks and blessed with a more than adequate acting capability. They were all Catholic apart from Sarah. In 1773 she married, aged eighteen, the middling 28-year-old actor William Siddons and he became her manager.

Sarah returned to touring the provinces, Scotland, Ireland and, following a triumphant season in Bath, she tried the capital again in 1782. Her first play was Garrick's *Fatal Marriage* at the Strand Theatre. This was her forte – she was a tragedienne *par excellence*. The dress she wore set off a fashion and she totally seduced the critics and public alike. Mme de Stael eulogised her. Byron was to state that 'of actors Cooke was the most natural, Kemble the most supernatural, Kean the medium of the two, but Mrs Siddons was worth them all put together'.

She and her brother John Philip Kemble, the actor-manager, were the monarchs of the time. She minted the role of Lady Macbeth and actresses since have modelled themselves on her creation. When she was sixty-one Hazlitt said that 'to have seen Mrs Siddons was an event in everyone's life'. The great portrait painters Sir Joshua Reynolds and her devoted admirer Sir Thomas Lawrence painted the toast of London.

In the late 1790s she suffered from severe back pains. She took the bold step of trying out the then innovative electric shock therapy (the first high profile personality to have this done), and was cured.

Sarah Siddons resolved to retire once she had amassed £10,000. This she did by the end of the eighteenth century. But tragedy struck. She lost two of her children and had her last one, Cecilia, when she was forty-three.

In April 1805 the tragedienne Mrs Siddons moved into a cottage at Westbourne Green, (pictured) now part of the Paddington Canal. Westbourne Farm was in the country. It was, as she put it, 'that dear little spot my home', with its green laurels, wooden palings covered with trailing plants, clinging honeysuckle that climbed over her lattice windows.

It was idyllic for the middle-aged actress. She and her daughter Cecilia were to live there until 1817. Mrs Siddons had had a very busy life and needed to be kept occupied apart from the token appearances she made on the London stage. She took up clay modelling, built a studio on to the house and made busts of her family and friends. She entertained her friends, such as Mrs Piozzi (the widowed Mrs Thrale), and distinguished members of the gentry. Her idyll was more a state of mind, not the rural delights of this backwater. Her weight ballooned and chairmen were beginning to grumble when they had to carry her. Some three years later she got stuck in her armchair when she played Queen Katherine in *Henry VIII*. She was vegetating, and felt she had to leave to rejoin the buzz of London's West End.

She left for 27 Upper Baker Street where she lived the rest of her long life in spartan but articulate splendour. She lies buried at St Mary's Church, Paddington, her old parish church where the only non-Catholic Kemble worshipped.

A Duel of Wits

THE POET THOMAS MOORE'S AFFAIR OF HONOUR IN CHALK FARM

'The harp that once through Tara's halls' and ''Tis the last rose of summer' are two Irish ballads that are forever part of the English language. These were penned by an Irish genius, Thomas Moore (1779–1852), who made London his home and Chalk Farm his nadir.

Thomas Moore is no longer an Irish icon. Yet, once, after Daniel O'Connell, he was the greatest Irishman of his day. He was born to please; he supported himself by the pen and spent much of his life in great houses where ministers of state talked politics, history was discussed by historians and poetry by poets. This Dublin poet, like many Irish of the day, realised that London would be his pot of gold, so he matriculated at the Temple to read for the bar and settled there in 1799. By the end of the year this piano virtuoso (for he was that too) had his songs performed. No mention was ever made of his legal studies! He was in London for the duration.

His first publication *Anacreon* appeared in July 1800 to encouraging press comment and he was dubbed 'Anacreon Moore' by the *Morning Post*. This young man whose 'eyes were dark and brilliant; his nose was slightly upturned, giving an expression of fun to his face; he was fair and somewhat ruddy with rich dark brown hair curled all over his head; his forehead was broad and strongly marked; and his voice, not powerful, was exquisitely sweet, especially when he was singing', was the model of the young gallants of the period. So were his friends, Robert Emmet, Lord Byron, Samuel Croker, William Spencer and a host of others.

By 1806 Moore was one of the most famous men of his day. His poems, his wit and his writings were giving him a comfortable lifestyle. The *Edinburgh Review* was one of the foremost journals of the day. Each time Moore published, its editor, Francis Lord Jeffrey, delivered his comments. His first book was judged 'remarkable

Thomas Moore.

Chalk Farm.

for its precocity'; the second was a 'succès de scandale'. His third, *Epistles, Odes and Other Poems* was harshly criticised as a 'style so wantonly voluptuous it is at once effeminate and childish'. Jeffrey went on to say that the poems were an insult to women's delicacy. Moore, offended, challenged Jeffrey to a duel.

Moore takes up the account. 'I must have slept pretty well; for Hume, I remember, had to wake me in the morning; and the chaise being in readiness, we set off for Chalk Farm.' Seconds were appointed and a surgeon was called. It was the first time the two men had met. They took to each other at once. The inefficient seconds fumbled with the bullets and Hume, Moore's second, was asked to load both pistols. The antagonists waited uneasily. 'What a beautiful morning it is', said Jeffrey. 'Yes, a morning made for better purposes', Moore replied.

The seconds then placed the two in position and retired. They raised their pistols and awaited the order to fire. It never came. Police officers rushed out from behind a hedge, disarmed the opponents and took them to Bow Street. They stayed there and talked literary matters, and this sealed their friendship. Bail was eventually met and the two left. On his return to Bow Street the officer gave Moore a nasty reception. There was no bullet in Jeffrey's pistol. The magistrate suspected foul play. It was very embarrassing, as Hume, who had been in charge of loading the pistols, had had to absent himself for a few moments. Hume accompanied Moore back to the magistrate who was mollified by his statement.

The report reached Fleet Street and an official statement was required to avert the ridicule. The offending newspaper agreed to publish but Hume refused to sign, saying that he didn't know who Jeffrey's second was!

Why did he fail Moore? Was it devotion to Moore? Whatever the motive, Moore was the buffoon, but his works continued to sell.

The Intrigues of Antraigues

THE BRUTAL DEMISE OF A FRENCH ARISTOCRATIC SPY IN BARNES

It was to England that a particular European émigré arrived with his wife and young son on 3 September 1806. Emmanuel Henri Louis Alexandre de Launay, Comte d'Antraigues, was no ordinary European emigrant. The Comte d'Antraigues (1753–1812) was huge, tall, handsome, arrogant and hot-tempered. He was moreover a member of France's elite, a provincial noble with Court connections. His early life had been plagued by the fact that he was intelligent, but not as bright as he wanted to be, and he was a noble, but not of the upper nobility. These combinations proved dangerous in the extreme. The impressionable young man needed direction – army life did nothing for his massive ego, but the writings of Jean-Jacques Rousseau directed the vain, egocentric and envious young man to a position of power in the dying days of the French monarchy. By 1789 he had become one of the most famous, outspoken and detested Reformist MPs in France – a revolutionary. But the

Revolution was not for him. He fled to Switzerland, married an opera singer, and started plotting and scheming among the royalist émigrés in Prussia and other German states. His connections, his name and his intelligence enabled him to become one of the most effective counter-espionage agents of the period . . . and one of the most feared and loathed men in Europe, with a unique spy network.

He was employed by Spain, Russia (for whom he had created a treatise on national schooling, later adopted by France) and Sweden, acquiring ministerial appointments and honours from different governments. His and his family's Pimpernellian escape from the clutches of Napoleon in Italy gained him a formidable enemy, Bonaparte himself. Escape was necessary, indeed mandatory. Robert Canning, the English foreign secretary, valued d'Antraigues' information, particularly his use as an agent who could represent Britain's interests with the Russians. George III, on the other hand, did not like the idea of a French intriguer on English soil.

The count lived at 45 Devonshire Street and later at 7 Queen Anne Street West. He also purchased a country retreat in the small village of Barnes, on Barnes Terrace. It was a property overlooking the Thames to Chiswick Meadows. He and his family would spend four days a week, Sunday to Wednesday, in Barnes,

Emmanuel, Comte d'Antraigues.

which was sufficiently removed from Richmond and Twickenham, two émigré strongholds whose members mistrusted the count. D'Antraigues did prove useful to the British government, albeit in dribs and drabs. His London properties were burgled in 1808, making him suspicious that his enemies were looking for his invaluable documents.

Mme d'Antraigues became more harsh and demanding, taking it out on the servants, their son and the count himself. Several servants left her employ. Finally a friend recommended Lorenzo, a Piedmontese cook and general servant, who arrived in April 1812. This new servant was hot-tempered and resented being told by his mistress how to cook Italian dishes. The countess threatened him with deportation, a threat which would have disastrous consequences.

On the morning of 22 July 1812 Lorenzo had had a few drinks at the White Hart pub. The count and countess had ordered a carriage for 8 a.m. The count was seeing Mr Canning at 10 a.m. The ensuing catalogue of events is somewhat blurred. Lorenzo refused to do his mistress's bidding, and ran into the house, hotly pursued by her. The count heard the commotion and ran down the stairs only to be shot at several times by Lorenzo. Lorenzo missed and stabbed the count for good measure, also stabbing the countess on his way down. The countess seems to have dragged herself out to try to call someone – but it was too late. The count and his wife died soon afterwards and Lorenzo shot himself.

The count and his wife were buried in St Pancras old church, while Lorenzo was buried only 100 yards away, much to the disgust of the locals. His body was hung on a gibbet for a short while. The government impounded all the count's papers and the European politicians heaved a collective sigh of relief!

La Dame Mal Gardée!

MARY ANNE CLARKE, THE COURTESAN, OF HAMPSTEAD

In 1807 a pretty and vivacious 35-year-old lady, her brother and her three children sought refuge in the quiet and discreet village of Hampstead. Their lodgings were on Heath Street and belonged to William Nicholls, an Overseer of the Poor. Mr Nicholls hadn't banked on so many bedrooms being used and complained that 'she occupied the whole house almost'. The 'lady' was none other than Mary Anne Clarke (1772–1852), the celebrated mistress of the Duke of York. She was to live in Hampstead for nine months, not as previously thought ten years. After two years of peregrination she had come to hide, lick her wounds and try to kick-start her life again. This would never happen. She would die impecunious in France.

Mary Anne Clarke, born Mary Ann Thompson, spent her youth in Bowl and Pin Alley, Chancery Lane, with her family and stepfather Robert Farquhar. It was a tough area where some of the most hardened prostitutes plied their trade. Her stepfather, a compositor for a printing firm, taught her to read and write and would often ask her to read copy for proof correction. No doubt this helped her to increase her general knowledge and her understanding of the English language.

This high-spirited girl was already putting out feelers on how to advance herself at the tender age of thirteen! She was a good-time girl, one who saw life as a game of chance and who boldly bid for the highest stakes. She had nothing to lose. Poverty was hard and odious and was a stranglehold to be broken, whatever the cost. Her escape route was to elope with the second son of a wealthy builder, Joseph Clarke. They had two children before they married in 1792. Joseph did not inherit, nor did he work; he played and drank and finally disappeared from sight well before 1800.

Mrs Clarke, the single mother of three children, was alone and virtually penniless. She was at a crossroads. Domestic work was out of the question so she decided to find a rich lover who could look after her and her children. Her first conquest was a barrister baronet with whom she lived in Wiltshire. But he refused to make a financial settlement. They soon parted and back in London she embarked on a string of affairs with London knights, none of whom wished to part with money.

It galled Mrs Clarke that it was easier to get into the beds of the aristocracy than to get money out of their pockets. She even made the mistake of falling in love with an aristocratic gigolo who had no money but taught her much about life in the upper echelons of society.

How Mary Anne met Frederick, Duke of York, in 1803, is a matter for conjecture; it could have been through a mutual acquaintance. It was, nevertheless, the start of an embarrassing friendship, for the duke anyhow. Frederick Duke of York, of 'The Grand Old Duke of York' fame, was twelve years her senior, fat and bored. The duke's duchess was not gay and scintillating – but Mary Anne was. She was the antidote to the German protocol of Court life and made him forget his army duties, which he took as seriously as his wine and gambling. He had eyes only for her, and when the affair became public property the Lampoonists had a field day:

> To gaze and kindle at thy charms,
> And life to spend in thy fond arms;
> And if it would not be too heavy,
> I there would always hold my levee.

Mary Anne was placed in a house in Park Lane, then one at 18 Gloucester Place. Here Madame received and used her influence with the duke to procure commissions in the army.

The affair lasted just over two years. By then the duke realised his mistress was too expensive and too demanding. A broken promise of £400 p.a. for life for Mrs Clarke and a Public Inquiry into the Duke of York's army conduct in 1809 revealed the connection, much ribald comment followed and this ensured that Mme Clarke's reputation was never restored.

The Man Who Walked Alone

THE PECULIAR TRAVELS OF GENERAL JOHN REID

The silent, tall, thin, elderly angular man dressed in a dirty drab coat, a small cocked hat, black breeches, his hair in a pigtail and holding a cane in one hand, the other hand slipped into his coat, would never alter his constitutional from 1788 until his death in 1807.

General John Reid (1722–1807) never changed his daily walks. He would walk melancholically down one side of Piccadilly, through Hyde Park, along Kensington Gardens and return up the other side of Piccadilly on to the Strand, Fleet Street, and St Paul's Churchyard, walking on to the Bank of England; and then the solitary figure would then retrace his steps back to his lodgings on the Haymarket, ignoring all those he chanced to meet.

The 'Walking Rushlight' as he became generally known, was deemed a poor man, judging by his worn and dirty garb. No-one knew his name until he died in 1807. It was then established that he had been an army general and had left £50,000 to found a professorship in music at Edinburgh University.

Just who was this eccentric loner who perambulated the City and the West End? He was born John Robertson, the son of a Scottish laird, Alexander Robertson of Straloch, and his wife. He was educated at Edinburgh University where he read law, and, adopting his mother's maiden name, Reid, obtained a commission in Lord Loudun's regiment of Highlanders in 1745. He served on the Hanoverian side in the '45 rebellion and saw active service in the Netherlands, Martinique and British North America. He served under James Wolfe in Canada as a lieutenant colonel and distinguished himself in several battles.

Reid purchased some 35,000 acres of land in Vermont which were subsequently seized by New England settlers in 1774 and despite having recourse to the law he lost his claim to his acres at the outbreak of the American War of Independence. This committed professional soldier was also a very good amateur flautist and combined this with his army life, composing some very competent pieces for wind bands, with a very distinct Scottish air about them, for he incorporated Scottish folk tunes into his marches. He was a member of the secret society of composers known as the Temple of Apollo, and was helped with the harmonisation of sonatas by a fellow musician, James Oswald. His best-known piece is 'In the Garb of Old Gaul'.

His will was as curious as his London lifestyle. He first described himself and his previous lodgings in Woodstock Street, then gave a potted autobiography stating that he was the last male heir to a very ancient family that would be extinct at his death. Apart from the Chair of Music at Edinburgh University, he stipulated that out of the general funds left in his bequest a concert should be played annually on 13 February (his birthday) at which the following had to be performed; one solo for the German flute, clarinet or hautboy, one march and one minuet. This was to show the style and taste of music during his adult years. He also requested that the amount of his estate be not published and asked that he be buried in a vault under St Margaret's Church, Westminster, close to a very dear medical friend.

The Chair was established in 1839 on the death of his daughter who had a lifetime interest in his estate, and £400 was set aside each year for the purchase of rare and costly books for the university library.

The Doctor & the Bodysnatcher

THE CURIOUS ALLIANCE OF SIR ASTLEY PASTON COOPER AND BEN CROUCH

'The Resurrection man [the Bodysnatcher], the Cracksman [the housebreaker] and the Buffer [the perjurer] hastened rapidly along the narrow lanes and filthy alleys leading towards the Church. They threaded their way in silence, through the jet-black darkness of the night. . . . Those men were as familiar with the neighbourhood as a person can be with the rooms and passages of his own house. At length the bodysnatchers reached the low wall of the church cemetery . . .'

This extract from a Victorian magazine was typical of the fear and loathing engendered by the professional body-snatchers of the eighteenth and nineteenth centuries. The 'profession' was reviled by the population but tacitly and privately endorsed by the medical establishment. In fact the bodysnatcher was essential to the surgeons. Without cadavers the emerging profession of surgeons could not study human anatomy nor make any advances in acquiring new surgical techniques. Sir Astley Paston Cooper, Bart (1768–1841), was one of the foremost surgeons of the day who readily dealt with the resurrection men, yet publicly despised them.

Surgeons were the natural heirs of the barbers. In England the barbers or barber-surgeons were the original saw-bones, and these, the crudest of medical men, were deemed socially and intellectually inferior to the 'physician'. Cadavers had always been intrinsic to the surgeons' advancement in their chosen field. By the early nineteenth century a vast increase in student numbers in London meant that the peripatetic supply of cadavers, executed felons or paupers, became totally inadequate. Some dozen bodies were annually made available to 500 students at a time when it was deemed that each student should work on at least two bodies before being licensed to practise surgery.

Sir Astley Cooper (left), nephew of a surgeon, son of a squire-parson, was one of the foremost surgeons of the time. He was a doctor at St Thomas's and Guy's hospitals as well as being twice elected president of the Royal College of Surgeons, and was a vice-president of the Royal Society. He was considered unsurpassed as a teacher and surgery lecturer. His lucrative private practice was to earn him an extraordinary £21,000 per annum from 1813.

This rich, elegant, superbly dressed, handsome and somewhat vain surgeon was the epitome of the successful professional in an age when the professional was regarded with disdain, especially when the professional happened to be 'gently' born. He was recognised as a very successful employer of bodysnatchers, intrinsic to his calling, despite calling them the 'lowest dregs of degradation . . . I do not know that I can describe them better; there is no crime that they would not commit . . . if they would imagine that I should make a good subject, they really would not have the smallest scruple, if they could do the thing undiscovered, to make a subject of me.'

Ben Crouch was the son of a St Thomas's carpenter. He was a 'heavy, hulking tallish man, with coarse features marked with the smallpox . . . his manners were always rude, coarse and offensive, even when he attempted to be civil', but he realised that huge amounts of money could be made by the common man in supplying the medical establishment with corpses from £2 to £14 per body. It was to Sir Astley that he apparently owed his start in the profession that would make his name. He headed a very organised gang that ruthlessly pillaged and ransacked cemeteries from the home counties to London to service the needs of Sir Astley Cooper and his team from about 1800 to 1818. Nobody, rich or poor, was safe from the clutches of the very efficient Ben Crouch gang. They would take the naked corpses without disturbing the graves too much – it was a criminal act to steal the corpse's clothes.

They would ferry them by river or by cart to the nearest hospital, leaving them, sacked, at the back door, and collecting their payment from the main entrance.

Magistrates turned a blind eye to the practice, as did the establishment in general. The promise of great financial reward meant that more outrages, such as deliberate murder, were committed to get bodies to the surgeons' dissecting tables. The trade spiralled out of control was eventually quashed by the Anatomy Bill in 1832, but the grim ballad of 'Mary's Ghost' is a timely reminder of the practice and its original 'godfather':

> The body-snatchers they have come,
> And made a snatch at me.
> It's very hard them kind of men
> Won't let a body be!
>
> The cock it crows – I must be gone!
> My William, we must part!
> But I'll be yours in death, altho'
> Sir Astley has my heart.

Robert Browning of Camberwell
ROBERT BROWNING'S CHILDHOOD INFLUENCES IN CAMBERWELL

Camberwell, Dulwich, Herne Hill and New Cross were, at the beginning of the nineteenth century, quiet farming communities quite separate from London. Rough-built old windmills were still a prominent part of the landscape. These were clusters of buildings around crossroads and miles of open country punctuated by the occasional estate or gentleman's villa.

The poet Robert Browning (1812–89) was born in this gentle, well-ordered environment, near Camberwell's 'fair Grove and verdant brow, The loveliest Surrey's swelling hills can show . . .'. From it could be seen

> The extensive peopled vale,
> From ancient Lambeth's west extreme,
> Beside the Thames' bending stream,
> To Limehouse glittering in the evening beam.

He was the gifted, bright second child and only son of Robert Browning, a senior clerk at the Bank of England, and his Scots wife Sarah Anna Wiedemann.

It was here, in this insular pocket, that a new breed of men, the professional middle classes, had comfortable lives in their commodious homes with large gardens, such as his neighbours Benjamin Jowett, later Master of Balliol, and James Silverthorne, Browning's cousin and son of a local brewer.

Camberwell had at least twenty different churches and sects. The Brownings' church was the York Street Congregational Church in Locks Field, Walworth, where Robert was baptised. The minister, George Clayton, had a profound influence on the young Browning (it was he who introduced him to Eliza Flower, the influence behind his first collection of poems), though not as great an influence as that of his father, Robert Browning senior.

The Browning family was very close. An adoring and adored pretty mother, whose interest in religion, gardening, wildlife and the piano she passed on to her children. The father, whose necessary work at the bank 'consumed his life in a fashion he always detested', was a scholar manqué, fluent in several languages including Greek, an accomplished caricaturist and painter, and a catholic reader.

Robert Browning senior was a gentle, well-educated, indulgent and facetious man who had rebelled against his own tyrannical and very successful father, forsaken a lucrative career in the West Indies because of his abhorrence of the treatment meted out to slaves,

Robert Browning.

and found a salaried position. His one great passion, that of book collecting, created a personal library of over 6,000 books on all subjects. It was this library that created the future poet's education and imbued him with an encyclopaedic knowledge that transcended conventional education. This father, furthermore, positively encouraged his inquisitive son to read all he could and answered questions readily and humorously. He even re-created the siege of Troy with the household chairs and tables for his son's benefit!

Camberwell and its environs was a perfect backdrop to Browning's future work; Guy Fawkes Day was a perfect excuse for the boys to go foraging for firewood in Norwood and the Dulwich woods. Bowyer Lane, the 'tough' part of Camberwell, was also an eye-opener, as was the traditional yearly Camberwell Fair on the Green until 1855. Its strange show-people and its appeal to all classes provided Browning with a great opportunity to know his fellow man.

Browning's education was initially a conventional one. He was sent at five to the local Dame's School where the teacher particularly favoured the bright child and then, aged seven, on to the Peckham Collegiate School, 'the very respectable establishment opposite Rye Lane', near the Brownings' Camberwell home. There, in the lower school run by two spinster sisters, the Misses Ready, sisters to the Master, Browning boarded weekly and was taught the obligatory 'three Rs'. He directed and acted in school productions and his pen and ink caricatures were remembered years later. This conventional education did not suit him. He found more knowledge in his father's library. It was therefore home tutoring from the age of fourteen.

By 1828, Robert was ready for 'that godless institution in Gower Street', the newly formed progressive London University. Here was 'A key to a new world, the muttering of angels of something unguessed by man.'

And it was from there, only two years later, that the poet emerged pupa-like from its shadows. It would be some time yet before his greatest works, 'Men and Women' and 'The Ring and the Book', and some time before he met Miss Barrett . . . but this would come.

A Death in the House
THE TRAGIC DEATH OF PRIME MINISTER SPENCER PERCEVAL

My grandmother, Annabel Grant Duff, remembered Ealing well. She was nine and visiting *her* grandmother at North Lodge. The large garden boasted a monkey puzzle tree, a status symbol in the England of the 1870s, and the two old Misses Perceval from the house opposite visited often.

These Misses Perceval were the spinster daughters of Spencer Perceval (1762–1812), the prime minister, whose assassination shocked the nation in 1812. Their home was then Pitshanger Manor and they had lived, it seemed, most of their lives in Ealing. One of their homes had been Elm Grove, a house near Ealing Common which was demolished at the end of the nineteenth century but in which they and their large family had lived between 1808 and 1812.

Spencer Perceval, a younger son of the Earl of Egmont and his second wife, was born in 1762. Cambridge was to mould his character. There he first identified with the small group of Cambridge evangelicals; there he developed his love for literature, made many friends, honed his debating skills and embarked on his legal career. The Percevals may have been grand but they were certainly not rich. An 'excess of modesty, which at that time almost amounted to timidity', and competition with such formidable barristers as Romilly and Vaughan was difficult. Perceval may have been slightly blinkered by his evangelical roots and his work the result of research and hard work rather than a natural talent, but his heart was in the right place. This man with 'the head of a country parson, and the tongue of an Old Bailey lawyer' was 'by his excellent temper, his engaging manners and his sprightly conversation, the delight of all who knew him'.

In 1796, very happily married with a large family becoming larger, Spencer Perceval was returned by the constituents of Northampton as their Whig MP. He represented the borough for sixteen years, coming to the House of Commons as a confirmed party man: for the constitution and Pitt; against Fox and France! His evangelism coloured his political beliefs: a politician was to be a model for the people, adultery was a sin, probity was the tenet. His zeal helped the abolition of slavery yet Catholicism was not tolerated.

The Perceval family rented Belsize House for their growing family. Perceval became Chancellor of the Duchy of Lancaster and, in 1807, prime minister. In 1809 the family moved to the more salubrious Elm Grove by Ealing Common where, escaping from the political arena for a while, Perceval would spend almost idyllic times with his eleven children and his adored wife.

This particular day, 11 May 1812, had been unusually quiet in the House of Commons. Yet it was an unusually fraught time. The wars with France had seriously depleted the nation's coffers; there was high unemployment and the controversial Orders in Council, attempting to counter Napoleonic decrees by increasing blockades and imposing severe restrictions on neutral shipping, were destroying many business ventures. At 5.15 p.m. the diminutive, dapper Perceval briskly mounted the steps that led into the lobby of the House of Commons. He was late for yet another heated debate on these Orders in Council. He

The assassination of Spencer Perceval.

handed his greatcoat to a doorman and made his way through the doors of the lobby. A small group of men, including William Jerdan, a journalist for the British press, and several MPs were making light conversation.

A single shot rang out in the near deserted lobby. Cries of 'Order, order' and 'Shut the door – let no one escape' created pandemonium. Perceval was carried into the office of the Speaker's secretary and placed in a sitting position on a table. He was dead within five minutes. The assassin, John Bellingham, a ruined merchant with a mistaken belief that the government was the cause of all his calamities, went to sit on a bench beside the wall by the fireplace. He made no attempt to escape.

The family in Ealing was inconsolable. It was, however, provided for, although the 'blood money' paid to them turned ultimately into a bone of contention. In the eyes of some, it was unnecessary; others more loyal to Perceval's memory viewed it as parsimonious in the extreme.

London's Mother of Christ

THE STRANGE STORY OF JOANNA SOUTHCOTT THE VISIONARY

On 19 October 1814 the messiah should have been born, at 38 Manchester Street, Marylebone. The 65-year-old visionary virgin mother, Joanna Southcott, and her thousands of followers patiently waited for the miraculous birth. She was the 'Bride of Christ' and the 'Mother of Christ'. She had always rejected sex but averred that she shared her bed with a 'most beautiful and heavenly figure'!

The nation waited. Gifts began to arrive at the door: a silver cup, a gold font, a £200 satinwood crib and many others including quantities of money. Shops brimmed with Joanna Southcott cradles and dolls representing Shiloh, the expected Saviour. Noble visitors to the place of the eagerly anticipated birth included the Russian ambassador and the Tsar's aide-de-camp. Doctors were sent for and the faithful kept vigil by her bedside. 'Excitement could not have been more intense had the dome of St Paul's collapsed', screamed the headlines.

The day passed with no birth and, despite seventeen doctors affirming that this corpulent matriarch was indeed pregnant; October came and went with no sign of a baby. So did November and most of December. The long wait ended on 28 December 1814. Joanna died. An autopsy revealed that internal flatulence and glandular enlargements of the breasts had given the appearance of pregnancy. She was buried in St John's Wood Chapel cemetery.

Her tens of thousands of followers certainly believed she was divine, as was one of her faithful lieutenants, a certain Brothers. Brothers had pretended to teach the mysteries of animal magnetism and deluded people into the belief that they had received spiritual circumcision through his special powers. Joanna Southcott (pictured) confirmed the authenticity of this individual's mission and acknowledged him as the 'King of the Hebrews'. One wonders whether he was the 'most beautiful and heavenly figure' she had described! Was Joanna Southcott deluded – a visionary or an incredibly clever religious impostor? Who was she and where had she come from?

She was born into a strictly religious Devon farming family and received little or no formal education. By her late teens she was in domestic service and came under the influence of a Methodist preacher, Sanderson, who often stayed with her employers. His strong personality and undoubted mesmeric qualities led the household staff to 'acts of madness' and hallucinations, and Joanna to believe she was surrounded by spirits. She became a Wesleyan Methodist in 1791 under the tutelage of the Reverend Mr Pomeroy. Her first confused announcement of her religious mission was at a class meeting in 1792 when she reported hearing voices telling her she had been chosen as the Bride of Christ.

Some of Joanna's strange pronouncements became reality, and this attracted a lot of people. Mr Pomeroy was so taken with her that he gave her money to advertise her prophecies – one of which was that many of them would perish in the impending Napoleonic invasion. Some were more down to earth: 'I am the Lord thy God and Master. Tell [name] to pay thee five pounds for expenses of thy coming to London; and he must give thee 20 pounds to relieve the perplexity of thy handmaid and thee, that your thoughts may be free to save me, the Lord in the care of my Shiloh.' The Calvinists became interested and after several interviews in Exeter she was invited to London. Her mission was to battle with the Devil. Thousands flocked to her chapel in Duke Street at the Elephant and Castle.

Although almost completely illiterate, Joanna managed to write and publish her predictions in prose and doggerel. She was a prolific writer, publishing sixty-five books and innumerable pamphlets. She also had a thriving trade selling about 150,000 signed letters with a celestial seal that promised a lifespan of a thousand years – Byron thought one was cheap at half a guinea.

Her followers' excitement reached fever pitch when she told them of her divine pregnancy; and the story of a sealed box, whose contents would save the nation (and her strict instructions that the box should only be opened in the presence of twenty-four bishops when the nation was in peril) sustained interest in her long after the non-birth – and after her death.

In the 1930s the Panacea Society campaigned vigorously to have the box opened. Its whereabouts were unknown but other boxes appeared. One contained a woman's nightcap, a pistol, a lottery ticket and a novelette. It was opened in front of one bishop – not the twenty-four of Joanna's request!

A Quiet Affair

THE CATO STREET CONSPIRACY

On 23 February 1820 the well-known Bow Street Runner, Constable George Ruthven, was provided with a warrant for the arrest of one Arthur Thistlewood and thirteen other named individuals. Ruthven and his men arrived at Cato Street, off Edgware Road, leading through an archway into John Street, and made his way to the loft above a stable, the address stated on the warrant. The Runners stormed the loft at 8.30 a.m., led by Ruthven. Ruthven was confronted at the door by a man with a blunderbuss who was immediately seized. They then rushed into the loft.

The small loft was crammed with about twenty bedraggled people and filled with bags of gunpowder, pikes, firearms, swords and home-made grenades. Thistlewood, the leader, was immediately recognised and chased by an enthusiastic Runner, one Richard Smithers. Thistlewood turned on him, and stabbed him with his sword. Smithers was to be the only fatality of the day. Thistlewood escaped but was found the following day in Moorfields with his pockets crammed with cartridges. Finally the detachment of Guards led by Lieutenant Frederick FitzClarence, 'a young officer well-known for his gallantry and gentlemanly conduct' arrived, surrounded the building and began rounding up the hapless insurgents.

In all, about twenty were captured. Six weeks later Thistlewood and eleven of his supporters were put on trial. Five were sentenced to death by hanging: Thistlewood, James Ings, Richard Tidd, John Brunt and William Davidson. They were condemned to death on 28 April, a Friday, informed of the date of their death on Saturday evening, and by Monday afternoon were in their coffins – swift retribution indeed! When the bodies had been hanging for half an hour the executioner cut off their heads to remind the crowd they were traitors. But the desired result was not achieved; the crowd showed sympathy, not loathing. It was fortunate that the sentence was only partly carried out as Lord Tenterden, the judge, had determined that the bodies were also to be quartered. The Cato Street Conspirators almost became martyrs.

The Prime Minister Lord Liverpool, the Home Secretary Lord Sidmouth and the Cabinet, whose popularity was waning, enjoyed a brief spell of sympathy created by the intentions of these desperate men, particularly when a public service was stage-managed to give thanks for their escape.

But what were the true intentions of these desperate men? They were to have slaughtered the prime minister and his whole cabinet while at supper. Who were these desperate men? They were poverty stricken, totally ignorant individuals. Some had started life well but circumstances had reduced them to penury and oblivion. They were ill-led and badly organised. Yet one of their aims was to capture the Bank of England, distribute the coins among the poor and burn the paper money which they held largely responsible for all their misery.

Arthur Thistlewood (1770–1820) (pictured), the leader of these would-be assassins, hailed from Lincolnshire. He was a well-educated lieutenant in a marching regiment. He had married well, but when his young wife died he resigned his commission and moved to France where he soldiered for a time. On his return to England he immersed himself in radical reform politics, meeting, eventually, his co-conspirators.

A more shadowy character emerges who figures on the warrant yet was never arrested. George Edwards had taken a prominent part in all the stages of the planned assassination. He even announced the cabinet dinner upon which the plan revolved. But he was not at Cato Street, nor was he at the trial. He informed on Thistlewood, who had the presence of mind to denounce him as a government spy at his trial. Edwards completely disappeared.

The Home Office certainly agreed that it had received hints of a forthcoming plot. It became clear that the Crown was carefully hiding Edwards during the trial and it seems that he formed part of a network of government spies specifically used to disseminate false information which could be used to the government's advantage as and when it was needed. Could it be that the government had decided that its popularity was so low it needed a welcome morale booster? We shall never know.

A Ghostly Influence
WILKIE COLLINS, THE MAN BEHIND THE MODERN DETECTIVE STORY

'On Hampstead Road there stood the figure of a solitary woman dressed in white . . . her hand pointing to the dark clouds of London as I faced her.' This is one of the most famous fictional episodes ever written.

It was in Pond Place that Wilkie Collins (1824–89), the author of *The Woman in White*, was born. He was the elder son of the successful portrait and landscape painter William Collins and his wife Harriet. William set great store in 'it's not what you know but who you know'; a belief he tried to imbue unsuccessfully into his sons Wilkie and Charles.

Wilkie's life was spent, for the most part, in a small area of north-west London, around Regent's Park. He also spent two highly formative years in France and Italy with his family where he spoke both languages, loved French food and acquired a taste for his favourite tipple, champagne. He was very sensitive about his physical proportions; he was short-sighted, had a slightly deformed head and a bulge on the right side of his forehead, was small and had tiny hands and feet. He always thought he was subject to a 'ghostly influence', or someone standing behind him. This manifested itself in all his writings as a double or hidden identity. It was further aggravated by his increased use of opium for his arthritis.

He wrote a biography of his father shortly after the latter's death. This was very well received and he followed it with his first novel, *Antonia*, in 1849. This was the story of an intelligent forceful woman in revolt against subjection to the conventional. This theme was a recurrent one, as well as his fascination for the macabre.

Collins's private life mirrored in part his novels; he refused to marry, considering the idea and purpose a miserable and narrow one; he championed women's rights, and those of servants and prostitutes; and questioned both the legal and social system which sanctioned the sale of a woman's body in marriage but not outside. He also despised conventional organised religion. He put his ideas into practice when he started living openly with Caroline Graves, in Harley Place, in 1858. It was a lifelong attachment. She was beautiful, youthful and with a daughter. She was also from a poor background (although she sought to hide this) – a lady was, in her opinion, 'a woman who wears a silk gown and has a sense of her own importance'.

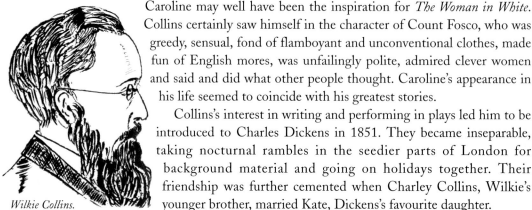

Caroline may well have been the inspiration for *The Woman in White*. Collins certainly saw himself in the character of Count Fosco, who was greedy, sensual, fond of flamboyant and unconventional clothes, made fun of English mores, was unfailingly polite, admired clever women and said and did what other people thought. Caroline's appearance in his life seemed to coincide with his greatest stories.

Collins's interest in writing and performing in plays led him to be introduced to Charles Dickens in 1851. They became inseparable, taking nocturnal rambles in the seedier parts of London for background material and going on holidays together. Their friendship was further cemented when Charley Collins, Wilkie's younger brother, married Kate, Dickens's favourite daughter.

Wilkie Collins.

Wilkie's novel, *The Moonstone*, published in 1864, deliberately flouted conventions. He had initiated and created a new convention, a new format – that of the detective novel. *The Moonstone* sold better than Dickens's *Great Expectations*. Dickens was flabbergasted and his massive ego deflated. Some say he deliberately set out to undermine Collins's work. Whatever the case, relations between them cooled. It was in the same year that Wilkie met Martha Rudd, a strong independent-minded 24-year-old working-class girl who never hid her origins. She and Wilkie had two daughters and a son.

The eventual ménage à trois seemed to suit all parties. Collins was already known for his relaxed attitude to sexual relations. This didn't seem to affect his popularity. He was witty, unpretentious, amusing and loved women. Despite remaining unmarried he revelled in the bourgeois virtues of family responsibility and hard work, doting on and providing for his children and his two loves.

This little man had a prodigious appetite and output. His dark, brooding, intense and shocking stories spawned generations of imitators. He was, however, not humourless. After his successful American tour, an American horse was named after him. On seeing the advert, 'Wilkie Collins covers mares at $75 each', he burst into gales of laughter.

Wellington's Last Stand

THE DUKE OF WELLINGTON'S DUEL IN BATTERSEA FIELDS

Religious bigotry has played a major part in many conflicts around the globe, though few can be deemed as silly as Wellington's duel with Lord Winchilsea on 21 March 1829. The Duke of Wellington (1769–1852) had reluctantly become prime minister in 1828. The new prime minister and King George IV both held very strong anti-Catholic views, yet in

Ireland the County Clare elections in 1828 had been won by Daniel O'Connell, the Catholic politician. Wellington's own Protestant candidate, Vesey Fitzgerald, was trounced. A Catholic could not, as the law then stood, take his seat in the House of Commons, but there was nothing to prevent him being elected to it!

During that summer Wellington had to put aside his opinions and view the Catholic problem in context – civil war was threatening in Ireland and one way to bring this troublesome nation to heel was to grant some major concessions to the Roman Catholic majority. George IV was intransigent; he insisted that his coronation oath bound him inextricably to Anglican precepts and that his 'conscience must not be disturbed upon this painful question'. By the beginning of 1829 Wellington's persistence paid off and he got the king's agreement that at least the Cabinet should discuss the Catholic question. The Duke of Cumberland, the king's brother and a Protestant bigot, stepped into the argument, forcing Wellington to play his last card – that of requesting the government's resignation. This was granted immediately and then retracted when the king realised that the Tory opponents of the dreaded Bill were not strong enough to form an alternative government. The king, after much argument, had to consent to the Roman Catholic Relief Act.

The Iron Duke.

There were casualties. He had to contend with the Lord Chancellor, Lord Eldon, the ultra-Protestant Attorney General Sir Charles Wetherell, whom he sacked, and Lord Anglesey, the Irish Lord Lieutenant. Two Protestant peers, the Duke of Newcastle and the Earl of Winchilsea, proposed leading a march to Windsor Castle. The Earl of Winchilsea had been particularly offensive to Wellington in 'Letters to the Editor' in the *Standard* and to the secretary of King's College, London, which had been founded by Wellington. He withdrew his subscription to the college fund, alleging that Wellington's motives in establishing this institution were highly suspect and that he was carrying on 'an insidious design for the infringement of our liberties and the introduction of Popery into every department of the State'.

Winchilsea refused to apologise, so Wellington asked him to give him satisfaction on the field of honour. Sir Henry Hardinge was Wellington's second and Lord Falmouth Winchilsea's. Dr John Hume, Wellington's physician, was sent a detailed message by Hardinge to be in attendance with a brace of pistols in Battersea Fields at 8 a.m. on Saturday 21 March, as persons of quality would be duelling.

Hume arrived and was astounded to find the duke riding up. 'Well, I daresay you little expected it was I who wanted you to be here', Wellington joked. 'Indeed my Lord, you certainly are the last person I should have expected here', replied Hume. Wellington and Hume waited for Winchilsea and his second. Hume paced the ground out only to be reprimanded by Wellington for placing Winchilsea's firing position 'so near the ditch. If I hit him he will tumble in.' But Wellington was a notoriously bad shot! Hardinge could not load the pistols because he had lost his left hand at Waterloo. Falmouth was shivering so badly with nerves and cold that Hume loaded both pistols. Hardinge gave the order to fire. Winchilsea's arm remained straight at his side so Wellington deliberately aimed well to the side. Winchilsea shot in the air and apologised. The duke bowed to his opponent, touched his hat, said, 'Good morning, my lords' and rode away.

The participants had been careful, so they thought. The pistols were hidden under a bush until the duel and their journey was anonymous. But all London seemed to know. The Duke of Newcastle, a die-hard Protestant, opined that 'one is almost tempted to wish that a life so dangerous [Winchilsea's] had been taken away, but one must not indulge in so unchristian feelings . . .'.

By Hook or by Crook
OR THE FORGOTTEN THEODORE HOOK'S LAST YEARS IN FULHAM

In 1831 the financially depleted Theodore Hook began to look for a house for himself, his common-law wife and his large brood of children away from the hustle and bustle of central London, where his strained purse could give him a semblance of prosperity! In March it was to Putney to view a couple of properties, then to Fulham and Barnes to look at some more. It was only in April that he decided on a waterside house with a garden running to the river's edge, in Fulham right by Putney Bridge. In fact Egmont House, as it was called, lay between Putney toll-bridge and Fulham Palace. It was a good-sized house with hall, butler's pantry, kitchen and library on the ground floor with stairs to the first floor, with a master bedroom and drawing room, and a second floor with a further two bedrooms and a sitting room. There was also a cottage in the garden.

The house and the village of Fulham proved a haven for the somewhat turbulent and hectic social life of the most famous novelist of the day. It was his very social life that had cramped what would have been a comfortable existence. 'Honest' John Phelps, the waterman who ferried people across to Putney and a close neighbour, said that Theodore was 'a curious gentleman who turned day into night, lived up to his income and died poor'.

Who was this Theodore Hook (1788–41) who was a stranger to moderation? He was a largely forgotten English genius who founded and edited anonymously the ferociously satirical and hugely successful Sunday newspaper, *John Bull*. He was England's best-selling novelist before Charles Dickens and the only successful 'improvisator' that the English language has known, instantly composing witty poems and songs on any subject.

Theodore was one of the children of the successful composer and musician James Hook. Educated at Harrow School, he then joined his father in a successful partnership creating musical comedies for the West End. These were derided by the literati but lauded by the paying public. He then wrote his first novel, so full of smutty jokes that society shunned it.

This young, witty master of the English tongue who burst on to the literary and fashionable scene of Georgian England captivated everyone, including the Prince Regent who found him a job as accountant to the Crown Colony of Mauritius. Unfortunately his rumbustious career there was cut short by avaricious employees who stole funds. The disgraced Hook was returned to England and spent two years in jail. Once out he continued his cavalcade through life, writing and performing for the jaded Georgian society. He was an inveterate practical joker whose jokes sometimes went too far.

He stole a life-size model of a kilted Highlander from a tobacconist. He wrapped it in a cloak deposited it in a coach and told the driver to take the inebriated gentleman home to a fictitious address. But his most successful hoax-cum-joke was the Berners Street Hoax where the unfortunate recipient of the farce, a widow living on Berners Street, received thousands of unwanted callers in one week – ranging from suppliers to peers of the realm and the Duke of Gloucester who had received a letter saying that one of his girlfriends was dying at this address. This joke caused such a furore that Hook had to leave town for a few weeks.

Excess followed by bouts of genuine hard work wreaked its toll on the irrepressible Theodore Hook. He was a popular figure in Fulham and his early death in 1841, almost a bankrupt, came as a blow to this tight-knit village. Friends and neighbours clubbed together to give him a decent funeral and burial at nearby All Saints' Church. He left his family destitute. Byron called him a man of genius but a chary critic said he was a 'man of unfeeling wit, a heartless lounger at the clubs, and a humbly born flaneur, who spent his life in amusing great people, who in their turn let him die at last, a drunken, emaciated, hopeless, worn-out spendthrift, *sans* character, *sans* everything'.

The Pineapple Gate Torso

JAMES GREENACRE – MURDERER

The shift in population brought about by the Industrial Revolution dramatically increased the population of major cities. In 1801 London had just under a million souls. In the next fifty years the population was to double.

The immediate surroundings of the West End were the first to be built up by developers, followed by the gradual urbanisation of the Edgware Road, specifically by the canal. The Hero of Maida inn was opened shortly after the Battle of Maida in southern Italy in 1806. Soon afterwards select houses and villas were built in this sector and the suburb of Maida Vale was born. Yet the area retained its rural atmosphere and there were stag hunts until at least 1829. In the same year George Shillibeer introduced a French invention, the omnibus, on to the new road from Paddington to the City.

The outcome of this early commuting was more development. It was in the mid-1830s that a new row of detached houses, Canterbury Villas, was built across from the Edgware

Road from Pineapple Place parallel to what is now called Sutherland Avenue. This quiet, select and leafy suburb was ideal for the emerging professional classes. But its very seclusion would also be the stage for one of the most blood-curdling crimes of the century.

At about midday on 28 December 1836, a labourer, Robert Bond, was walking to work via the Pineapple Toll Gate. He spied a large hessian sack tied up at the top outside one of the Canterbury Villas. His curiosity piqued, he opened the bag and recoiled in horror, for inside was the torso of a woman. He rushed to the nearest policeman, a Samuel Pegler of 'S' Division, who happened to be doing his rounds on the Edgware Road. The torso was conveyed to the Paddington station house in Hermitage Street, an inquest was held and 'wilful murder' was established. Despite newspaper coverage no one came forward. There were no clues whatsoever to the woman's identity.

On 6 January 1837 a bargeman was trying to close the lock gates in one of the stretches of the Regent's Canal near Stepney, but something was obstructing them. He and the lock keeper used a hitcher (a long pole with a hook at the end) to remove the obstruction. It was a woman's head with only one eye, a fractured jawbone and a slit ear.

The head was presumed to belong to the torso. It was preserved in alcohol at Paddington police station. On 2 February a young man discovered dismembered legs in a similar sack in Camberwell. These were deemed to belong to the rest of the body and were also taken to Paddington.

William Gay, of Goodge Street, visited the police station at his wife's insistence, to view the head, and recognised it as being that of his missing sister, Mrs Hannah Brown. The slit ear confirmed it. She was to have been married on Christmas Day to a James Greenacre of Lambeth. They had not seen her since a week before the proposed wedding. Her intended had come to see them after Christmas to explain that the wedding was off because Mrs Brown had deceived him about her personal wealth. Mr Greenacre had also visited a friend of Mrs Brown's, a Mrs Davis of Smithfield, whose daughter was to be a bridesmaid, and told her of the deception which forced him to cancel the wedding. It was fairly obvious that Greenacre was the culprit.

James Greenacre.

He was arrested along with his live-in girlfriend, Sarah Gale.

Greenacre was a serial widower. He admitted that they had quarrelled. He had hit her with a stave, breaking her jaw and popping her eye out. He had panicked and decided to quarter her and dispose of the parts of her body in different areas of London – he had been carrying her head when he visited Mrs Davis.

Both Miss Gale and Greenacre were tried. He was hanged on 2 May and she was deported to Australia. Greenacre's crime remained long in Londoners' memories – until Jack the Ripper appeared on the scene.

Howard's Way

THE LIFE AND TIMES OF MISS HOWARD OF ST JOHN'S WOOD

Who was this delightful vision that so beguiled the Prince Louis-Napoleon? 'She with the exquisite figure, at once stately and graceful, with a head and features such as only one of the great Greek sculptors could have chiselled'? She was 23-year-old Miss Elizabeth Howard (pictured). Her portrait reveals an undeniably attractive woman, with an intelligent and forceful beauty. This Brighton belle was born to a shoemaker called Harryett. She was determined to use her brains and beauty to better herself from the outset.

She went into service and by 1836 had already embarked on her chosen career. She became mistress to a steeplechaser and then to a well-connected officer, Major Martin, by whom she had a son. It was then that she began calling herself Miss Howard, acquiring many more admirers. Among these was the Duke of Beaufort, who not only lavished upon her his affections, but also part of his fortune. Other admirers abounded, and so did their gifts. One gave her a single present of £5,000, about £200,000 nowadays.

Louis-Napoleon was 5ft 5in tall, had chestnut hair and beard, grey eyes, rounded shoulders and a very large nose. He was also sickly and had just made a remarkable escape from the fortress of Ham in Picardy. He had served only six years of a projected life sentence – the result of an abortive coup d'état in France and an equally futile defence in court.

He arrived in London in May 1846, dishevelled, dispirited and dead broke. He became a *cause célèbre* and was lionised by London society. Elizabeth and Louis-Napoleon supposedly met at Lady Blessington's house. He was struck by her beauty and her wit, and she by his total belief in himself and his star. They settled in Rockingham House, 23 Circus Road, St John's Wood, a noted road for rich men's mistresses. She also shared her now great wealth with him, especially in 1848 when she lent him £80,000 to assist him in his successful return to French politics.

One potential solution to Louis-Napoleon's financial problems would be marriage to a rich heiress. Elizabeth Burdett-Coutts, the richest heiress in England, was ideal but rejected him, and undoubtedly Miss Howard actively dissuaded him. Miss Howard followed Louis-Napoleon to Paris in 1848. When he became president she was placed in a house near the Elysée, under the strict instructions that she could attend public functions, but not main receptions.

On Louis-Napoleon's re-election in 1851 Elizabeth moved to the Palace of St Cloud. She was a perfect consort. She distracted his mind from affairs of state and never pried nor meddled. She never even bothered to learn French! She demanded fidelity and got it. Her motives were self-serving. While she undoubtedly loved her man, she was determined to keep him and, if possible, marry him. Louis-Napoleon became emperor in 1852. His senators hoped that he would find a suitable consort, as his irregular liaison displeased them. He never contemplated marrying her although this was the happiest time of his life. His letter to Odilon-Barrot made this clear: 'I own that I am guilty of seeking in illegitimate bonds the affection my heart requires. I may be well forgiven, I think, for an affection which harms no one and which I do not seek to make conspicuous.'

His choice of Eugénie de Montijo made Elizabeth furious. She plotted in vain to impede and stop all matrimonial negotiations, but to no avail. She was lured out of Paris on a pretext four days before his marriage. Eventually protracted negotiations and threats made her accept the situation. She was given the Estate and County of Beauregard. She wrote to a friend: 'His Majesty was here to pay me off, yes, an Earldom and a decent French husband.' Her son was also created Comte de Becheret. She married Clarence Trelawney in 1854, and divorced him in 1855. Apart from the occasional *grande sortie* she retired to Beauregard and died there alone and forgotten, on 19 August 1866.

Tooting's Human Farm

THE EXPOSURE OF MR DROUET'S CHILDREN'S HOME IN TOOTING

Nineteenth-century parish councils and the established church were highly involved in the day-to-day running of every parish. They were the precursor of the modern London Borough Council. One painfully difficult aspect of its administration was the housing and upkeep of the parish poor, particularly the pauper children. The monies needed for the assistance of the poor and needy was levied from the parish as a whole in the form of a community tax, and from church funds.

Parishes would set up establishments to deal with this expanding problem. Some of these were highlighted by novelists of the era, particularly Charles Dickens, whose crusade for the poor led to an eventual wide reform of the system. His novel *Oliver Twist* aptly describes the tortuous and precarious life of the workhouse inmate. Some enterprising and less than honest individuals set up 'academies' or 'farms'. These were sub-contracted by the parishes to look after their paupers. The object was to feed, clothe and educate the inmates to enable them to procure some worthwhile trade on their eventual departure. Their *raison d'être* was the convenient removal of undesirables of the parish. Subsequent lack of adequate supervision by local administration led to a wide abuse of this system, and one particular case was that of the establishment of Mr Drouet of Tooting Broadway.

Mr Drouet had started a 'Farming Establishment for Pauper Children' on Tooting Broadway in about 1843, to cater for the poor children of the parish. He was paid 4s 6d per child per week for full board and lodging. In all respects he was deemed a pillar of the local community and an enterprising businessman. Unfortunately for Mr Drouet, cholera hit his establishment in 1848. So many of his wards died that 'Tooting Churchyard became too small for the piles of children's coffins that were carried out of this Elysium every day'. An enquiry was set up and virtually whitewashed the whole affair. The Surrey county coroner thought an inquest would serve no purpose, deeming that Mr Drouet's farm was the best of all possible farms in the best of possible worlds. The Board of Health and Charles Dickens became involved and it transpired that Mr Drouet was not the 'gentleman' everyone had thought.

The esteemed Mr Drouet thought fit to put four cholera patients in one bed and left the sick to look after themselves. He ensured that the food was basic and scarce as well as

Drouet's Farm on Tooting Broadway.

piling as many children into his establishment as he possibly could. There was neither adequate sanitation nor basic health requirements. The children under his care were beaten on a whim and virtually starved to death. Charles Dickens was so sickened and incensed that he published an article in the *Examiner* on 20 January 1849 criticising the report on the incident and stating that the disease had broken out because 'the Farm was brutally conducted, vilely kept, preposterously inspected, dishonestly defended, a disgrace to a Christian community, and a stain upon a civilised Land'.

In one particular example a Mr James, solicitor and clerk to the Board of Guardians, who kept minutes of the 'official' visits to the farm, had asked (in front of Mr Drouet) some of the boys if they had any complaints. If in the affirmative he recommended that they be flogged forthwith!

A coroner's jury eventually convicted Mr Drouet of manslaughter. Charles Dickens was to immortalise Tooting in *Bleak House* two years later, when an inmate of Mr Drouet's establishment, Guster, became a servant to one Mr Snagsby. Guster was a lean young woman supposed to have been christened Augusta. Originally from a workhouse she had been contracted or farmed out in her youth to an 'amiable benefactor of his species resident at Tooting' and could 'not fail to have been developed under the most favourable circumstances'! This young woman had fits and went about in 'fear and trembling' and was 'so apprehensive of being returned to the hands of her patron saint, that, except when she is found with her head in the pail, or the sink, or the copper, or the dinner, or anything else that happens to be near her at the time of her seizure, she is always at work'.

Hip! Hip! Hooray!

OBAYSCH THE HIPPOPOTAMUS, DENIZEN OF REGENT'S PARK

The *Dictionary of National Biography* has but a small mention of Sir Charles Augustus Murray (1806–95), second son of the Earl of Dunmore. Sir Charles was a minor diplomat and author. His main claim to fame, so he later wrote, was to win a silver racquet at tennis at Oxford: 'this is the only incontestable distinction that I can claim to have achieved in my long life'. This life would have been relegated to his family archives and the dusty tomes of some provincial library had it not been for three incidents; one was a stupid and misguided mistake on his part which precipitated an absurd Anglo-Persian War in 1856; the second was his part in the building of the Cairo–Alexandria railway in Egypt and the third, arguably his only real claim to eternal fame, was the reintroduction of the first hippopotamus into Europe after 1,500 years!

After a stint as secretary of the British Legation in Naples in 1844 Charles Murray was sent to Egypt to act as Britain's consul general in Cairo in 1846. He was to stay there until 1853. Britain was then caught up in a craze for natural history and exotic animals. The Zoological Gardens at Regent's Park already had an enclosure for giraffes. The gardens' council thought it would be a great coup to have a live hippopotamus, which would also be a phenomenal money-spinner. They quite reasonably surmised that if these had been transported to the circuses of Rome, a thousand or so years before, then why could they not be transported to the world's greatest city in the world's greatest empire since the Romans?

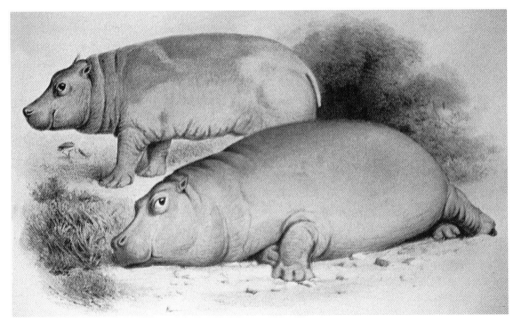

Adhela with Obaysch in the foreground.

In July 1849, through Charles Murray's influence, the Viceroy of Egypt, Abbas Pasha, sent hunters to the White Nile, to the island of Obaysch, to capture a hippopotamus calf. While he awaited transport to England the little hippopotamus not only bonded with his keeper, but with Charles Murray. The year-old Obaysch (named after his birthplace) was packed on to the P&O steamer *Ripon* and arrived, amid a blaze of publicity, on our shores on 25 May 1850.

Giraffes had caused a furore, but Obaysch created public dementia! The Zoological Gardens had had 168,000 visitors in 1849 and would have 360,000 in 1850. People lined up in their thousands each Saturday to visit him. Mr Murray would visit his four-legged friend as often as possible, whenever he got a home leave. He was nicknamed 'Hippopotamus Murray' because of this, not for his plodding diplomatic skills! *Punch* chronicled every event in the life of Obaysch or HRH (His Rolling Hulk). Queen Victoria wrote copious notes in her diaries about the hippo's behaviour, silver hippo necklaces were made in his honour and the 'Hippopotamus Polka' became a big hit at about this time. Macaulay was to write that he had 'seen the hippopotamus, both asleep and awake; and I can assure you that, asleep or awake, he is the ugliest of the works of God'.

Sadly, like all novelties, his popularity dwindled by 1851, leaving *Punch* to ruminate:

> I'm a hippish Hippopotamus
> And don't know what to do.
> For the public is inconstant
> And a fickle one, too.
> It smiled once upon me,
> And now I'm quite forgot;
> Neglected in my bath,
> And left to go to pot.

In 1853 Adhela the female hippo entered his life. They were to mate successfully, but despite this the public soon lost interest. In 1872 Sir Charles Murray purchased a large property, Oaklands near Kilburn Grange Park, with a view to retiring there. The now elderly Sir Charles often visited his friend at what was now the Zoo, shouting to him in Arabic as the hulk lumbered up to him bellowing welcoming rumbles. Obaysch died in 1878 largely forgotten, except by *Punch*:

> URM'P! Urm'p! A feeble grunt! I fail apace.
> Old Hippo's mighty yet melodious bass
> Sinks to a raucous whisper, short, not sweet! . . .
> I dreamt of (the White Nile) last night, the unctuous ooze
> Whereone might take one's ease, and bask and snooze . . .
> Ah, well! I've had my triumphs, and am yet
> A Public pet!

The Bottle, the Artist & the Man

GEORGE CRUIKSHANK'S YEARS IN HAMPSTEAD ROAD

A tall stuccoed house, marked by a circular tablet, stands at 263 Hampstead Road, halfway up from Euston Road. The plaque is to George Cruikshank (1792–1878) (pictured), the nineteenth-century caricaturist. He and his second wife lived here from 1850 until his death.

Here the artist, 'a broad-chested well-built man, rather below the middle height, with a high forehead, blue grey eyes, a hook nose and a pair of fierce looking whiskers of a decidedly original pattern' illustrated *Uncle Tom's Cabin* and did his twenty etchings for Robert Brough's *Life of Falstaff* including the wonderful death of the knight. The house, however, was famous not for the work he achieved, but for Cruikshank's crusade against the evils of drink he conducted from here.

George Cruikshank was the son and the brother of an artist. He was the strangest of men almost to the point of dottiness, and this was mirrored by his appearance. Charles Dickens, his friend and for whom he illustrated the *Sketches by Boz*, said that his whiskers when wet stuck out in front of him 'like a partially unravelled bird's nest'. His Regency Buck period saw him as a 'bruising, gig-driving, badger-baiting, rat-catching, dog and duck-hunting pet of the Fancy', where he was wild at parties 'singing all manner of songs, coming home (six miles) in an open carriage of Dickens', on his head to the indignation of the police'! His drinking was equally monstrous: in one spree his friends left him trying to climb up a lamp-post. By the 1840s his drinking purportedly landed him in police custody in the small hours of the morning.

Cruikshank's particular genius at political lampoon was coloured by his own inconsistent opinions. In one instance he represented George IV as a drunken debauchee, yet in another the king appears as Coriolanus at his most noble. He condemns government brutality at the Peterloo Massacre and then denounces radical agitators. His sympathy for the condition of the poor (a stance he adopted all of his life) is balanced by ridicule for their pretentious aspirations. He was an original who shifted his ground like the best of politicians. He was brave and had a nature that was childlike and was completely transparent, for an enormous amount of his art was inspired by the impulse to try to do good.

He nearly did not go into caricature. He followed his father and brother into the army, and then followed his father Isaac into drink. Isaac, an accomplished caricaturist and miniature painter, sank into alcoholism from 1797. His art suffered, not in quality at first but in quantity. One night in April 1811, just as George was starting to get commissions, Isaac accepted a challenge to a whisky-drinking match. Isaac won, fell into a coma and died, aged forty-eight. George, the younger son, was more affected; he missed his gentle inebriated father, his tutor in his craft, but this also gave him the impetus to carve his own niche in his chosen field and to find some solace in the bottle! His drinking lurched dangerously close to his father's.

Dickens witnessed him walking into the library of his home in Devonshire Place after a night's celebrating, stinking of tobacco, beer and sawdust, afraid to go home to his wife.

Opinions differ as to why he took up the campaign against drink. Was it because his first wife was diagnosed with the fatal tuberculosis? The marriage, like his second, was childless, and he felt remorse? A friend's alcoholic death? The selling-power of his name was fading and commissions were falling? His taking the pledge was preceded by his completion of *The Bottle*, a set of eight plates beginning with a husband urging his wife to drink and ending with the ruin of the family. All his work was influenced by his new crusade. The ills of the poor he now put down to drink. Even on the occasion of his silver wedding, in 1875, it was with tea that the toast to Mr and Mrs Cruikshank was drunk!

Yet Victorian values are barbed! After his death, a mere three streets away, a much younger woman and ten children were established as his secret family.

The Last of the Romantics
THE EARL OF KILMOREY'S TWICKENHAM AFFAIR

Francis Jack Needham, 2nd Earl of Kilmorey (1787–1880), was fifty-three when he arrived in Twickenham. His life until then had been tinged with bitterness and regret. He was married and had procured himself the obligatory heir, but his life was one of duty. His presence in Twickenham was due in part to his separation from his wife and the need to find a new purpose to his life. He embraced the quiet life, away from the petty intrigues and high japes for which he had been known. Indeed, until his arrival in Twickenham this handsome, witty and gallant gentleman was quite a rake. He had run away from school, joined Wellington's army in the Peninsular War, been a member of the notorious Hellfire Club and had had more punch-ups than a professional boxer!

Jack Needham had been a friend of the Hoste family for some years. The father, Captain Sir William Hoste, Baronet, was a contemporary of Jack's. His death in 1828, five years after the birth of his youngest daughter, Priscilla, brought the families much closer. But it came as a huge shock to discover that the 56-year-old Earl of Kilmorey had eloped with the twenty-year-old Priscilla in 1843! Her brothers tried in vain to find the couple.

The earl's marital arrangements were sufficiently cold to enable him to leave his wife. The youth and the promise of devotion to an ideal in Priscilla must have awakened the sentimental and romantic dreams of the middle-aged peer. However much society may have condemned it, theirs was a devoted and passionate affair. It was sealed with the birth of his adored son Charles, on 19 July 1844 in Cross Deep House, Twickenham. The fact that Kilmorey's name appears on his son's birth certificate shows that theirs was quite an open liaison.

In 1846 the couple moved to Orleans House. Here, as with all his future houses, he indulged in his passion for change. He altered, added to, adorned and planted, often with his own hands. Once everything was completed to his satisfaction he would purchase another house and do the same. They lived in Orleans House for five years. In 1851 he purchased St Margaret's House – and then Gordon House.

It was Gordon House that the earl made his home. Here he built a new house, designed by Lewis Vulliamy and built by Messrs W. Cubitt & Co. Here he was to live with his beloved Priscilla and seven-year-old Charles. Shortly after 1851 it became apparent that Priscilla was suffering from a terminal illness. In September 1853 Kilmorey wrote to the Brompton Cemetery Company requesting a select site for her burial. The mausoleum was to be a central feature in the cemetery. It was built in polished pink and grey granite, 15ft square, and designed in an Egyptian style by H.E. Kendall (senior). The proportions of this little Egyptian temple are perfect. Inside, on the back wall, Kilmorey commissioned

a large marble relief showing the dying Priscilla recumbent on a day bed with the earl kneeling at its foot and their son Charles standing at the head. From when the mausoleum was first built there was a space beside her, ready for the earl. Kilmorey also had his coffin prepared, covered with crimson velvet.

Priscilla died on 21 October 1854, the day the grant of the plot for her mausoleum (pictured) was finally sealed. Here she was laid to rest, only to be moved together with her mausoleum to the earl's new house, Woburn Park in Chertsey, in 1862. Wherever the earl moved, his dead consort followed. In 1868 the mausoleum moved once again to Gordon House. Here he would often lie in his coffin rehearsing his own funeral. He had an underground tunnel built from the house to the little temple, so that when the whim took him he would dress in white garb and pace the tunnel to his resting-place.

When he finally died, aged ninety-two, the desolate Earl of Kilmorey joined his beloved in a dressing gown of rats' fur, in this testament to his undying passion for his Priscilla.

Girls Count Too!

FRANCES MARY BUSS OF CAMDEN, INSPIRED FOUNDER OF NORTH LONDON COLLEGIATE SCHOOL FOR GIRLS

Frances Mary Buss (1827–94), or Miss Buss as she was later to be known, was born at a time when the Industrial Revolution was drastically altering the life of the English. It was creating immense wealth but was also exacerbating the negative aspects of urban life. The man went to work and the woman stayed at home. Marriage was no longer a working relationship. The general consensus of opinion was unhappily compounded by Ruskin's own views, 'that a woman's function was to guide and uplift spiritually her intellectually superior husband'. Teachers were hopelessly incompetent and untrained. The intellectual development of a girl, once a matter of concern, had become a matter of indifference. This was about to change. Three women were to dominate women's education in the nineteenth century: Miss Emily Davies, Miss Dorothea Beale and Frances Mary Buss (pictured).

Miss Buss proved that women were able, mentally and physically, to benefit from quality education. She also evolved the methods and set the standards for providing that education. She had no option but to educate. She was the eldest of ten children (five of whom survived childhood) of Robert and Frances Buss. Undoubtedly, being the eldest, the future Miss Buss developed her gravitas and sense of purpose quickly. They lived, for the most part in genteel poverty, in Mornington Crescent – an area populated by retired gentlemen, doctors, and lawyers: the aspiring professional classes.

Robert Buss was an unsuccessful artist, but he had exhibited at the Royal Academy. He was kind, unassuming and fun with no business sense. Frances was altogether different, obstinate, an efficient administrator and organiser with plenty of energy. Frances Mary went to a local mixed school, and at ten went on to a 'higher' school kept by a Mrs Wyand at the corner of Rutland Street, Hampstead Road. Sometimes she was left in sole charge of her class, her first taste of teaching!

Encouraged by her daughter's success as a student, and desperate to increase the family's meagre income, Mrs Buss went on a rudimentary training course for teachers at the Home and Colonial School Institute, Gray's Inn Road. She and other students successfully petitioned this institute to start a school for secondary school teachers.

Mrs Buss and her daughter opened a small school at 14 Clarence Road, Kentish Town, in 1845 and early success encouraged them to move to larger premises in Holmes Terrace four years later. Miss Buss, meanwhile, had developed a strong desire to improve the standard of her teaching and enrolled in evening classes at the recently established Queen's College in 1849. The principal, Frederick Denison Maurice, gave a stern warning at his inaugural lecture: 'the vocation of a teacher is an awful one . . . she will do others unspeakable harm if she is not aware of its usefulness. . . . How can you give a woman self-respect. . . . Watch closely the first utterances of infancy, the first dawnings of intelligence; how thoughts spring into acts, how acts pass into habits.'

Inspired by her diploma in French, German and historical geography, Miss Buss opened a new school at their new family house at 12 Camden Street, near Oakley Square, NW 1, the North London Collegiate School for Girls, on 4 April 1850. It was 'to prepare pupils for any position in life which they may be called upon to occupy and which with a larger number of pupils can be afforded at a moderate fee of 2 guineas a quarter'. Thirty-five pupils, daughters of the local professionals, assembled on that day. Two years later there were over a hundred. The whole Buss family taught – her mother, her two ordained brothers and her father, who finally found his vocation! The school finally moved to Canons Park in 1926.

Reach for the Stars

JOHN CRAIG'S TELESCOPE

The variety and richness of the Victorian era created some architecture and intriguing monoliths that still form part of everyday London life, such as the Houses of Parliament, the Victoria and Albert Museum, most of the bridges that ford the Thames and some of the London Underground. Others have disappeared, such as the Crystal Palace and Craig's telescope on Wandsworth Common.

Nowadays giant telescopes can be found in mountains far away from cities with their atmospheric pollution. The cost of such telescopes is too great for a single individual even to entertain thoughts of paying for them. In the mid-nineteenth century the world's largest

reflecting telescope was in Ireland, on the estate of William Parsons, 3rd Earl of Rosse. He was a council member of the Royal Astronomical Society. It was affectionately known as the Leviathan of Parsonstown. The world's largest refracting telescope, however, was in an observatory on Wandsworth Common, in the heart of London!

Wandsworth Common formed part of the Spencer family holdings. A retired country vicar, John Craig of Leamington, devised a telescope which he hoped would enable him to discover whether Venus had a satellite and to confirm the discovery of Saturn's third ring. He was neither a member of the Royal Society nor a member of the Royal Astronomical Society, just an individual with a bee in his bonnet. The 4th Earl Spencer accordingly fenced off 2 acres of common land for the vicar's monolith, 'in perpetuity or so long as the telescope shall be maintained', near the present Herondale Avenue.

Craig's design for the telescope was highly innovative. The mount consisted of a massive 64-ft high brick tower from which were slung massive iron chains holding a 76-ft cigar-shaped tube. The various floors of the tower could be weighted to prevent any vibrations, and to point the 'cigar' in the desired direction the chains could be rotated around the tower. The end containing the eyepiece was fixed to a small wooden trolley running on a circular rail 52ft from the centre of the tower. A metallic hoop fixed to the centre of the cigar enabled the telescope (pictured) to move up and down, using a counterweight on the opposite side of the tower.

Refracting telescopes are difficult to make as a good objective lens needs to be free from rainbow-like edges in the image. These edges are created when a lens bends lights of different wavelengths or colour through differing angles. The Dollond brothers of Wandsworth had, in the preceding century, developed the idea of using two distinct pieces of glass to make a double lens. Each piece of glass had different colour-dispersing properties. In this instance the optical work was made by Mr Somers of Euston Square.

Work began on the telescope in May 1852 and it was finished in August. Initially the press gave it favourable reviews, extolling its virtues; 'a quarter-inch letter can be read at the distance of half a mile' and 'were such a building, for instance, as Westminster Abbey in the Moon, this telescope would reveal all its parts and proportions'. Problems arose when the claim was made that it could view Saturn's third ring. This was published in the press but the article raised the first doubts on the quality of the instrument: 'the Craig telescope is, in a small portion of one of its lenses, too flat by about the five thousandth part of an inch. This has to be stopped out when extreme accuracy of definition is required as when observing such a fine point as an object as Saturn's third ring'.

This virtual condemnation halted the public coming to view the telescope, although it remained a curious Wandsworth anomaly for a short time. Its poor optical quality seems to have been its death knell, combined with the death of Craig's wife in 1854. The broken and disheartened vicar returned to Leamington and the tower and the telescope were dismantled and sold. The exact date of the demise of this monolith is unknown but was probably between 1857 and 1858. This piece of the common remained enclosed and was subsequently developed.

An Inconvenient Way to Die

THE SUICIDE OF FRAUDSTER JOHN SADLEIR ON HAMPSTEAD HEATH

Hampstead was a very awkward place for a suicide. The lord of the manor had very extensive rights. One such was that of deodand. When a suicide was committed within the jurisdiction of the lord of the manor, and the jury had returned a verdict of suicide, the lord of the manor was entitled, as heir, to seize the goods and chattels of the deceased (except for his estate or his inheritance).

On the morning of 16 February 1856 a well-dressed body was discovered lying behind Jack Straw's Castle tavern, in a hollow on Hampstead Heath. A silver cream jug and a phial lay by the body. Death, it was established, had been caused by swallowing the contents of the jug. A search of the corpse's clothes revealed a piece of paper identifying, supposedly,

the identity of the bearer, 'John Sadleir, Gloucester Square, Hyde Park'. Sadleir (1814–56) had started his professional life as a Dublin solicitor, becoming a director of the Tipperary Joint Stock Bank and Chairman of the London and County Bank in 1848.

In 1847 Sadleir was elected MP for Carlow and in 1853 MP for Sligo. It was obvious from the start that he was destined for great things. He was ambitious, clever and ruthless. His legal background enabled him to deal in the lands sold in the Encumbered Estates Court in Ireland for a quick profit, and forging conveyances of these to raise money to finance his other 'get rich quick' schemes. The coming of the railways, and the potential immense profits to be made from them, enabled such astute businessmen as Frederick Huth, Richard Potter and William Jackson to realise immense fortunes. John Sadleir jumped on the bandwagon and actively financed the Grand Junction Railway of France, a Swiss railway, the Rome and Frascati Railway (co-financed with William Jackson), the East Kent Line and became chairman of the Royal Swedish Company, as well as Chairman of the London and County Joint Stock Banking Company – he was eminently successful in this last post and, it seems, well thought of by his contemporaries. His apparent business acumen enabled him to be selected as Junior Lord of the Treasury in 1853.

But his quest for riches and power caused him to make several mistakes. Of the 79,925 shares issued on the Royal Swedish Railway Company, 48,245 were held by him. He had a further 19,700 duplicate shares forged and sold to finance his various enterprises. His duplicity was discovered when Glyn's Bank, the London agent for the Tipperary Bank, returned cheques marked 'Return to Drawer' and 'Insufficient Funds'. The Bank of Ireland did the same. An enquiry was set up to discover the reasons for the failure of the Tipperary Bank.

Sadleir wrote to another director of the Tipperary Bank, Robert Keating, MP for Waterford: 'to what infamy have I come step by step – heaping crime upon crime; and now I find myself the author of numberless crimes of a diabolical character, and the cause of ruin, misery and disgrace to thousands – aye tens of thousands! Oh how I feel for those on whom this ruin must fall! I could bear all punishment, but I could never bear to witness the sufferings of those on whom I have brought this ruin. It must be better that I should not live.'

The *Nation*, a Dublin newspaper reviewing his suicide, said that he was a 'man desperate for nature . . . his fate seemed written in that sallow face, wrinkled with multifarious intrigue – cold, callous and cunning with an unscrupulous audacity and an easy and wily energy'. Such was the scandal that Dickens portrayed him as Mr Merdle, the London banker in *Little Dorrit* who became a bankrupt and committed suicide, 'immensely rich . . . a Midas without ears. He was everything good from banking to building. He was in Parliament of course, in the City necessarily. . . . He was tenacious of the utmost deference being shown by everyone, in all things to Society.'

Needless to say the lord of the manor of Hampstead seized the only tangible asset, the silver cream jug!

The Lady with the Lamp
FLORENCE NIGHTINGALE'S NURSING SCHOOL AT ST THOMAS'S

The appalling conditions in the hospitals in the Crimean War convinced the government that a suitable person should be found to supervise the nursing. Sidney Herbert, the minister for war, persuaded the Cabinet to employ Florence Nightingale and thirty-eight nurses – these were sent to the hospital at Scutari in 1854. Miss Nightingale was appalled at the lack of hygiene and the state of near starvation of the soldiers who arrived at the hospital. She took matters into her own hands and returned to Britain a national hero.

Florence Nightingale (1820–1910) (pictured) was a highly intelligent, articulate and cultivated woman born into extreme affluence. Her father was her teacher and gave Florence and her sister an unparalleled education. He taught her French, German, Italian, Latin, Greek, history and philosophy – not the usual education for a rich young woman! Her father realised he had gone too far when she asked to be taught mathematics at the age of twenty, as this was considered very unbecoming for a future wife. Despite several suitors, her education and her natural intelligence put paid to her matrimonial prospects: she did not wish to become an adornment, nor did she want to be part of the 'usual amount of Charity Balls, Charity Concerts, Charity Bazaars, whereby people bamboozle their conscience and shut their eyes. . . . England is surely the country where luxury has reached its height and poverty its depth.'

God supposedly called her to his service when she was seventeen and again seven years later. It was Sidney Herbert and his wife, whom she met in 1847 and whose interest in providing hospitals for the poor coincided with hers, who provided the catalyst for her burning ambitions. By the age of thirty-two Florence was superintending a charitable institution in Harley Street, organising supplies of goods and services, reducing staffing costs and bringing the dispensary in-house. She and Herbert had also conducted surveys of several hospitals and formed a working plan of how best to improve them and their ancillary services.

Florence wanted to create a nursing school in teaching hospitals but this was hampered by the perception of the establishment that this was too dangerous a profession for a young woman. She was stubborn, optimistic and had a total belief in herself and in God. Everything had a reason, even the gilded life of a caged bird of the first twenty-seven years of her life. Her experience in the Crimea enabled her to write a concise and instructive report to the War Commission. She used her skills and her energy to develop guidelines for modern hospital management and nursing care as well as hygiene – her consuming interest. This was put to good use in the American Civil War and to overcome the sanitation problems in India. Another aspect of her work was to write a booklet on nursing, *Notes on Nursing*, coldly received by the establishment but selling millions of copies worldwide. Her pioneering graphs and charts, used in the army hospitals, enabled her to give accurate information. They are used to this day.

The consequences of the Crimean War were far-reaching. A public Nightingale Fund was set up and raised £44,000. These funds were to be used to set up an 'institution for the training, sustenance and protection of Nurses and Hospital attendants'. The need to establish a school within an existing hospital was recognised. The ideal candidate, St Thomas's Hospital, about to be redeveloped, was chosen, though not without strong opposition from the medical fraternity. June 1860 saw the first intake of probationary nurses into the first nursing school, the Nightingale School of Nursing.

The Poet Painter

SOUTH LONDON'S PRE-RAPHAELITE PAINTER ARTHUR HUGHES

Dante Gabriel Rossetti, William Holman Hunt, Ford Madox Brown, John Everett Millais and Edward Burne-Jones are names to conjure up the richness and diversity that was the Pre-Raphaelite movement in the nineteenth century. One of this glorious brotherhood, however, is all too often omitted, not because he was a lesser artist, but because he was a little younger and thus on the periphery of that golden cabal.

Arthur Hughes (1832–1915) (pictured) was born in Dover Street, W1, and showed a particular talent for drawing from very early on. He was sent first to the government's School of Design, Somerset House, and then to the Royal Academy's Antique School where in 1850 he was introduced to Pre-Raphaelitism. He married in 1855, having vowed to get married 'after much billing and cooing . . . when he sold or completed a picture'. After a cramped studio in Belgrave Square, SW1, he and his young wife Tryphenia moved to her home town, Maidstone, where Rossetti and others would visit. Hughes was liked above all for his modesty and gentle nature. William Rossetti would say that 'if I had to pick out . . . the sweetest and most ingenuous of all, the least carking and querulous and the freest from envy, hatred and malice and all uncharitableness, it would be Arthur Hughes'.

Ruskin, the arch-critic of the time, praised Hughes' work for a 'sense of beauty that is quite exquisite'. Despite this Hughes found it quite difficult to sell his pictures because as he admitted he 'was trouble with that unaffected modesty which has always so stood in the way of my advancement'. Yet his was the life of a devoted family man, supremely happy with his beautiful wife and their eventual large brood of children, and an almost religious devotion to his other passion, Art.

Maidstone proved too far from London and the Hughes family moved to Staines in 1860, finally moving to 12 Oberstein Road, Wandsworth, in 1863. It was from this house that he finally got the commissions he needed to feed his large family. Each patron was very well received – one in particular was told that 'you are really paving my way into this house with gold'!

This was a poor reward, though, for a man with an undeniable talent, more talented than some of his contemporaries. Not only were his works more often than not rejected by the Royal Academy, he was never elected to it. His works were also ill-received in America. While the sales of his pictures were erratic, his meeting with the writer George Macdonald in 1859 was eventually to make him a household name. Arthur Hughes was to illustrate Macdonald's classics, *The Princess and Curdie*, *The Princess and the Goblin* and his masterpiece *At the Back of the North Wind*.

George Macdonald's inspiration to have Hughes as illustrator of his books was to provide Hughes with yet another author to illustrate for, Christina Rossetti. His illustrations of her nursery poems, *Sing Song*, were to be his most admired and successful illustrations – these involved children, for which he remains famous. One contemporary who was to view his pictures at a Royal Academy exhibition was to say 'how tenderly he can read the face of fair children, how beautifully he can paint them'. He would later illustrate Thomas Hughes' *Tom Brown's Schooldays*.

Hughes persevered with his painting, selling some at decent prices but not at the huge fees commanded by his contemporaries.

The family's house at Oberstein Road brought them into contact with Lewis Carroll, who became an honorary uncle for the Hughes brood, often taking them up to the West End for treats. The family moved once again in 1865, to Windsor Lodge, by the river at Putney, where many of Hughes' friends visited to watch the Boat Race. From here, he and Tryphenia often attended Rossetti's parties, held at his house in Cheyne Walk. Hughes was to leave the South Bank in 1869 for Fulham and then Wallington, eventually living out his days at Kew Green from 1891. His death in 1915 brought a telling comment, that 'while artists with not one-half of his charm and ability have risen to popular success, this poet amongst artists has been content to work quietly'.

Cooking the Books

MRS BEETON'S LAST RESTING PLACE

Cookery today is all the rage – in the papers, the magazines, on the television and on the net. Restaurants and all manner of eateries are mushrooming all over Britain's hotspots as the British become a café society, and food is king.

The doyenne of English cooks is Mrs Beeton (1836–65). She was known as the mother of English cookery and her books – including the bible, *Mrs Beeton's Household Management* – are still incredibly popular. This lady is largely remembered wrongly, for the ridiculously large amounts used in her recipes – 'take ten eggs' – but to accuse her of extravagance is inaccurate as her aim was to promote efficiency and economy in the household.

Isabella Mary Beeton, née Mayson, her husband Sam and her second son Samuel Orchart are buried in West Norwood Cemetery. Exactly why they are buried here remains something of a mystery. West Norwood Cemetery was one of the grand cemeteries of London, vying with Nunhead and Highgate. It was nearer Epsom, where the Beetons lived. One theory is that the couple was so distraught at the loss of Samuel that a relation in Epsom was left to make the arrangements to have the child buried there; and that Sam and Isabella subsequently chose to be buried with him.

Isabella, one of four children, started her life in the shadow of St Paul's and lost her father at the age of four. Her father's best friend, Henry Dorling, clerk to the Epsom

Racecourse, was a widower with four children. Dorling married the widowed Mrs Mayson, taking the family to live in Epsom in 1843. Theirs was to be an idyllic life but no sinecure for the new Mrs Dorling, for she started her second marriage with eight children and ended up with twenty-one!

Isabella now had a secure and prosperous home which, however, was not without its negative aspects; she was the eldest, was in charge and was sometimes regarded as an interloper in her own home. Her education, however, was first class. A short spell in a school in Islington was followed by further education in a boarding school at Heidelberg. Germany took girls' education far more seriously than England. There Isabella was taught to speak German and French fluently, became an accomplished pianist and learnt the values of diligence and German Methodism that she would apply in her career. It was also there that her burgeoning interest in cookery was encouraged. She continued her pastry lessons on her return to England.

How she met Sam Beeton, the aspiring young publisher, can only be an educated guess. The Beetons and the Maysons lived in the same area, had the same style of life and Sam's mother became a close friend of the widowed Mrs Mayson. Sam and Isabella were married in 1856.

Sam Beeton, like Isabella, was a firm believer in good education for girls, a liberal and an optimist. By the time of their marriage the reading population had expanded by millions but most could not afford the prices of the current magazines and books. Someone of Sam's energy and drive was needed to create a cheaper alternative. W.H. Smith's bookstalls were springing up and Sam cleverly serialised *Uncle Tom's Cabin*, eventually creating a de luxe volume which made him and his partner, Charles Clarke, a lot of money. Sam then embarked on *The Englishwoman's Domestic Magazine* and Isabella came in on the editing and contributed articles on cookery. Her epigrams, 'a daily supply is a daily waste' for example, became a byword. This publication became the precursor to *Household Management* and indeed to all women's magazines. It was cheap (2*d*), very informative and deliberately encouraged its readers to use their minds – a controversial attitude in the Victorian patriarchy.

What is all the more remarkable is that Isabella continued working during her first pregnancy and after her son's birth. His early death seems to have precipitated Sam's plan of a book, *Household Management*, and certainly galvanised Isabella into researching for it. The book was partly influenced by Dr Kitchener's *The Cook's Oracle* (1811), and Elizabeth Acton's *Modern Cookery for Private Families* (1845). Brillat Savarin, the cook's philosopher, was also a profound influence. It was primarily written for the middle-class housewife for whom "to understand the Economy of Household Affairs is essential to a woman's proper and pleasant performance of the duties of a Wife and Mother".'

Household Management took four years to write. The recipes were tried and tested by the author and were accompanied by colour plates of the dishes. It was not an immediate success but was to sell consistently from the 1870s onwards. Sadly Isabella died of puerperal fever after the birth of her son Mayson; the popularity of her books is an enduring testimony to Mrs Beeton's profound influence on modern cookery.

Flushed with Success

THOMAS CRAPPER, SANITARY ENGINEER OF CHELSEA AND BATTERSEA

Thomas Crapper is a name one smirks at, an odorous name that reminds one of schooldays, school pranks and toilet humour. The English and the entire Anglo-Saxon world have had a long infatuation with bowel trouble and this Victorian plumber, Thomas Crapper (1836–1910) (pictured), retains the dubious and possibly spurious honour of inventing the flush toilet.

Thomas Crapper was born in Yorkshire long after the first lavatory flushed. The first patent, taken out by the watchmaker Alexander Cummings for a mechanically flushing toilet, was in 1775 at the beginning of the Industrial Revolution. Crapper was first apprenticed to a plumber and moved down to London with his brother George in the early 1860s. He lived at 1 Buckmaster Road, SW11 (formerly Middleton Road) from 1867 to 1874 and at no. 8 from 1874 to 1886. George lived at 19 Gorst Road, SW4. The brother also took a hand in developing and building 8–10 St Mark's Villas in Buckmaster Road and installing, no doubt, their own toilets!

Thomas set up shop on the King's Road in an age of extreme moral propriety where the mere mention of a toilet brought a flush to the young Victorian damsel's distressed face. His shop was revolutionary and rather disquieting – it had a glass front where the water closet paraphernalia could be plainly seen. He set up shop in the golden age of the toilet, and these were on everyone's mind. Architects started to incorporate flush WCs into building plans. Inventors and entrepreneurs scrambled on to the loo bandwagon to corner the new market. George Jennings, one of the three 'musketeers' of plumbing (the other two were Thomas Twyford and the hero of this story), had provided WCs at a price at the 1851 Great Exhibition, and the price was one penny – hence the expression to spend a penny.

The Victorian era was awash with smells and perfumiers had a field day. But Thomas Crapper did not invent the 'valveless lavatory cistern', although he did take out nine patents in his lifetime, four for improvements to drains, three for water closets, one for manhole covers and the last for pipe joints. A patent was granted to Albert Giblin for 'the silent valveless water waste preventer' in 1898, however, and Giblin worked for Thomas Crapper. This product was a siphonic discharge system that allowed a toilet to flush effectively when the cistern was only half full. Crapper may well have bought the patent rights and marketed the device himself.

Early models of the new lavatories were less than perfect. Crapper himself once suffered from concussion when a mixture of air and sewer gas exploded. Some fifty years earlier a plumber suffered a similar fate when he lit a candle in the smelly sewage drains under the flagstones of a London house and did not live to tell the tale.

Thomas Crapper's roll of honour, though, was his winning the contract to install his porcelain toilet bowls with valve-controlled cisterns in the royal cloakrooms of Sandringham House. The goddess of the Roman sewers, Cloacina, after whom the cloakroom is called, was eulogised by a Victorian wag:

Oh Cloacina goddess of this place
Look on thy servant with a smiling face,
Soft and cohesive let my offering flow
Not rudely swift nor obstinately slow.

The Thomas Crapper factories lasted well beyond his death. In fact the company has recently been revived. The Thomas Crapper legend continues in the belief that the term 'crapper', brought back to the States in 1920 by US soldiers who had noticed that all London toilets bore the legend 'Thomas Crapper – Chelsea', returned to its roots when their children returned to fight in the Second World War. The brand name, like that of Hoover, became a new word.

They were built like Emporia in the reign of Victoria
In the Castle, Manor or Grange.
With their seats made of wood, which have gamely withstood
Pressures greater than mere winds of change . . .
But forget all the strain, pull the gleaming brass chain
(With a porcelain handle no less)
And, released by a piston, from within a vast cistern
Comes a roar – and you're flushed with success.

Tea, Travel & Treasures
THE GREAT COLLECTOR, FREDERICK HORNIMAN OF CRYSTAL PALACE

The High Victorian era of the British Empire brought the profits of its far-flung reaches home. The successful Victorian entrepreneur was a very lucky man. The capital, the City and all the other large British cities were a testament to the wealth of the individuals – imposing mansions, office buildings, government offices and museums. The Victorian mania for accumulating wealth was matched by its great merchants using some of their profits to found charitable institutions to assist those less fortunate – a largesse that reaped other benefits. Another craze equal to these fortunes was that of collecting from the outer reaches of the Empire – Cleopatra's Needle made its way from Egypt to the Thames Embankment, the Parthenon Marbles made their way to the British Museum and esoteric collections found new homes in private residences. One such collector was Frederick John Horniman (1835–1906), tea merchant extraordinaire, whose Quaker father, John, had reputedly been one of the first tea importers to sell tea in packets and one of the last men to ride to work on a black horse in full Quaker costume!

Frederick John Horniman was typical of his breed; he ran his business personally, was a member of the LCC, MP for Falmouth and a collector of 'curios and specimens of insect life'. How he got the bug is a matter for conjecture, but contrary to popular opinion he did not purchase most of his collection on his travels – he bought it from other collectors, travellers and foreign institutions. The collection of natural history and tribal arts and crafts, including musical instruments, was stored in his large house in Forest Hill. The collection grew so large, and visitors to his 'museum' became so constant, that his wife gave him an ultimatum. The family accordingly moved in the early 1870s to Surrey Mount, 'midway between Forest Hill and Lordship Lane Stations' and close to the Crystal Palace, the site on which the present museum stands.

Horniman only started his travels in the late 1880s, visiting Canada and the United States and opening his museum to the public at about the same time. His world tour began in 1895. His diaries and accounts of these vividly convey the Victorian lust of the collector, the big-game hunter and the scientist. He travelled to India, Burma, Japan, China and Egypt. His stay in Egypt is reminiscent of the modern traveller's journey. He travelled on a P&O steamer to Ismailiya and took the train to Cairo, then boarded a steamer to Luxor. His

The Horniman Museum.

observation that 'rapid and easy travelling is attracting a great number of travellers to this interesting country' was based on the efforts of Thomas Cook and Son.

In 1870 John Mason Cook (Thomas Cook's son) was appointed sole agent for passenger traffic on government-owned steamers. By 1875 he had established his own steamer service and by the late 1880s had added hotels to his empire. The Shepheard Hotel in Cairo, one of F.J. Horniman's stops, was a Thomas Cook hotel, as was the one in Luxor. Horniman's description of the Shepheard was that of an 'immense building with palatial accommodation', whereas he viewed the 'primitive and squalid' lower quarters of Cairo with an anthropologist's detached air, and the 'squalid mud houses' in the 'Arab village' by Ismailiya were also noted as 'interesting'. John Mason Cook's efforts at keeping the tourists isolated from the less acceptable realities of Egyptian life worked – even for F.J. Horniman!

While in Cairo Horniman met and was guided by Howard Carter (of later Tutankhamen fame), who introduced him to officials of the Cairo Museum. Cairo Museum had mummies and artefacts for sale in a separate room. Carter took him to Luxor and Karnak. He purchased some 'very fine mummies in magnificently ornamented inner cases' from the Gizeh Museum.

Horniman stayed two weeks in Egypt, returning sated and with an overburdened museum. A new museum, the present one, was opened in 1901.

When Irish Eyes Are Smiling
SOCIETY ARTIST JAMES TISSOT IN ST JOHN'S WOOD

Joseph Jacques Tissot (1836–1902) moved from Paris to London following a disastrous association with the Paris Communards at the end of the Franco-Prussian War in 1871. He had been one of the more successful young Parisian artists, portraying the Beau Monde of the capital and being effortlessly integrated into Parisian society. He could number among his friends James Whistler and the journalist and founder of *Vanity Fair*, Thomas

Gibson Bowles. His military service with the Garde Nationale during the war was a departure for any artist, but his espousal of the cause of the Communards earned him the enmity of other former friends such as Degas.

James (he had started to affect this anglicisation of Jacques in the late 1860s), on first settling in London, drew a series of caricatures for *Vanity Fair* and then branched out into depicting life in the upper echelons of London society, particularly the nouveaux riches, whose ready purses and yearnings to be accepted by the established order made them purchase anything that would aggrandise them.

He lived in London for a very successful decade, earning enough to purchase a large house in St John's Wood, 7 Springfield Road, with a waiting room where his customers were plied with a constant flow of champagne. His immediate success lay in the fact that he depicted modern subjects with all their accompanying colours and with an underlying languid nuance, particularly when painting women. He was in many ways ahead of his time, as one could see that the artist more than appreciated the female form, and even fully clothed his subjects were almost erotic in their expressions and poses – a subject that caused hot gossip in prurient London society. Tissot was particularly occupied with the minutiae of the woman's toilette, the angle of her hat, the fall of a flounce and the fabric of her clothes. John Ruskin delivered a back-handed compliment on viewing some of his paintings when he said that 'Mr Tissot's paintings require a special notice, because their dexterity and brilliancy are apt to make the spectator forget their consciousness. Most of them are, unhappily, mere coloured photographs of Vulgar Society.' By 1873 Tissot had moved to larger premises at 34 Grove End Road. This 'charming, very handsome man, was always very well groomed and had nothing of artistic carelessness, either in his dress or demeanour', and always used attractive models, one of whom was Kathleen Newton.

They had met in St John's Wood when she was posting a letter. She was a young Irish divorcée, with an infant child, who lived with her sister. She became a sitter and then his mistress by the mid-1870s. It was a passionate affair that raised many eyebrows. They were both Catholics living in an age when girlfriends, let alone married or divorced mistresses, were a delicate subject; they were accepted as long as it never became official knowledge. But James brought a divorcée into his house and openly lived with her, which was unpalatable for the delicate mores of high Victorian society. It seems, furthermore, that her second child was his.

Once ensconced with his beautiful muse, James Tissot obsessively painted his 'mavourneen' whose effect would make him pen 'She will bring in spite of frost, Beauties that the earth has lost' under one of her portraits. Before her arrival he would hold lavish dinner parties and be seen everywhere. Now that Kathleen was with him he became more reclusive, partly because he was shunned by the very society that he sought to emulate and paint. Their affair lasted six years. In 1882 Kathleen was diagnosed with tuberculosis, and despite trips to the seaside she died in St John's Wood on 9 November. He never got over her loss, painting her delicate features over and over again, fleeing their love-nest to Paris, where his religious predilection combined with his sense of utter loneliness drove him to paint religious and biblical subjects to the end of his life.

Portrait of the Artist as a Young Man

VINCENT VAN GOGH'S VISIT TO STOCKWELL AND SOUTH LONDON

It was at the end of August 1873 that Mrs Ursula Loyer welcomed a new lodger to her house at 87 Hackford Road, SW9. She was the widow of Jean Baptiste Loyer, an ex-minister of the French Protestant Church and professor of languages. Mrs Loyer ran a small school for boys in her home, aided by her young daughter Eugénie, and took in lodgers.

The new lodger, Vincent van Gogh (1853–90), was a shy twenty-year-old Dutchman 'with an ugly face, a mouth more or less awry, his face densely covered with freckles and hair of a reddish hue'. He had come to London to work as an assistant to the art dealer Goupil & Co. at 17 Southampton Street, near Covent Garden. His father, Theodorus van Gogh, was a Reformed Church priest who had decided that his shy son would benefit from a more worldly occupation and had sent him to The Hague to become an assistant to his art dealer brother, a partner in Goupil & Co. Four years later the young man was sent to London, embarking on what would be a self-destructive short life that would transform the art world.

Vincent's first impressions of England were mixed. He loved the London houses with their carefully tended and colourful front gardens, but found English art bad and uninteresting with a few exceptions such as Reynolds, Gainsborough, Constable, Turner and, above all, a largely forgotten artist George Boughton. Vincent sketched a lot. In fact he had always been encouraged to sketch, and his earliest known English sketch is one of his new lodgings at Hackford Road.

87 Hackford Road.

His new room was completely different from the attic bedroom he had had as a child. He wrote to Theo, his younger brother, that his room had no 'slanting ceiling and without blue paper with a green border'! The landlady's daughter also mesmerised the impressionable youth. It seems he became besotted with Eugénie. He wrote to his sister Anna saying that Eugénie was a 'girl with whom I agreed we should be brother and sister. You should also consider her as a sister. . .'. Vincent's infatuation with Eugénie, was, unfortunately, not reciprocated. She was secretly engaged to another lodger, an engineer, Samuel Plowman. He implored her to break off her engagement but she refused. Anna meanwhile was looking for work in England and was offered a room at the Loyers.

A morose, depressed and melancholic Vincent returned to his family for the summer holidays in 1874, when he spent a lot of time sketching. He came back to England with his elder sister, Anna. Their stay at the Loyers continued to be friendly. He took Anna to the Dulwich Picture Gallery and showed her the sights. Relations with the Loyers then became frosty, possibly because Eugénie's twentieth birthday heralded a formal engagement to Samuel Plowman. It may have also been because of Vincent's somewhat libertarian views on sex before or without marriage, which would be likely to offend an English Victorian miss.

In August 1874 Vincent and Anna had decided to move. Vincent wrote to their brother Theo telling him that the new house was covered with ivy. In fact they moved to Ivy Cottage at 395 Kennington Road, the home of publican John Parker and his family. It was little more than a mile from Hackford Road. Anna finally found a job teaching in Welwyn, a village some 25 miles north of London. Vincent was once again alone and prone to depression.

In November Vincent was transferred to Goupil's in Paris for a month. He was back in London in the new year, still living with the Parkers, working at the gallery and sketching in his spare time. In April he walked to Streatham Common, sketched it and sent it to Theo, saying that the common was 'a large grassy plain with oak trees and gorse. It had been raining overnight; the ground was soaked and the young spring grass was fresh and green.'

He left for France this year, but returned to Isleworth in 1876 for a year. He became ever more inverted and melancholic, and his emotions appeared to be released only through his painting.

Play it Again, Sam
BRITAIN'S FIRST BLACK COMPOSER, SAMUEL COLERIDGE TAYLOR

'Those whom the gods love die young' is a sad description of the gifted young people whose early death, in the prime of their lives, has robbed the world of yet another creative genius. This natural culling seems to be the way nature reminds the world of the ideals of youth. Nothing, though, prepared the musical world for the early and tragic demise of one of its rising stars, who died at the age of thirty-seven on 1 September 1912, after collapsing at West Croydon station.

Samuel Coleridge Taylor (1875–1912) (pictured), whom Elgar ranked as one of the greatest exponents of his art, was the only child of Daniel Hughes-Taylor, a black man from Sierra Leone, and an Englishwoman. Daniel was himself a man of no mean accomplishments. He had come to England to study medicine at Taunton College, Somerset, and then at King's College, London. He became a fellow of the Royal College of Surgeons and obtained a licence from the Royal College of Physicians. He then became an assistant, and heartened by his apparent popularity sought to have a practice of his own. He couldn't. The reason for this, it seems, was that the white population, particularly prospective patients, resented being told what to do by a black person. Disheartened, the young doctor left his wife and their infant son in Holborn and returned to his homeland in 1876.

Samuel and his mother moved to Whitehorse Road, Selhurst, SE25, opposite the Tabernacle. The young Samuel sang in the choir of St George's Presbyterian Church, under the tutelage of the musical director H.A. Walters, who realised that this child had a prodigious musical talent and encouraged him to learn the violin. Samuel went to the British Boys' School in Tamworth Road, West Croydon, and Walters guided his young protégé to a place at the Royal College of Music in 1890.

While studying at the Royal College, Samuel's interest in composition grew and such was his talent that he was recommended for tuition with Sir Charles Villiers Stanford, who was held to be the finest teacher of composition in London. During this time Samuel competed for one of the nine open scholarships at the college and was awarded the fellowship in composition in 1893. Sir George Grove, who had admitted him to the college, wrote 'now you are a scholar . . . you are before the world'. These early years were some of the most productive for young Samuel. It was in the shed at Whitehorse Road that he composed the *Song of Hiawatha*, one of his greatest achievements. The Royal College of Music regarded this as 'one of the most remarkable events in English musical history'. He premiered this work at the Royal Albert Hall and became a celebrity overnight.

In his final year at the college he met Jessie Walmisley, a student of singing and a white woman. They were married at Holy Trinity Church, Selhurst, and had two children, Hiawatha and Gwendolen. They then settled at 30 Dagnall Park, South Norwood.

During his short life he wrote prolifically and achieved much. He was appointed a professor at Crystal Palace School of Music and Art, conducted the Croydon Conservatory Orchestra, the Bournemouth Symphony Orchestra and was appointed Professor of Composition at the Trinity College of Music and at the Guildhall School of Music.

His achievements were, however, tempered with racial abuse. A fellow student at the college assaulted him on the same day he was lauded by his principal. One day he would be working, the next he would be spat at in the street. For these reasons Samuel became an active Pan-Africanist. He was a close friend of John Archer, the black mayor of Battersea. Samuel toured the United States where he held workshops for black musicians and composers, and was received at the White House by President Roosevelt. Evidence of his influence on the public was demonstrated by the sales of sheet music in the early 1900s – the three most popular works by British composers were Sullivan's cantata *The Golden Legend* and two by Coleridge Taylor, *Hiawatha* and a *Tale of Old Japan*.

A Worthy Gentleman

AN INVESTIGATION INTO FORMER CLAPHAM RESIDENT, ADAM WORTH

In early 1875 Henry J. Raymond, a quiet American gentleman, purchased a handsome late eighteenth-century villa, Western Lodge, on the west side of Clapham Common, for himself, a business colleague and his wife.

On Friday 26 May 1876 Gainsborough's celebrated portrait of the Duchess of Devonshire, recently purchased by Sir William Agnew, the art dealer, was stolen from his Bond Street gallery. The portrait had achieved star status – its subject encapsulated Victorian values and failings. Its theft gave the thief celebrity status, yet his identity remained an enigma for a quarter of a century. The rolled-up painting supposedly remained in the coach house in the grounds of Western Lodge for a decade.

Who was this American, who also possessed a spacious West End flat, a string of racehorses, a yacht, had Savile Row suits and entertained lavishly in both his residences?

Pinkerton's Detective Agency had warned Scotland Yard that Adam Worth, the notorious American arch-criminal and forger and his henchmen had arrived in England. Scotland Yard even knew his alias, Henry J. Raymond, and posted uniformed constables outside his Clapham mansion – to no avail.

Adam Worth was born in 1844 in eastern Germany to German Jewish parents. They emigrated to America when he was five. His tough impoverished childhood was the catalyst to his eventful career. A soldier in the Civil War, he then graduated to the criminal fraternity of the New York underworld, becoming a successful pickpocket and by the age of twenty-one organising gangs of pickpockets and supplementing his income with minor burglaries. He was different from the average criminal. He dressed like a dandy, avoided heavy drinking and abhorred violence. He controlled his growing empire with his steely intellect. His forte was meticulous planning.

'Piano' Charley Bullard was his partner in crime; he was everything Adam aspired to, cultivated, multi-lingual, a musician and of an old establishment family. Within four years Adam and his confederates were so successful that Pinkerton's Detective Agency began to take a very active interest in them and even tried, unsuccessfully, to nab them. Ironically, despite their fierce professional antagonism, William Pinkerton and Adam Worth had a high regard for each other which eventually turned into a deep friendship.

The move to England followed a highly successful gambling venture in Paris. Worth's supreme organisational skills gave him a phenomenally successful British venture. He 'farmed out' contracts so that no one knew who the boss was. His control was rigid but fair and his skills were also used in masterminding other European heists and forgeries. Despite Scotland Yard's efforts (which seemed amateurish by comparison with his), Adam's career continued unabated. He was nicknamed the Napoleon of Crime. This quiet gentleman became very rich. His annual expenditure averaged £20,000.

Worth had, it seemed, finally achieved his ambition: beautiful residences, nodding acquaintance with the great and the good, a 'mascot' rolled up in Clapham which showed his contempt for the British police, most notably his adversary Inspector John Shore. His contempt for the English criminal was equally damning. Maybe his acquisition also gave him the comfort of at least the semblance of a 'born' gentleman – a status he so patently craved.

Undoubtedly his exploits influenced a generation of writers. Conan Doyle's Moriarty might have been inspired by Worth. Moriarty, though, was tall and cadaverous, treacherous and coldly evil – Worth on the other hand was short, loyal, generous, a 'gentleman thief' whose style was more Raffles or the 'Gentleman Cambrioleur' of French fiction, Arsène Lupin. One of Adam's exploits, however, did give Conan Doyle the basis for the plot of the 'Red-Headed League'; he tunnelled into a bank from an adjoining property, netting $450,000 !

Adam Worth was the most successful criminal of the nineteenth century and Pinkerton's Agency regarded him as the cleverest. His life was the stuff of legend and dissemblance. His partner's wife was the mother of *his* children; his children reputedly never knew their father. He certainly spent brief stints in prison and eventually 'returned' the Gainsborough for a price: the broker was his old adversary William Pinkerton. Adam Worth was buried in Highgate Cemetery in 1902; the tombstone reads Henry J. Raymond. Western Lodge is now a home for homeless men, most of them ex-offenders.

The Forbes Road Tragedy
THE TERRIBLE FATE OF HARRIET STAUNTON IN PENGE

It was a strange quirk of fate that brought Louis Victor de Casabianca to the post office in Forbes Road, Penge, at that time on the evening of Friday 13 April 1877. Someone came in to enquire where he could register a death that had taken place at no. 34 that afternoon. The boundary line between Kent and Surrey ran through the centre of Forbes Road – was no. 34 in Kent or in Surrey? Mr de Casabianca discovered that the deceased woman was from Cudham in Kent. How extraordinary! His wife's sister was supposed to live in that area and her family were very anxious to trace her but had had no success.

He asked more pertinent questions and discovered the name and address of the doctor who had signed the death certificate. He subsequently identified the filthy, lice-ridden, emaciated body as that of his sister-in-law, 36-year-old Harriet Staunton. The police were called and a post-mortem ordered. It established that Harriet had died of 'starvation and neglect', and her husband, Louis Staunton, an auctioneer's clerk, his mistress, Alice Rhodes, his brother Patrick and Patrick's wife, Elizabeth, were arrested. What was the story behind this gruesome death?

Harriet Staunton, née Richardson, was born in 1841. She was the youngest of four children. Theirs was a comfortable life. Her elder sister, Eleanor, later Mrs de Casabianca, was the widow of the Hon. William Howard. The family was living in New Kent Road in 1873. Harriet frequently visited her aunt and cousin Thomas, in Walworth. Thomas had married a widow with two daughters, one of whom – Alice – had recently married Patrick Staunton, an artist and brother to Louis. On her aunt's death Harriet moved in with Thomas rather than move to the country with her mother.

Harriet was thirty-three, a bit dim and not particularly good-looking, but she wanted to get married. She also had, unfortunately as it turned out, £4,000 (about £155,000 nowadays) in her own right and was due to inherit more. She was a perfect catch for an opportunist. Louis Staunton was ten years younger and, much to her mother's horror,

Harriet married him on 16 June 1875 in Clapham. Under the law as it then was, Louis became entitled to all his wife's property and any future property she might inherit. This he took advantage of as quickly as possible.

The newlyweds settled at Loughborough Park, Brixton, in the same road as his brother Patrick. Harriet's mother tried to see her daughter but was rebuffed. Before long Alice

A contemporary newspaper's version of Harriet's death.

Rhodes had moved in with the Stauntons and Harriet became uneasy about the familiarity between Alice and her husband. This feeling was well founded as it transpired. Harriet's son Thomas Henry was born on 23 March 1876. One Clara Brown, Alice's cousin, was employed as a general servant. They moved to Upper Norwood in May and by the end of 1876, Harriet and her little boy were imprisoned and starving in a small cottage in secluded Cudham, Kent, while Louis Staunton lived openly with his mistress down the road. Harriet's mother's attempts to see her daughter were continually thwarted.

Harriet's weight plummeted to just over 5 stone. Staunton must have realised that his wife's death in the country would bring about an inquiry. So, one dark April night he brought the dying Harriet by train to Penge East station and moved her into pre-rented accommodation in Forbes Road. She died the following day.

The 'Gang of Four' were tried and sentenced to death. There was, however, widespread debate about how much Staunton was to blame. After the case was reopened, Alice Rhodes was pardoned, Patrick Staunton died in prison, Elizabeth was released a few years later and Louis was sentenced to twenty years' penal servitude. House prices in Penge suffered and Forbes Road was renamed Mosslea Road. Had Mr de Casabianca not been in Penge on that fateful day, Louis Staunton might well have got away with it.

Bear Necessity

E.H. SHEPARD'S EARLY LIFE IN ST JOHN'S WOOD

Ernest Howard Shepard (1879–1976) is best known as A.A. Milne's illustrator. This partnership was an immediate success, mirroring that of Lewis Carroll and Tenniel or Dickens and Phiz. It is a tribute to the two collaborators that the clumsy Pooh Bear, despite Disney's slickness, remains very much part of the nation's childhood.

E.H. Shepard was born at 55 Springfield Road, St John's Wood, moving with his family to 10 Kent Terrace when he was about four years old. His was an idyllic childhood. He was the youngest of three children whose father was an architect. His was the London one recalls in storybooks, of the 'pea soup' fog and the gas lamp-posts, lit every evening by the gas-men. His godmother, Aunt Alicia, had given him a tricycle shaped like a horse he named Septimus, which he would ride down the pavements clanking over the coal-hole covers. A milkmaid would lumber down the street carrying two buckets suspended from a wooden yoke, tipping milk into the jugs left outside the houses. The dustmen would come once a week in a horse-driven four-wheeled cart and the buses would sometimes stop outside the Windsor Castle pub on a hot summer's day to let their horses have a drink at the trough there!

Park Road, now a busy rat-run, was almost countrified with a neat row of shops that have since gone – Kensit the greengrocer, White the chemist, Mr Grahame the cabinet-maker and Maltby the tailor – and by the top of Gloucester Place, Coles the linen draper.

The maiden aunts lived in Gordon Square, WC1, where the children would go when their parents were away. Here life was somewhat more frugal but just as exciting, with a hip-bath in the bedrooms although there was a bathroom at the top of the house. Despite the aunts' attempts to make the house child-friendly, its dark furniture made it gloomy and it smelt of dinner and mahogany polish.

Queen Victoria's Golden Jubilee, in 1887, was the high point of Shepard's childhood. Coles had a riot of flags in its windows. The children trooped up to Park Road to watch the band of the Boys' Brigade and in the evening the family went out to watch the fireworks and the illuminations. Most of the houses had fairy lights on their window-sills and Oxford Street was ablaze with lights, music and dancing.

Sadly, their mother's death of an unspecified illness not long afterwards brought an end to that carefree childhood. The boys

E.H. Shepard.

were sent to an 'Academy for Young Gentlemen' known as Oliver's, on Acacia Road. The walk to and from school was fraught with danger, as the local boys would try to pick fights with the young gentlemen. At least, as Ernest recorded in his autobiography, he learnt the art of self-preservation. This was not to last long, however. After his wife's death, their father decided that a house in Hammersmith would be the best for his work and for the boys' next school, St Paul's.

Shepard's talent showed exceptionally early. At the age of five he would draw soldiers and battlefields with a maturity that belied his young years. He would eventually record such scenes for real when he served in the Royal Artillery in the First World War, and his pictures vividly brought out the horrors of that disastrous period. He is justly famous for his association with A.A. Milne, but his talent was also put to good use with illustrations for such books as *David Copperfield*, *Tom Brown's Schooldays* and *Aesop's Fables* in the pre-First World War years. His drawings were first accepted for *Punch* in 1906 and he became a member of staff in 1921, a situation that continued virtually until his death.

He was a gentle, kindly man whose illustrations mirrored his personality. While his drawings in *The Wind in the Willows* were affectionate caricatures, they depicted the lost innocence of youth, and the child's straightforward view of his world in *Winnie the Pooh*. It was in this collection of stories that Shepard returned to his gentle, late Victorian childhood, re-creating a timelessness where, even in the rain, all children have fun.

The Beloved Enchanter

ARTHUR RACKHAM, THE ILLUSTRATOR, IN SOUTH LAMBETH ROAD

Britain dominated the world in one particular aspect of art in the late nineteenth century – illustration. Among its proponents were Kate Greenaway, Edmond Dulac, Aubrey Beardsley and Arthur Rackham (1867–1939) (pictured).

Rackham was and remains one of the finest illustrators of his genre – science fantasy. His illustrations litter our favourite childhood books; from *The Wind in the Willows* to *Peter Pan in Kensington Gardens*, *Rip van Winkle*, *Alice's Adventures in Wonderland* and *King Arthur and the Knights of the Round Table*. He illustrated over 150 books, many of which were re-published *because* of his illustrations. He was born in South Lambeth Road.

The Rackhams were, as Arthur later proudly proclaimed, 'Transpontine Cockneys'. This, he later claimed, endowed him with intense powers of observation and with a fascination for the fantastic and the weird. His predecessors had all been in the teaching profession – in fact not only was his grandfather the owner-headmaster of his own school south of the river, but so was his great-grandfather.

Arthur's father, unlike his forebears, did not become a teacher. Instead he became a clerk at the Doctor's Commons and then at the Registry at the Admiralty Court, rising to the top of the civil service. He was a genial, fun-loving, God-fearing and relaxed man whose marriage to Annie was a happy one.

Their first home was at 210 South Lambeth Road, 'the next house to the corner on the South side of Mawbey Street', so Alfred wrote in his diary. They lived there for over twenty years, begetting a brood of seven children, and attended the local dissenting church, presided over by the controversial minister and pamphleteer James Baldwin Brown. The house, now demolished, was opposite Stamford House and Turret House, both also gone, with their extremely large and untended grounds with gnarled and wizened old elm and yew trees: a perfect place for the young Arthur to be imbued with the magic of nature, which he made his own in later life. The family then moved round the corner, to a larger house at 27 Albert Square.

Arthur, like his siblings, was encouraged to cultivate his talents, and like every little boy of his time was given a shilling paint-box before he was able to read or write. It never left his side. He was sent to the City of London School where he excelled in mathematics and was encouraged in his burgeoning interest in art. Unfortunately the relaxed mischief-maker had to cut his schooling short, aged sixteen, as his ill-health required a few months' absence in the warmer climes of Australia. On his return he became an insurance clerk by day and enrolled at Lambeth School of Art in the evenings. For his holidays he travelled Britain *en famille* or with friends, developing his sketching and painting techniques.

The family moved to 3 St Ann's Park Villas, Wandsworth, in the mid-1880s. Arthur continued with his watercolours and landscape painting during his spare time. It was from there that some of his paintings were sold to friends of the family. It was also from this address that he had his first picture accepted for the Royal Academy Summer Exhibition in 1888. He started to submit some of his drawings to the illustrated magazines of the time, such as *Scraps & Illustrated Bits*.

The future illustrator of the weird and wonderful graduated from his art college in 1890 and began to look tentatively towards the possibilities of illustrating as a commercial enterprise. He finally left home in 1892 to live in Lincoln's Inn Fields.

He illustrated his first book in 1893, settled in Hampstead and married. His craft would make him revered as 'Le Peintre Sorcier' or the 'Beloved Enchanter' whose drawings could humorously suggest the mysteries of nature:

> With a courtly bow, the bent tree sighed,
> May I present you to my friend?

Ice Cold in the Antarctic
SIR ERNEST SHACKLETON'S FORMATIVE YEARS AT DULWICH COLLEGE

The successful Antarctic explorer and adventurer, Sir Ernest Henry Shackleton (1874–1922), admitted that he had not discovered himself when a day-boy at Dulwich School. Indeed his three years at the London public school had not shown the world his mettle, but it did show him what he did not want to do!

Ernest Shackleton was the second child and elder son of an Irish farming family that eventually numbered two brothers and eight sisters. He was a male in an overwhelmingly female household. This might have crushed some, but he seemed to revel in all the attention, and soon learned that he could charm his womenfolk totally. His was an irrepressible spirit and learned to manipulate early.

When Ernest was six his father gave up farming, enrolled at Trinity College Dublin and qualified to be a doctor. On qualifying in 1887, he moved his whole family to 12 Westwood Hill, Sydenham, and practised as a homeopathic doctor for the next thirty years. The young Ernest was sent first to Fir Lodge in Croydon and then at thirteen to Dulwich College.

Ernest would have walked to school. The distance was short compared with those he covered in his native Ireland. His single hindrance was his soft Irish burr, which he retained all his life. This was to make him feel something of an outcast among the 'Anglos' of the College, and to give him the determination to drop the shackles of conventional education. He was a well-built youngster with an easy smile who did little academic work but made up for this on the field of sport. He would also step in to deal with bullies and gravitated to the role of protector – he was a natural big brother known for getting into scraps.

He found academic work tedious and hard to grasp despite being quite a bookworm. Geography, he complained, was 'names of towns, lists of capes and bays and islands', and dissection and interpretation dulled poetry. In fact he was unutterably bored, whether because he actively wanted to leave the school or because he was genuinely confused is a matter for conjecture. His later career was to show, however, that he could grasp all forms of theories and break them down to exercises anyone could understand. An early biographer joked that the only sign in his childhood that he was destined for higher things was a class ranking that was more 'south of the equator and sometimes perilously near the Pole'! He was invariably castigated in his reports as being a boy who wanted 'waking up' and who had 'not yet fully exerted himself'. This healthy good-looking boy with slate-blue eyes and dark hair, this humorous, imaginative and mischievous child could also be kind

and gentle, quick to forgive and generous to a fault. He was aware of this and used his duality of nature to convince his father to allow him to leave the school early for a life on the seas. He was to use this ingenuous appeal to great effect with countless women in later life.

Once he had decided what he wanted he began to excel as a student, showing that once he had fixed his sights on a goal he was motivated to apply himself. At the end of the spring term of 1890 the sixteen-year-old travelled to Liverpool and joined the crew of the *Hoghton Tower* as a cabin boy. This was hands-on learning where his stamina was tested to the extreme for the next four years, as was his resolve; it was life in the raw far away from the halls of Academe, and one he relished as a challenge.

Dulwich College (above) provided the catalyst for his undoubted abilities and matured the plans of the youngster. His genuine regard for others would mark him out as being ahead of his time, but would also blight his success with the hierarchy of the day. He was what everyone would have liked to have been, if they had had the courage to follow their dreams.

The Great Detection

CONAN DOYLE IN SOUTH NORWOOD

South London has had its fair share of gruesome murders and ghastly deeds. One cadaver was discovered at 3 Lauriston Gardens in Brixton in 1887. A corpse was discovered at Pondicherry Lodge, Norwood, in 1890. Yet another gory episode in the annals of Scotland Yard recalls a boxed pair of severed ears on their way to Croydon police station in the 1890s.

One of the sensational mysteries was that of the Beryl Coronet, a scandal causing high dudgeon among the greatest in the land and threatening the reputation of the second largest bank in the City. The mysterious happenings took place in Streatham in 1886, and would have had national repercussions had not the greatest of detectives solved this case in twenty-four hours!

Yes, Sherlock Holmes did venture south of the river! So did his creator, Sir Arthur Conan Doyle (pictured), to 12 Tennison Road, South Norwood, from 1891 to 1894. The fell deeds described above will be found in *A Study in Scarlet, The Sign of Four* and 'The Cardboard Box' respectively.

What brought the famous detective and his creator here? Conan Doyle no longer needed to live in central London. Although a practising GP, he was earning more from writing than doctoring. He had just had 'flu and decided that Montagu Place was not for him. South Norwood abutted on the open Surrey countryside and had streets of comfortable middle-class homes. It gave him peace to write, yet still allowed easy access to central London by train – and his new house, much to his delight, was next to a cricket pitch and shared tennis lawn. The house had sixteen rooms on three floors, stood back from the road, and the front garden was approached by a short drive.

In the afternoons Conan Doyle walked, played tennis or rode his tandem tricycle with his wife Louise. It is quite probable that these journeys gave him ideas for his stories; like many fiction writers, he based his fictional locations on real ones. For instance Lauriston Gardens, Brixton, feature in *A Study in Scarlet*. While these do not actually exist by name the description of the houses tallies almost exactly with 329-335 Brixton Road. In another adventure, that of 'The Blue Carbuncle', the imaginary Mrs Oakshott fattened geese at her premises, 117 Brixton Road.

The location of Fairbank, the house central to the story of 'The Beryl Coronet', remains a mystery. Come back, Sherlock Holmes, to help us solve the problem of its whereabouts! It's proving far from elementary although clues are plentiful: Streatham, in the last twenty years of the nineteenth century, was one of south London's most fashionable and expanding suburbs. 'The Beryl Coronet' describes 'a good sized house, standing back from the road. . . a double carriage sweep . . . large iron gates . . . on the right side a narrow path . . . leading to the tradesmen's entrance'. One could walk to the house from the station – but which station? Leigham Court Road still boasts some large Victorian houses and, while there is no Fairbank there is a Fairfield, and this house loosely fits the description. Another house, Leigham Holme, used to stand at the junction of Mount Nod Road and Leigham Avenue. This one fitted the description better, but so did Streatham Lodge, which used to stand between Heybridge Avenue and Hilldown Road. It had large iron gates and its owners were *bankers*. . . .

While living in South Norwood and absorbing locations for his mysteries, Conan Doyle visited Switzerland – in particular the Reichenbach Falls in 1893. This was the scene of the spectacular fight between Holmes and Moriarty and genesis of 'The Final Problem'. In 1894 Louise was diagnosed with tuberculosis. There was no cure and she was given only a few months to live. A short notice in the *Streatham News* informed readers that the couple was moving to Davos, Switzerland, and that Conan Doyle was then to undertake a lecture tour of America.

High Adventure

THE VICTORIAN NOVELIST G.A. HENTY

In the Victorian age in Britain writers were gods. Their stories were the stuff of legends. Their tomes were kept dusted on everyone's shelves. Modern critics, however, consider the themes somewhat old-fashioned and basic, particularly the adventure stories.

The British Empire ruled. Battles were fought and won by 'honourable' men who knew their duty to their country. Victorian writers reflected the glory and pride of Great Britain. Captain Marryat's delightful *Children of The New Forest*, recently adapted for the BBC, was an example of a stirring adventure with derring-do written by one such writer. The story delighted young and old, was full of Christian ethics, the bad were bad, the good, good.

Another writer of the Victorian age was G.A. Henty (1832–1902), whose works seem to be enjoying a welcome resurgence of popularity. George Alfred Henty (pictured) was larger than life. His big, burly frame could often be seen in the West End clubs – he lived at 33 Lavender Gardens from 1892 until his death, with his second, much younger wife. His first wife had died many years before, as well as two of his four children. His new home, he wrote to friends, was minutes from Clapham Junction 'which is only eight minutes from Victoria'!

He had always lived in the general area of Putney, first in Upper Richmond Road, then with his sister in Ravenna Road. On her death he moved to Lavender Gardens. He married his second wife at St Paul's, Clapham, in 1889. This huge man with a full beard and a bluff hearty face was the 'Edgar Wallace of the juvenile story'. His life story was as ripping as his yarns.

Henty attended Westminster School and then Cambridge, then moved swiftly to the Army Hospital Commissariat and went to the Crimea. His letters to his father reporting on the events that took place were published in the *Morning Advertiser*. Illness, most probably glandular fever, forced him to be repatriated, but once recovered he was sent to Italy as a purveyor to organise hospitals. He learned Italian to boot. He then managed coal mines in Wales and Sardinia, and went to America on business.

His knowledge of Italian and his previous experience as a war correspondent in the Crimea enabled Henty to return to Italy in 1866 to cover the Austro-Italian War for the *Standard*. There, after the Battle of Custozza lost by the Italians, he was discovered among the Italian troops and assumed to be an Austrian spy. He successfully talked his way out of a hanging.

Henry continued to work as a war correspondent for the *Standard* for a decade, covering the Italian campaigns, the Carlist uprising in Spain and many smaller wars in the African continent. He shot big game, and had some hair-raising escapes from some of the more dangerous wildlife. It was in Africa, too, that he met Henry Morton Stanley of Doctor Livingstone fame.

He became a full-time writer in 1867. His first novel, published in 1867, was one for adult readers, *Search for a Secret*. His first for children was in fact his fourth, *Out on the Pampas*, published in 1871. This was a story he originally told his children and subsequently published. All the children involved were named after his own, Charles, Hubert, Maude and Ethel.

Henty wrote 122 books and countless articles. He is best remembered for his stories for children. These adventure stories spanned the Roman Empire to the Victorians. The heroes were boys who were not always good, usually because of their lack of judgement. They were 'blood and morality' tales where honour is a real quality of human life – adversity is worth facing for a good cause, and when faced with courage and strength can yield great reward. His research was methodical; his battle scenes were extraordinarily detailed and can still bear the scrutiny of the historian. He relished criticising government policies, especially with his stories set in the colonies. He also had an interest in the Women's Movement. Were his ideas on Christianity and his beliefs 'passé and simplistic'? Has the world changed that much? One hopes not.

The Baboo from Bombay

DADABHAI NAOROJI, FIRST INDIAN MP IN NORTH-WEST LONDON

The arrival in England of Dadabhai Naoroji, a young Parsee, to take up a partnership in the Indian commercial firm of Cama and Co. in 1855 was unspectacular inasmuch as increasing numbers of Indians were moving to Britain, the hub of the Empire. Naoroji, an articulate, highly intelligent linguist, believed strongly in the apparent values of the Empire. He retained the British idea of 'fair play' to the end of his life. He lost no time in setting up his own cotton company and devoted himself to voice the political and economic grievances of his fellow countrymen. He set up a centre for the Indian civil service examinations, the London Indian Society, the East India Association and the London Zoroastrian Association.

Naoroji's speeches and writings attracted many influential Britons, John Bright, Henry Fawcett MP, W.S. Caine, H.M. Hyndman, the British socialist leader Keir Hardie and Ramsay Macdonald. He became convinced that if Indian reforms were to be realised he would need to become a member of the British Parliament.

In 1886 he started to canvass for a British constituency. The Liberal Party was the obvious choice. He contested the Holborn seat and lost. His next chance was for Finsbury Central in 1892. He won this seat with a majority of five over his Tory opponent. He became the first black to sit in Parliament.

Dadabhai Naoroji's candidature and subsequent election aroused the strongest passions within his own party and without. The Liberals were divided. John Bright warned that constituencies wanted 'local men or men of distinction'. Another colleague suggested that he should discard his Parsee head-dress for an English hat as it was 'better to appear altogether like an Englishman'. Some advised him to try a Scottish seat as the Scots had the reputation of being more liberal than English Liberals.

Some assets conspired to help him. His long residence in England, a western education and a lighter skin than even Lord Salisbury, one of his most outspoken critics, helped him, but provoked some of the more racist comments. Salisbury declared, 'I doubt if we have come to a point when a British constituency will take a black man to represent them . . . at all events

he was a man of another race who was very unlikely to represent an English community'. Sir Lepel Griffin, Chairman of the East India Association, declared that Naoroji (left) was 'an alien in race, custom and religion. . . . As to the people of India, Mr Naoroji no more represents them than a Polish Jew settled in Whitechapel represents the people of England. He is a Parsee, a member of a small foreign colony, probably semitic in origin, settled in the west of India. The Parsees are the Jews of India; intelligent, industrious and wealthy. . . . But they are quite as much aliens to the people of India as the English rulers can possibly be.'

The Times dismissed Naoroji's entry into Parliament as a 'romantic event'. The *Bristol Times* sounded a warning that this was the thin end of the wedge and one fine morning 'the British would wake up to find that English members are in a minority in the Imperial Parliament'. *St Stephen's Review* was pleased that Finsbury had not returned a 'Bengali Baboo'. Another tabloid thought that it was unwise to allow a 'Baboo from Bombay enter the British House of Commons'.

Not all comments were adverse, although most of the British forgot the principle of equality behind the Queen's 1858 proclamation. Some, like the *Warrington Examiner*, tried to remind people, declaring, 'It is a monstrous doctrine that 250 million Indian people are not to have as much as one representative in the House of Commons. The right policy is to strengthen Parliament by admission of men who know something of the pressing wants of people who were advanced in civilisation. . . . They do not ask for Home Rule yet; but they do demand, and have a right to demand, that they shall have some voice in the government of their country.'

Naoroji remained in Parliament till 1895, but his hopes for India were not realised, not until half-way through the next century!

A Blighted Spirit

MARGARET RUTHERFORD'S EARLY YEARS IN SOUTH LONDON

That shapeless, endearing comedy actress Margaret Rutherford (1892–1972) was offered the part of Miss Marple in 1960 by MGM. It was a timely offer, for the Inland Revenue was hot on her heels. For many years Miss Rutherford had refused to take any role connected with crime. She hated violence of any kind, and murder in particular! Her eventual decision was swayed by the sporadic terse reminders from the Inland Revenue, and the director of the film, George Pollock, suggesting that solving a murder was like playing chess.

What was the reason behind this almost pathological refusal? Could the answer to this riddle be in her life, in her early years? Certainly these were always delicately glossed over. Did her father really die in India tending the sick? Rutherford's father, William Benn, was an aspiring silk merchant, a romantic with a tendency towards depression. He assisted his father, the Reverend Julius Benn, in bringing comfort to the poor and the dying of the East End. In 1882 William married Florence Nicholson at All Saints, Wandsworth. Florence was also a romantic. Both her parents were dead and an older sister, Bessie – another having committed suicide – looked after her.

William had a nervous breakdown shortly after their marriage, went on to convalesce and seemed to improve. The doctors suggested that he stayed apart from his wife for a short time. He and his father went to Matlock, Derbyshire, for a further break. A week after their arrival a blood-soaked William was found in his father's bedroom standing by his father's corpse, trying to commit suicide. John, William's brother and a future MP, arranged for his unstable brother to be committed to Broadmoor Criminal Asylum. Seven years later, William was released, returned to his wife, changed his surname to his middle name, Rutherford, and moved to a quiet London suburb, Balham, to a world of anonymity where the media could not pry. There, ably assisted by Bessie, Florence gave birth to Margaret Taylor Rutherford at 15 Dornton Road (right), on 11 May 1892. Five years later the family left for India, ostensibly for William to continue his interrupted trade. They seemed to be very happy, doting on their small daughter. Florence became pregnant again. William asked Bessie to come and look after her sister. Florence's mental health had always been precarious and this pregnancy seemed to make her more irritable and disturbed. The strain was too much. Florence committed suicide before Bessie had time to pack her bags, and a distraught William returned to England, leaving six-year old Margaret

to the tender care of her aunt. His mental instability worsened and he was sent from one mental hospital to another until his death in 1921. The powerful Benn clan decided that it was in their interests that Margaret remain with her Aunt Bessie in her house, 4 Berkeley Place, Wimbledon. Moreover, Bessie had known the child since birth.

Margaret was thirteen when she found out about her father, and this from a bearded, dishevelled stranger who knocked on the door and told her that her father sent his greetings from Broadmoor. She remonstrated with her aunt that both she and 'Uncle' Benn had told her that her father was dead, and what was Broadmoor? This news would affect her all her life. She would often be plagued with the fear that her own mind would suddenly snap, and sometimes needed periods of complete rest in nursing homes in times of stress and overwork.

Wimbledon proved perfect for Margaret as a girl. Bessie doted on her adopted daughter, ensuring that she wanted for nothing. Margaret went to Wimbledon High School where she edited the school magazine. She also started to learn the piano, something that stood her in good stead when she later relied on this as a source of income, teaching locals the rudiments of music. Margaret had little contact with the Benns. It was only much later in life, when she was a successful actress, that there was a 'rapprochement', when the stigma of a 'murderer and madness' in the family was a less immediate source of distress.

Poisoned of Sydenham

THE CURIOUS DEATH OF ELEANOR MARX IN SYDENHAM

In late 1895 no. 7 Jews Walk, Sydenham, was purchased by a forty-year-old woman, Eleanor Marx Aveling (pictured). Her 'husband', Dr Edward Aveling, was only there peripatetically. She was to live there for only three years, her tragic death being her exit.

Eleanor Marx (1855–98) was the youngest surviving, and the prettiest, of the children of the celebrated Karl Marx. She was a child prodigy, speaking French, German and English fluently before the age of eleven and was the apple of her domineering father's eye. Imbued in her father's social doctrines from a very early age, she espoused his cause with fervour, accompanying him as his private secretary to conferences all over Europe from the age of sixteen. It was at one of these that she fell in love with a French journalist twice her age, but her father refused to allow her to marry.

Embittered and determined to show her independence, she took a teaching job in Brighton on her return to England, co-writing her first book. In 1880 Eleanor moved back to London to nurse her ageing parents. She assisted her father in preparing the manuscript for his life's work, *Das Kapital*. Her colleague was a certain Dr Edward Aveling.

Within a few months of her father's death in 1884 she started an affair with Dr Aveling. They shared the same views. It was what she called 'a free love liaison'. Beatrice Webb described her as having 'curly hair . . . fine eyes . . . otherwise ugly features and expression showing the signs of an unhealthy excited life, kept up with stimulants and tempered with narcotics. I should think she has somewhat "Natural" relations with men! Should fear that the chances were against her remaining long within the pale of "respectable" society'.

Aveling (1849–99) was a man of great capacity, a magnificent speaker with a wonderful voice – but a philanderer, selfish and domineering. Armed with a doctorate in medical sciences and involved from the outset with the socialist movement, it was only natural that he and Eleanor should meet. Superficially he was very like her father. Through Edward Aveling Eleanor met the social reformer Annie Besant, and both Aveling and Eleanor joined the Social Democratic Federation.

In the late 1880s Eleanor worked with a vengeance for various strike actions and organised the National Union of Gas Workers and General Labourers. She also took an active interest in the theatre, particularly Ibsen's plays, even toying with the idea of becoming an actress. She made several lecture tours to America and wrote several books on the socialist movements of both England and America.

In 1895 Friedrich Engels, her father's close collaborator, died, leaving her enough money to make her financially independent and to purchase a property. Why did she choose Sydenham – the name of the road, the fact that Annie Besant lived nearby, or to try to keep her errant boyfriend from having yet more affairs? Whatever the reason, it was a disastrous move. Her friends warned her that Aveling had affairs, but wasn't theirs a 'free love liaison'? And as long as he didn't marry she felt safe in carrying his name as a semblance of married life. She may have added a codicil to her will benefiting Aveling to try to keep him from straying, or perhaps he had influenced her to write this codicil. He had left her to move in with a 22-year-old actress a few months before her legacy from Engels, only to return when penniless and suffering from a kidney disease in 1897.

Eleanor nursed Aveling through his illness, paying for the various operations. One of her friends hoped that the surgeon's knife would slip – but it didn't. In March 1898 Eleanor was horrified to discover that Aveling had secretly married. Had he engineered this discovery knowing that for Eleanor to be a common-law wife, not a legal one, would precipitate her into a profound depression? She took some prussic acid he had ordered from the local chemist and was found dead on 31 March. Her epitaph could be her own quotation: 'by the time your life is finished you will have learned just enough to begin it well'.

The Devil Rides Out

DENNIS WHEATLEY'S EARLY LIFE IN BRIXTON

Mention Dennis Wheatley and the reply may very well be, 'Who's he?' The master storyteller of the 1940s to the 1970s is largely forgotten. Yet, mention *The Devil Rides Out* and there will be the glimmer of a response: 'Oh yes, that black magic film.'

Yes, Dennis Wheatley was largely famous for his highly readable and ultimately terrifying books on the occult, some of which were made into films. Teenagers would read them with a torch under the covers for fear of being discovered, but the dark was not a place to digest the black side of nature! Wheatley wrote other books whose heroes and villains were just as exhausting: the Chevalier de Breuc, aka Roger Brooke, masterspy to William Pitt the Younger, who triumphed against the Napoleonic forces; Gregory Sallust and his beautiful lover, Erica, pitting their wits against the evil Obergruppenführer Grauber and the might of the German armies in the Second World War, the Duc de Richleau, suave aristocrat and master of the occult who does battle with the forces of evil in the twentieth century.

Yet there were no obvious predictors of such prolific writing and storytelling in the upbringing of the author. Dennis Wheatley (1897–1977) was born into relative affluence in the family house at 10 Raleigh Gardens at the bottom of Brixton Hill, midway between Aspen House (where his maternal grandfather lived) and Brixton town centre. Albert Wheatley, his father, was a wine merchant with a thriving business in Mayfair.

The house was semi-detached and in a row of about twenty similar properties, screened from the road by a line of tall trees and a hundred yards back from it. Aged five, Dennis was sent to a kindergarten half a mile away on top of Brixton Hill, run by two sisters, the Misses Pierce. It was there that he experienced his first calf love. Honor, the object of his devotion, had chestnut ringlets falling to her shoulders. She completely bowled him over when one day she bent down to tie his bootlaces. His whole body was one huge blush and he took days to recover from this shattering experience.

Dennis was given a penny a week for his pocket money. He usually spent this on toys and sweets. One day he spied a children's magazine, *Chums*, priced at one penny. Its front page had the picture of a Red Indian creeping up behind a cowboy sitting on a fallen tree.

He bought it, only for his father to take it from him and throw it into the fire saying that this was trash and he shouldn't have been allowed to buy it! This festered in his young mind and turned his love of his father to hatred, despite the *Chums* annual being his favourite Christmas present in his teens.

There were also shopping expeditions to the centre of Brixton. The Bon Marché, the largest local store, was his favourite. Other shops, long since gone, such as Quin and Axtens, intrigued him even more because of the way in which customers' payments were dealt with. The money and the bill were put into a wooden container, which was then attached to a system of overhead wires. A lever was pulled and a bell rang and the container disappeared from sight, only to return with the receipt and the change.

Dennis Wheatley.

Another highlight was Electric Avenue at Christmas time when the street was decorated with Christmas trees, garlands and chains of coloured lights.

Three days a week were spent at Grandpa Baker's house, Aspen House, at the top of Brixton Hill. There he would play in its large garden bounded by two great mulberry trees, gaze in delight at the splendid flower gardens, the peach house, the tomato house and two hot-houses containing only orchids. There he also played in the coach-house loft, admired the horses in the stables, practised archery and swung on the great swing.

In 1905 the family moved to a much bigger house, Wootton Lodge on Streatham Hill. There his only sister was born, and it was from there that Dennis was sent to boarding school, which marked the end of his golden childhood.

J'Accuse

THE REASON FOR EMILE ZOLA'S STAY IN NORWOOD

On 15 October 1898 a middle-aged bespectacled Frenchman arrived at the Queen's Hotel, Norwood. This particular Frenchman was to stay for about a year in this leafy suburb, quietly taking photographs of the area and keeping in touch with his beloved France. Emile Zola, the writer and journalist, had fled France accused of libel, and could only return when the charges were dropped.

Emile Zola (1840–1902), friend of Paul Cézanne and Alphonse Daudet, was part of the emerging 'Naturalistic' wave introduced by the painter Gustave Courbet and a band of writers, Gustave Flaubert, Daudet and Zola. His vast study of a family under the Second Empire, *Les Rougon-Macquart*, had brought him some financial security. His depiction of working-class squalor and life in *L'Assommoir* in 1877 propelled him to contentious stardom, thereby assuring him of a settled financial future.

In 1894 Captain Alfred Dreyfus, an obscure army officer, was accused of treachery, and found guilty by a court-martial of passing military information to the Germans. But for Zola's intervention the poor captain would have remained interned on Devil's Island for the rest of his life. The Affaire Dreyfus divided France completely. Some said that the army officer was a pawn in a bigger game, had been framed and was totally blameless, while others (the conservative Right) were convinced that this Jewish officer in an otherwise Catholic and aristocratic Army Officer Corps, had deliberately passed on information to Germany.

Returning to Paris in 1897, Zola was determined to prove that the whole story and the ensuing court case were a complete charade. It was a closed case as far as the law and the anti-Semitic General Staff were concerned. But in 1895 the then head of the Intelligence Service, Commandant Picquart, a self-confessed anti-Semite, reported that his subsequent investigations showed that another officer was a more likely suspect. Further evidence also surfaced indicating that Dreyfus had been framed. Zola was convinced that this had been a miscarriage of justice, and a calculated lie. He wrote his famous open letter to the President, aptly titled by his editor, Georges Clémenceau, *J'accuse.*

Emile Zola.

His action would trigger appalling violence and an enormous wave of political and intellectual brouhaha. The all-powerful, censor-free and highly political French press flared up, playing on public emotions: racism, public manipulation, traditional values and their impact on justice as well as probing the secretive intelligence warfare. It was a massive soap opera involving double agents, planted evidence, anonymous letters, recriminations and set-ups.

Zola was summoned to stand trial in the Palais de Justice on 7 February 1898. He was being sued for libel. He had stated in his open letter that he was fully aware that this 'defamation' was open to a case being made against him but hoped that his own trial would reawaken the conscience of French public opinion and lead to the reopening of the Dreyfus case.

Zola accused a certain Lt Colonel du Paty de Clam of creating this judicial error and General Mercier of compounding it. He also accused one general of deliberately hiding the truth and another of colluding in this crime. He accused another brace of officers of conducting a completely opinionated and one-sided enquiry as well as accusing the handwriting experts of lying. He accused the War Office of deliberately hiding evidence to cover their own ineptitude and the Council of War for condemning an individual with a 'proof' that could not be made public! During the whole of his trial the media denigrated Zola and the baying mob spat on him, threw rocks and rotten food at him. Defence witnesses were forbidden to make any reference to Dreyfus, as this was 'irrelevant' to this case. Zola was found guilty, but not before a foolish prosecution witness had revealed that there was new evidence. He appealed, lost again, was fined heavily and got a year in jail – a sentence he escaped by leaving for England.

Emile Zola returned to France eleven months later when he was granted an amnesty. Captain Dreyfus was pardoned in 1899, and only officially exonerated in 1906. It was four years too late for Zola who died of carbon monoxide poisoning in his apartment in 1902 – another suspect death? No, in this case his servants' mistake.

A Queen for Life

THE TUMULTUOUS LIFE OF THE LESBIAN RADCLYFFE HALL

Marguerite Radclyffe Hall (pictured), or John, as she preferred to be called, was born into a materially secure background in 1880. There is no doubt that her emotionally atrophied childhood contributed enormously to the almost Frankenstein creation of John Radclyffe Hall, the poet, the writer and the very public lesbian. The product of an irresponsible,

upper-middle-class, dilettante, rich English father and a 'selfish brainless, vain' American divorcée, Marguerite was handed over unconditionally into the sole charge of her mother (along with a large annual allowance) aged three, while her father decamped, and subsequently divorced her mother.

Mrs Radclyffe Hall had never wanted children, and, her first daughter, Florence, died in infancy. She tried vainly to self-abort by consuming vast quantities of spirits. From the moment Marguerite was born her mother tried to crush her. She hated her daughter as much as her husband, frequently telling her that 'your hands are like Radclyffe's; you're the image of your father'. Her mother's violence was all-consuming. Marguerite's nurse found huge welts and bruises on the child's body and remonstrated with her mother, and was sacked for her troubles.

This single child had an adored canary, Pippin. The canary once went on holiday to Belgium accompanied by Marguerite, her grandmother, her governess, her mother and her mother's new Italian husband, Alberto Vissetti. They were staying in a hotel when Mr Vissetti decided that the bird should be given to a waiter. Her mother, only too pleased with this edict, took great delight in handing it over to the staff.

The Vissettis moved to a large house in Earl's Court. This marriage was equally disastrous and violent. Marguerite consoled herself with dalliances with some of her stepfather's female students. She desperately sought affection, wrote poetry and retreated into her own world.

In 1898 her father, Radclyffe Hall, died aged forty-nine. Marguerite was to inherit £100,000 on her twenty-first birthday (about £5.5 million nowadays). Her mother screamed but it did not stop Marguerite bolting when she finally inherited. She leased a house in Church Street, Kensington, and, with her new-found freedom, changed her image, cut her hair short, wore suits, used money to seduce generally and seduced her mother's cousin. She rode with the hounds, wrote more poetry – now her time had come, 'life's but a game, love is the same'.

On 22 August 1906 Marguerite met Mabel Veronica Batten at the Savoy Hotel. Mabel was a colonial expatriate who viewed marriage as a necessity and affairs as a matter of course – she'd had several flings, one with Edward, the Prince of Wales. She was married to a man twenty-five years her senior. She was bored and fifty with a penchant for mauve silk housecoats and long earrings.

It was mutual admiration. Mabel saw in Marguerite the promise of youth and a burgeoning literary talent which she encouraged. Marguerite found the almost maternal love which she craved. Mabel christened Marguerite John because she resembled her great-grandfather, John Hall. Mabel became 'Ladye'. John had her poetry published, and it was subsequently kindly reviewed.

On 24 October 1910 George Batten, Ladye's husband, died. Marguerite and Mabel moved in together. Their life was decadence in the South of France and 'marital' bliss in Cadogan Square. John was the husband – she paid the bills, gave presents and had affairs. The irony was that Ladye knew John's next great love and noted all their meetings in her diary. Una, Lady Troubridge, was Ladye's cousin. John met Una in 1915. Una was twenty-eight, John thirty-five and Ladye fifty-eight. It broke Ladye's heart. She died in 1916. John was to lead a tumultuous life with Una until her own death in 1943 when she was returned, at last, to rest with Ladye in Highgate Cemetery.

Where the Sun also Rises

A JAPANESE IN CLAPHAM

On several occasions, while on Clapham Common, I've noticed an unusual number of Japanese strolling towards Clapham Common North Side. It was only later that I realised that one of Japan's greatest writers, Natsume Kinnosuke (1867–1916), better known as Soseki, studied in London from 1900 to 1902, and lived for the last 'miserable' eighteen months, prior to his return to his homeland, at 81 The Chase (pictured), on Clapham Common North Side, as a lodger of Miss Leal from 20 July 1901 to 5 December 1902.

Although we are ready to acknowledge the existence of societies and museums perpetuating the lives, personalities and writings of such Europeans as Goethe and Zola, it is much less well known that London also houses the first Japanese literary museum outside Japan, the Soseki Museum, at 80b The Chase: an improbable setting perhaps, but directly opposite Soseki's last residence in London.

Who was Soseki? He was a student, one of the few sent abroad to study their chosen subject in Europe. He was one of the Japanese intellectuals who came to England in pursuit of vocation, but also endured privation and hardship. He lived in no fewer than five different lodgings, Gower Street, NW1, near University College where he briefly studied for two months, West Hampstead, Camberwell, Tooting and finally Clapham.

Soseki described the two years he spent in London as the most unpleasant of his life, as 'a poor dog that had strayed among a pack of wolves'. It may have been that had he come to England of his own volition and not government orders he might have been less unhappy; nevertheless his first futile months culminating in his pursuing his studies at home, purchasing second-hand books and closing himself off from the world, his tutelage under W.J. Craig, the editor of the Arden Edition of Shakespeare, had a profound effect on him and his writings.

Soseki certainly studied too much. It may have been this that gave credence to the rumour that he had gone mad. An anonymous telegram was sent to the Ministry of Education in Japan stating his neurosis. The culture shock of life in the West and mental fatigue combined with the very real duty imposed by the Japanese government and his wish to live up to their exacting standards caused him to become melancholic and withdrawn.

What Soseki did learn in Britain was individualism. Before he arrived he said, 'I was not so sure where I was standing. I felt I was walking in the mist. However, after I learnt the word "egotism", the mist vanished.' His first successful novel, entitled *I am a Cat*, was published in 1905. It was followed by the humorous *Botchan* in 1906. His novels were essentially deep psychological studies of urban intellectual lives. His later works are reminiscent of those by Henry James. His face is also on the 1,000 yen note!

The museum dedicated to Soseki was opened in August 1984 by its owner and curator, Mr Tsunematsu. It houses items relating to his life in London, his entire writings, critical works on Soseki and an impressive collection of books on modern Japanese culture. There is also an important exhibition of photographs, magazines and periodicals of that period – invaluable source material for students of the late Victorian age.

Two other Japanese culture icons are also featured; the natural historian and folklorist, Kumakusu Minakata, and the painter, Yoshio Markino. The latter endured similar hardships in England, but his was a more outgoing personality. He made a point of talking to all the English people he came across. He is best remembered for his watercolours of London fog and as a unique essayist.

One of Soseki's most intriguing short stories is that of 'The Tower of London'. Here, paradoxically, is the classic example of the Japanese fascination for England, particularly London. The Japanese interest in symbolism is its pervading theme. Soseki feels like a 'hare from the country' and his imagery portrays the Tower of London as a symbol of English nationhood.

His fascination for the British overrode his distaste for London, if indeed there was any. Yet, like D.H. Lawrence, Thomas Hardy and George Eliot who also despised our city, it profoundly influenced his psyche.

These Old Shades

GEORGETTE HEYER'S PATERNAL INFLUENCES IN WIMBLEDON

It was my Latin master, Frank Heyer, who suggested that his pupil should read books at the back of the class while the others struggled with Caesar. He lent me a book, *The Quiet Gentleman*, by Georgette Heyer (pictured). I had read all her books by the time I sat the exams. I never realised until much later that 'our' Mr Heyer was Georgette's brother!

Georgette Heyer (1902–74) wrote with a style and humour that put her in a class of her own. Her elegant romantic comedies were a refreshing change from the detective story, and, despite being slanted towards women readers, were read by all. These stories were the façade she wished the world to see. Her private world remained private.

She was born at 103 Woodside, Wimbledon, on 16 August 1902. George, her father, was the son of a Russian émigré. His education was that of an English gentleman, for he was sent to King's College School and then Trinity College, Cambridge. He was to have followed his father into the fur business, but times became hard, and instead he went to teach at Weymouth College.

In 1897, George was invited to teach French at King's College School on its removal to Wimbledon. He was a great success, with a gift for class management. His marriage to Sylvia Watkins, a student of cello and piano at the Royal College of Music, produced three children, Georgette, the eldest, followed by George and Frank. The family stayed in Wimbledon until at least the 1920s, moving to 11 Homefield Road in 1918 and again to a modern house at 5 Ridgway Place in 1923.

George Heyer was a profound influence on his children, most notably his daughter. She later wrote that 'boys tell their mothers and girls tell their fathers'. He was widely read, had a great sense of humour and rarely got into a temper. His talents lay not solely in teaching: he found he had a flair for fund raising. One of his most notable successes was to find the finance to relocate King's College Hospital to its present location. He wrote for *Punch* and translated French books and even managed, despite being over age, to secure a commission in the army!

Georgette's education, unlike that of her brothers, was not mapped out. Her schooling was peripatetic. She studied briefly in Paris, then at the socially conscious The Study in Wimbledon. Her father encouraged her to read and among her favourite authors were Jeffrey Farnol and Baroness Orczy.

In 1919, a fateful year for Georgette, she met two slightly older girls, Joanna Cannan and Carola Oman. All three had the writing bug; all three would become successful novelists, all writing under their maiden names. It may have been this mental stimulus that prompted Georgette to write a serial story to amuse her sickly brother George to relieve his boredom while convalescing. Her father, hugely impressed, asked her to prepare it for publication and arranged for it to be sent to his literary agent Christy. The outcome was that this nineteen-year-old woman had her first book, *The Black Moth*, a romantic story set in the middle of the eighteenth century, published in 1921, both in the United States and England. She never looked back!

Georgette Heyer is best remembered for her Regency tales. She wrote, however, on a variety of different subjects ranging from the medieval to the detective novel. Her research, particularly in diction and terms used for the periods of which she wrote, was meticulous. Her own strong views came over clearly, particularly in *The Black Moth* when the main protagonist is told, 'For God's sake live clean, Belmanoir!' Her views on marriage were refreshingly practical. But could it have been, despite her own happy marriage, that she lusted for the romance and tumult of her own creations? Alas, this question evades public scrutiny.

Her father's sudden death in the 1920s made her the major breadwinner of the family, supporting her husband, assisting with the education of her two younger brothers and helping her mother through her widowhood. To this day her fans are legion, particularly in America.

An Officer and a Gentleman

MONTGOMERY OF ALAMEIN'S CHISWICK CHILDHOOD

'Cherchez la femme' is an apt saying for the will to succeed in a man. For some it is the wife, for others the mother. In Field Marshal Viscount Montgomery of Alamein's case, it was undoubtedly his mother.

Bernard Law Montgomery (1887–1976) (pictured) was the fourth child and third son of the Reverend Henry Montgomery, Vicar of St Mark's, Kennington, a man 'of fair ability common sense and industry', and his wife Maud Farrer. Both parents had a distinguished ancestry and large families. At the time of his marriage Henry Montgomery was thirty-four, his wife sixteen. They were to have eight children.

In 1889 Henry Montgomery was appointed Bishop of Tasmania. The family remained there for twelve years. There while the bishop tended his dispersed flock his abandoned lady wife ruled the Episcopal house, the household, the children and the budget with a rod of iron (she gave her husband 10 shillings allowance per week, and this remained the same throughout his long life). If, for instance, one of the children, invariably Bernard, dared drop into the Australian vernacular, he was beaten and made to enunciate his words until they sounded correct. Bernard was, it seems, the only child to rebel against his mother's indomitable will, something that would stand him in good stead in later life.

The bishop's exceptional missionary work and his succinct and full reports sent back to England ensured that the post of Secretary of the Society for the Propagation of the Gospel in Foreign Parts was offered to him. It was a post he did not necessarily want, but despite his reservations the family returned to England in 1902 and the family settled in a roomy house in Chiswick, 19 Bolton Avenue, with the apt name of Bishopsbourne. It was a marked contrast to the Episcopal Palace, Bishopscourt, in Tasmania. It was half the size and, although the garden was large by London standards, it wasn't by Tasmanian standards. A small room was turned into a chapel where the family worshipped, as did some of their neighbours. It was here that the bishop and his wife entertained visiting missionaries – a sober start for the youngsters! There was no carousing either, as both parents were teetotal. It was also in this house that the youngest son, Brian, was born.

The elder children's education was sorted. The eldest, Harold, went into the army, the second and brightest, Donald, went as a scholarship student to St Paul's in Hammersmith. Bernard tried the scholarship entry but failed. Both boys turned up on their first day, in 1902, wearing bowlers, a privilege reserved for the seniors. A school porter removed the offending headgear before this infraction was noticed.

While Donald triumphed at school, Bernard was academically challenged. His poor performance in Divinity, a subject he might be naturally gifted in, was a blow to his aspiring parents, for they had thought he would make an admirable cleric. His decision to become a soldier further anguished them! He was fourteen. His mother was the loser for the first time in one of their many arguments. Bernard excelled at sports. The wiry 5ft 7in boy was a natural sportsman and leader. This was where he could forget about the maternal hammer and revel in the intensity of contact sports. His studies, however, suffered. His abysmal penultimate report gave him the impetus to work towards Sandhurst and freedom from the parental yoke. Despite average marks he got in comfortably.

The family stayed at Bolton Gardens with long summer holidays at their country seat in Moville, Ireland. Bernard, however, moved on. His visits to his parents became fewer and fewer; the army had taken over.

The dapper, intense young man had found his vocation. He was a marshal in the making. In 1927 the 39-year-old Lieutenant Colonel Montgomery met a local widow through army connections. She was Betty Carver, née Hobart. They were married at St Mary's, Chiswick, on 27 July 1927. Bishop Montgomery officiated. It was with Betty that Bernard could finally lay all his ghosts to rest and concentrate on his destiny.

A Magnificent Man & his Flying Machine

HIRAM MAXIM, INVENTOR, OF DULWICH AND BECKENHAM

It is ironic that nowadays the ambitious flee England and go to America. In the last quarter of the nineteenth century the reverse was true. The American hawk came to Britain to seek his fortune. Such was the case with Sir Hiram Maxim (1840–1916), one-time Dulwich resident.

Sir Hiram Maxim, a partner in Maxim Vickers and Son, the emerging aeronautical engineering firm, was to choose Ryecotes House, just off Lordship Lane and now part of the Dulwich and Sydenham Golf Course, as his residence in 1910. It is possible that this larger-than-life figure chose this house because his grandson Maxim Joubert was to attend Dulwich Preparatory School as a day boy.

Known as the inventor of the machine gun that bears his name, Hiram (left) was born in Maine, USA. He was fascinated by machines from the moment his father showed him a model of a flying machine. He became an engineer, moved to New York, married and became a partner in a new company, the US Electric Lighting Company. He combined his knowledge of engines with a very real flair for innovation in all technical fields. It was he, for instance, who invented the process of producing a practical incandescent electric lamp. His failure to patent this in time meant that Edison, who readily admitted that it was not necessarily the inventor who patented an invention, pipped him to the post. This lackadaisical attitude to patents was to bedevil him throughout his life. His other problem was that he was an ideas man, totally driven – when his workforce went on strike for an 8-hour day he told them that this concept was not new to him because 'I used to work 8 hours in the forenoon and 8 hours in the afternoon'.

One colleague suggested that as Europeans were forever killing themselves, 'if you ever want to make your everlasting fortune, invent a killing machine'. He went to the Paris Exhibition in 1881 and settled in England by 1882. It was his patent for the Maxim machine gun in 1883 that made his initial fortune. He moved from Central London to Sydenham, near his factory, and continued his quest to conquer the air. At Baldwyn's Park he devised and developed his gargantuan flying machine with an 105ft wingspan and weighing more than 7,000lb, powered by steam engines. He also invented the world's first single-axis autopilot to ensure stability and a true propeller made of slender timber laminated with glue and shaped into a twist form. He set up an 1,800ft steel test track to ensure that the aircraft wouldn't soar away and started tests. National interest made the Prince of Wales want to try this monster out. He was the first British monarch to fly!

On 31 July 1894, in front of a huge crowd, the machine flew off the ground but a gust of wind proved too much and the aircraft tore free of the track and soared above, only to crash some 600ft away. Maxim had done it – he had flown! The Wright brothers' first flight did not take place until 1903.

Hiram Maxim took up British nationality and was rewarded for his work with a knighthood in 1901. His list of inventions was extraordinarily varied, from the patent of a bomb for use with aeroplanes, the patent for a gun silencer in the last year of his life, to the invention of the medical inhaler (to ease his own chronic bronchial problems), and a gas-powered vacuum cleaner in 1907. He was also a visionary theoretician, anticipating in 1912 the theory of radar. This, he propounded, was merely an extension of nature, watching how bats were able to avoid things in their path by the use of a basic sonar device. He had used the same principles with the plane – if a bird can fly, why can't a human?

He left Dulwich for Sandhurst Lodge, Streatham High Road, now the Streatham ice-rink, in 1913, and continued to invent until his last gasp.

A Talent to Amuse

NOEL COWARD'S CLAPHAM YOUTH

It was the death of Grandpa Veitch that made his widow and daughters move to genteel Teddington. It was there that Violet Veitch met and married Arthur Coward, a piano salesman. There the Coward family, fiercely musical and enormously active, almost ran the local church choir and embroiled itself in all things theatrical.

On 16 December 1899 Noël Pierce Coward was born, followed six years later by his brother Eric. Money was always tight and in 1908 the family moved to 70 Prince of Wales Mansions, Battersea, ostensibly for Papa's business, but also quite possibly because Uncle Walter Coward was a member of the Chapel Royal Choir, and young Noël might benefit from an education at the Chapel Royal School in Clapham.

Noël travelled daily to the school in two trams, finally alighting at the Plough on Clapham High Street and walking the rest of the way to his little 'hell'. His return journey from the school in the afternoons was 'on wings of song'. His mother was the driving force both in marriage and in the education of her precocious son. It came as a bitter blow to her that Noël was not considered good enough for the Chapel Royal Choir, despite his undoubted talents.

After a seven-month stint in Hampshire the family returned to London. Noël returned to the Chapel Royal School and its irascible headmaster, Mr Selfe. He occasionally sang in church but admitted he hated doing this as 'the lack of applause' depressed him. He much preferred to attend the annual church garden party at Teddington where he sang to an appreciative audience who clapped rather than scuffled to their knees murmuring gloomy Amens.

Mrs Coward encouraged her son's talents. He was taught dancing by a Miss Thomas who ran a dancing academy in Hanover Square and was taken to see the *King of Cadonia* for his ninth birthday. A chance advertisement for a talented attractive boy for an all-children fairy play, *The Goldfish*, prompted Noël's mother to answer, and Noël was taken on for a guinea and a half a week. His cavalcade had started! He would sometimes use this engagement as an excuse for playing truant from school, spending a whole day at Waterloo station or Clapham Junction watching the trains, sporting a penny-worth of crêpe hair masquerading as a red beard!

In 1912 the family moved to more spacious accommodation, Ben Lomond, 50 Clapham Common South Side (pictured). Two sisters, Mrs White and Miss Pitney, owned the house. They lived in the ground floor and the basement while the Cowards had the rest of the house.

Clapham hasn't altered in the last hundred years. The pond opposite the house where Mr Coward would indulge in his passion for sailing model boats is still used. Here he would take his younger son, Eric. The family would have tea under the trees in the summer and play bat-and-ball afterwards. Noël Coward's Clapham High Street was very lively on Saturday nights particularly at Christmas when the shop windows were 'gay with tinsel and crackers, and the poulterers' and butchers' and greengrocers' were glaring yellow caves of light, with the crowds on the shining pavements silhouetted against them'.

The refined 'suburban' houses secure in small prosperity still abound and the High Street from the Plough onward still retains a 'palpably commoner atmosphere'. Noël's journey to the West End is still made in the no. 88 bus or in the City and South London tube (the Northern Line) with a change at Elephant and Castle for the Bakerloo Line. This is Noël's uncomplimentary description of the train journey: 'it was unique in uncomfortable charm . . . rattled alarmingly and over it all there brooded a peculiar pungent stink.'

In an effort to create a larger family income, Mrs Coward decided that the family ought to invest in running a lodging-house. The family duly moved out of Clapham nearer the West End lights to 111 Ebury Street in 1917. It was from here that the polished, blithe, 'cool' spirit that was Noël Coward descended on the unsuspecting public.

From a Cygnet to a Swan
ANNA PAVLOVA, ONE-TIME GOLDERS GREEN RESIDENT

The sheer magic and make-believe of a performance of the ballet *The Sleeping Beauty* in that theatre in St Petersburg, enthralled the diminutive eight-year-old Anna Matveyevna Pavlova (pictured) in 1889. It was a world away from the pedestrian existence of a washerwoman's daughter. She could no longer see herself in any other role 'than that of a dancer on a big stage in front of a crowded audience'. She 'wanted to perform for them the perfect beauty of movement, to wait with bated breath and a convulsing heart for their applause'.

Anna Pavlova (1881–1931) was to continue her quest throughout her short but magical life. Her natural talent, the poetry of her body, was so outstanding that nobody could ignore it, especially Marius Petipa, the father figure of the St Petersburg Ballet Academy in which she was enrolled in 1891. In 1899, on her selection to join the Imperial Ballet at the Maryinsky Theatre, she met the influential balletomane and government official Victor Dandré, her future husband. Her debut in that same year was in *La Fille Mal Gardée*. She worked closely with Mikhail Fokhine, the rising young ballet star, eventually being paired with him.

In 1902 Anna was singled out as a major new talent, though one critic unkindly said that ' as a purely classical dancer Pavlova promises much, but I would advise this young dancer to look upon her art in a more profound manner. She lacks application.'

But the critic had noticed her and the publicity, unkind as it was, ensured that she remained in the spotlight. Anna Pavlova was an astute businesswoman who would look for any medium to sell her art.

She spent a vacation in Milan in 1903 studying with Caterina Beretta at La Scala. She would later, in 1907, visit both London and Paris. Pavlova started seriously thinking about the potential of touring Europe with the company. She was promoted to ballerina in 1905. Her first performance in her most famous role, the Dying Swan in *Swan Lake* (created by Fokhine, now a rising young choreographer) in 1905, gave Anna the necessary leverage to get the ballet management to accept the idea for the ballet to tour Europe.

The first tour of Eastern Europe and the Baltic in 1908 was a resounding success. A Paris season was to bring two tempting offers, one from New York and one from London. She performed in New York under the auspices of Sergei Diaghilev. Her first performance in England was at the Palace Theatre in 1910, followed swiftly by a protracted engagement in America. Her success was immediate and profound. She briefly returned to her beloved Russia before settling down in England in 1912, where she rented and then purchased her ideal residence, Ivy House, with its large garden and pond on North End Road, NW11. On seeing the pond she exclaimed, 'There I will have swans! I take the house.'

Ivy House was perfect. It was large enough for her plans for a ballet school, airy and close to Hampstead Heath. Ironically, she was resigned to the fact that she was irreversibly stuck with the swan image and when she was presented with a pair, the cob was bad-tempered and bit everyone in sight. Pavlova was determined to win him over. Whether she did is a matter for conjecture, but both swans fled the coop only to be returned to have their wings clipped.

Here at Ivy House Pavlova entertained and even took her turn in local events, such as opening the Ionic Picture Show in Finchley Road. This cinematic medium was one she would use in America. Ivy House was empty most of the time as she toured the world with her own ballet company, reaching Japan and Australia and becoming the richest ballerina of her time in the process. It was a punishing schedule that would kill any mortal, which it did. Her ashes were placed in the Golders Green Cemetery. Recently, however, it seems that the Committee for Russian and Slavonic Art has requested that her ashes be returned to Russia – Pavlova may yet return home!

A Life Before the Mast

DULWICH OLD BOY, C.S. FORESTER'S EARLY YEARS

Cecil Lewis Troughton Smith (1899–1966), the future writer C.S. Forester of *Hornblower* fame, was born in Cairo. He was the fifth and last child of an English schoolteacher teaching upper-class Egyptian boys the rudiments of an English education. Aged three, Cecil, his siblings and their mother were shipped back to England in the hope that the children could get a public school education. Their father remained teaching in Egypt, only returning home for one month in the year.

Money was tight. A teacher's pay was modest. Mrs Smith found a house, 37 Shenley Street, SE5, opposite the South London Gallery on Peckham Road. The area was insalubrious and the neighbours regarded the lone mother and her brood as strange. The Smiths in turn regarded the neighbours as beneath them. Cecil hoped against hope that he was the product of a secret liaison, such was his embarrassment at his family's predicament, especially when his lonely mother took to the bottle.

Cecil was never taught to read; he copied his elder siblings, reading it seems from the age of three, borrowing his brothers' annuals and reading about pirates, treasure and Spaniards,

C.S. Forester.

later graduating to *The Scarlet Pimpernel*. His first schooling was at the local council school where their better quality clothes, English and superior intelligence marked out the Smith children for bullying. His elder brothers and sisters gained scholarships to excellent local schools.

Lack of funds meant that only the ground-floor rooms of their house could be adequately furnished. The children played pirates on the upper floors. The local library fed him with his yen for escape; Rider Haggard, Henty and Ballantyne sated his thirst for adventure.

His second school was to have been Christ's Hospital, but this was conditional on his receiving a scholarship. His father, however, was deemed to have sufficient funds despite being the only breadwinner in a comparatively large family. Instead Cecil was sent to a local school within walking distance, Alleyn's, at eleven. Here he learnt that being bright had its drawbacks – he was bullied mercilessly: hit over the head with books, shoes dropped out of the window during classes and the occasional drubbing. This stopped after the first year and he settled into the daily routine very happily. He discovered, among other pleasures, that smearing a tiny trace of bicycle oil on the blackboard made it impossible to write on, and secreting a dead fish in the innermost reaches of a pupil's desk was a joy. Another was to smear glue over the door handle before the teacher came in. The pupil versus teacher battlefield had its victories!

In 1915 Cecil Smith was awarded a scholarship to Dulwich College. Here was a different atmosphere, a public school with rules largely dictated by the boys, a school that set standards of behaviour and a dress code involving starched detachable collars. The Master, as the headmaster was called, issued a request that starched collars were to be worn no longer owing to mounting laundry costs. Needless to say the boys stuck with their starched collars. It was here that Cecil continued his dalliances with the local girls and it was here that a major scandal blew up, but for once not of his making. Two girls at a nearby school were discovered to be pregnant. They were cross-examined by their teachers, parents, the local clergy and the police. They kept stoically quiet until the barrage of questions wore them down. The natural turn of events was that several boys at Dulwich College were asked to see the Master, and were never seen again.

The First World War barely impinged on the school apart from the continuous cavalcade of old boys' names being recited in Chapel as the latest casualties of the war. The tall,

6ft 5in seventeen-year-old gangling youth applied, like his peers, to join the army but failed the medical examination, as he had a heart condition. He dejectedly applied to be a medical student at Guy's Hospital – not out of a passion for the subject but because his brilliant older brother, a rising star in the firmament of medicine, could assist him financially. His medical studies were cut short by his venture into freelance writing and his first successful novel, *Payment Deferred*, later to be a major role for the actor Charles Laughton, was the beginning of an epic adventure.

It was only when his first writings were published that Cecil changed his name. While his schoolfriends knew his real name, very few of his later friends found out. His autobiography glossed over his early formative years, ultimately the hardest years of one's life. One can't help feeling that like his hero Horatio Hornblower he was very conscious of his somewhat disadvantaged early life, but also like his hero his name became synonymous with the most vivid sea adventures ever written.

The Bride in the Bath

A MURDER IN HIGHGATE UNCOVERS A SERIAL KILLER, GEORGE SMITH

Miss Margaret Lofty was a 38-year-old spinster of Bath. She lived with her aged mother and sister. On 15 December 1914 she went out for tea and never returned home. On 17 December, Margaret Lofty became Mrs John Lloyd. John Lloyd, aged forty-two, was a Bath estate agent. That same day the newlyweds went to London – the first stop before a romantic honeymoon in Scotland.

Margaret Lloyd wrote a letter to her mother about her marriage. Her husband was a 'thorough Christian man. . . . I have every proof of his love for me. . . . He has been honourable and kept his word to me in every thing. He is such a nice man.'

Mr and Mrs John Lloyd arrived in Highgate towards the evening of 17 December. Mr Lloyd found them a suitable furnished room in a terraced house at 14 Bismarck Road (now renamed Waterlow Road). Miss Louisa Blatch, the landlady, also directed them to a local doctor as Mrs Lloyd seemed, according to her husband, somewhat poorly. Dr Bates of Archway Road prescribed something to bring down her temperature. The following day they went to see a solicitor and Mrs Lloyd made a will – her life had already been insured for £700 (about £31,000 today). She also withdrew her savings of £19 (about £860) from the Muswell Hill post office.

Mrs Lloyd's death.

In the evening Mrs Lloyd still seemed to be running a temperature. Her husband suggested she had a hot bath to bring it down. Miss Blatch was ironing in the kitchen immediately below the bathroom. She heard a sound of splashing then the sound of someone putting wet hands or arms on the side of the bath . . . and then what she thought was a sound a child might make, a sort of sigh. The next thing Miss Blatch heard was the harmonium being played in the front room; the tune was 'Nearer My God to Thee'. A quarter of an hour later there was a loud knock at the front door. Mr Smith had just 'popped out to get some tomatoes for Mrs Lloyd's supper'. He asked if his wife were down yet. Miss Blatch said she had heard nothing. They both went upstairs. Margaret Lloyd was dead, drowned in her bath.

The hapless wife was buried on 21 December. Her husband disappeared. Her inquest was held on 1 January 1915. The case was widely reported in the press, particularly in the *News of the World* where the headline 'Bride's Tragic Fate on Day after Wedding' attracted the attention of a Mr Burnham and a Mrs Crossley. Both of them were struck by the similarity of the death of a Mrs Alice (Burnham) Smith and that of Mrs Lloyd. They contacted the local police and Scotland Yard. Meanwhile Mr Smith instructed an Uxbridge Road solicitor, Mr Davies, to have Mrs Lloyd's will proved and the insurance policy made good. While Mr Smith waited for the money to come in, the police were making exhaustive enquiries countrywide. After a month the police had enough to make a holding charge and Mr Smith was arrested at his solicitor on 1 February.

The whole grisly story began to unravel. George Joseph Smith (1872–1915) was a Cockney who started in crime at the age of nine. His one legal marriage was in 1898, and even then he used an alias, George Love. This was the prelude to a whole series of liaisons, seductions and bigamous marriages. He was a very sexually attractive man who realised that he could make money out of his marriages. He 'married' a middle-aged boarding-house keeper whom he milked of money; the next was a Worthing widow, Mrs Florence Wilson, whose savings he pocketed – he deserted her at the Franco-British Exhibition at the White City, quickly sped to their Camden digs and sold all her belongings! His bigamous marriage to a Bessie Mundy in Herne Bay ended in her murder-by-bath in 1912, and another bigamous marriage to Alice Burnham ended in the same manner in 1913. There were other unfortunate women who married him, but they somehow survived.

He was hanged on Friday 13 August 1915, unrepentant.

The Bolshie of Battersea

SHAPURJI SAKLATVALA, RADICAL INDIAN MP OF BATTERSEA

Who was 'one of the most anti-British agitators in England' who showed 'considerable interest in the extremist movement' but had not 'hitherto shown his hand openly as such' in 1911? The individual in question was Shapurji Saklatvala, a 37-year-old Bombay Parsee whose wealthy family had given him the best possible education in India. He had come to Manchester as representative of the family firm J.N. Tata and Co. in 1905. His early interest in emancipation for the poor was given a powerful boost when he arrived in England and noticed the extreme poverty in a supposedly affluent country.

An ardent anti-imperialist, Shapurji Saklatvala (pictured) believed that the Left in Britain was the only movement committed to anti-colonialism, an ideal dear to his heart.

His struggle for emancipation was not just for India, Africa and China, but for the working classes everywhere. It was in Manchester that he joined the Independent Labour Party in 1909, as well as the Workers' Union, the National Union of Clerks and finally the British Socialist Party.

The Russian Revolution stirred his imagination. It was the dawn of a new beginning. When the Communist International was formed in 1919 he argued that the ILP should join it. His defeat only served to make him join the newly formed Communist Party of Great Britain. Saklavala lived and breathed politics. His wife, an Englishwoman, remained very much in the shadows. His continued high profile lectures and speaking at political rallies for the trade unions. This brought him to the attention of John Archer, the first black mayor in Britain and an ardent pan-Africanist. It was Archer, the Mayor of Battersea, who suggested that Saklatvala contest the Battersea North seat.

It was a good choice, as Battersea was predominantly working-class with a large Irish population. Battersea had a strong, fiercely radical and independent tradition. It had elected Roman Catholics to its council and elected John Archer, a black, as mayor. The borough also declared itself against the jingoism of the Boer War, naming some streets after the Boer Generals, such as Joubert Street.

Saklatvala stood in the 1922 elections as a Labour candidate. He won with a majority of 2,000. He lost in 1923, but contested the seat in 1924 as a Communist with Labour support (despite Labour having recently outlawed Communists from party membership). The turnout was a record 73 per cent and Saklatvala beat his opponent with a majority of 542.

Walton Newbold had been the first Communist MP in the Commons, but Saklatvala was the first and only Asian MP to sit as a Communist. Despite having a virtually unpronounceable name, he had tremendous personal charisma and was a powerful orator. His personal magnetism was such that the press had to acknowledge that the 'Parsee might be a Svengali or an Indian Fakir with a knowledge of Black Magic, but he wields a magnetic influence over his audience that verges on hypnotism'. The *Daily Graphic* also said that 'nor is it only hysterical women that he captures, but solid British working men. A burly taxi driver stood for twenty minutes at his doorway arguing, politely but stubbornly, with Colonel H.V. Coombs, who had come up from the country to help his friend Hogbin. One of the taxi driver's arguments was that he had fought side by side with Indian Regiments, and that their soldiers were as brave as any white soldiers were. That the Oriental firm, of which Saklatvala is a departmental manager, pays very capitalistic dividends didn't matter to him – nor apparently to the rest of his supporters.'

That Saklatvala had enormous personal charisma is true, but one of the main reasons for his success was that he had the unswerving support of the Battersea Labour Party despite his membership of the Communist Party. The electors of Battersea North, it seemed, couldn't care less whether he was Asian or had Communist sympathies, as long as he had total backing from the local Labour Party. What mattered to his supporters, it seemed, was that he had declared himself willing to accept the Labour whip. His victory was owed to a 'moral enthusiasm, his passion for reform, for equal justice and for the uplifting of the underdog'.

A Moving Picture
THE LIFE OF ONE TIME MAIDA VALE RESIDENT, WILLIAM FRIESE-GREENE

On the morning of 5 May 1921, one of the luminaries of cinematography, William Friese-Greene (pictured), a frail 65-year-old, left his grotty flat in Portsdown Road, Maida Vale, to attend a meeting of the Cinematographic Society at the Connaught Rooms in the West

End. There he collapsed and died of a heart attack mid-speech. His passion, the moving-picture camera, had extinguished his financial independence, his home life, his health and finally his life.

What had happened to the young Willie Green of Bristol, the young man whose passion for cinematography spawned a million films? What had happened to that man who had taken out over seventy patents and yet never made a cent from any cinematographical ones?

He was born in Bristol in 1855 and the nineteen-year-old photographer's assistant married his first wife Helena Friese in 1874. They moved to Bath and Mr William Friese-Greene (the name change a professional ploy) with his good looks, smile and charm became a very successful photographer. It was in Bath that he met two men who were to shape his life, J.A.R. Rudge and William Fox-Talbot, the photographic pioneer. The latter, young Willie Green's hero, told him that 'if you want to keep in touch with the men who walk ahead on the road to knowledge, you should go to London'.

He arrived in London in 1885, alone. He soon set up a photographic studio with a partner in New Bond Street and his flair, originality and personality soon made him one of the most sought-after London photographers. Studio after studio mushroomed, which would ordinarily make most relatively affluent. Not William; he spent most of his profits experimenting with cameras, especially the concept of the roll of film that would enable unlimited snapshots to be taken, as his goal was to be able to photograph a continuous motion.

By 1888 Friese-Greene was the father of a daughter, Ethel, and rented 136 Maida Vale for his family. He closed down his now unprofitable provincial businesses and continued with his experiments. These were crowned with the prestigious award of the Daguerre Medal for the latest advance in photography.

The fruition of his work took place in 1889. He took his newly made box-like camera with side handle and a roll of 50ft clear celluloid film up to Hyde Park to photograph his cousin walking. This film still exists. He improved on the camera and took out the first patent for the use of celluloid film, patent no. 10131 of 1889. The rights to this he was to sell shortly afterwards. One other person, Louis le Prince of Leeds, had invented a camera to take moving pictures, but his patent bears no resemblance to the modern cine-camera, whereas Friese-Greene's patent did.

The first of three bankruptcies in 1891 showed his failings. He was an ideas man who could never keep his inventions secret. He was so naïve that the Official Receiver could only say, 'Really, Mr Greene, you are a very silly man.'

His next invention did make him rich, for a while. He made and patented a machine that printed pictures on cigarette cards. It was first used by W.D. and H.O. Wills of Bristol.

His wife Helena died in 1895. In 1897 he married Edith Harrison, a 23-year-old who produced him six sons. These were the high days where his x-ray exhibitions, his photographic rotary-printing patent and his inkless printing process made him money.

A brief spell in prison for breaking the terms of bankruptcy did not deter his spirit, but started breaking his wife's. She left the marital home to find work in 1918 because he lived 'in a world of colours where bread and butter don't count'. He moved back to Maida Vale chasing the dream of recognition.

Friese-Greene was treated appallingly by the burgeoning film industry. The cinema industry moguls belatedly gave him their respect. His best epitaph appears in a letter from his wife to his daughter Ethel: 'Let us all try to remember what a glorious death, and the greatness he achieved in life, a life all to one purpose with one fixed aim and ambition. . . . How grand it is that he is acknowledged at last. Wasn't it what he always prayed for?'

True to Himself

HOW EVENTS AT FINBOROUGH ROAD SENT RONALD TRUE TO JAIL

The end of the First World War saw a resurgence in serious crime caused by a demoralised country, the decimation of the youth of the nation and postwar deprivation. One of the first serious crimes in London was dealt with by the Flying Squad. This case was a murder that could have happened some years earlier.

The 25-year-old Olive Young was a successful prostitute. She had worked in a shop under her real name, Mrs Gertrude Yates, but found that her looks and youth attracted a better class of gentleman who would pay her better for more personal services. Her basement flat at 13a Finborough Road, Fulham, was well maintained and kept clean by her personal maid on a daily basis. She had money in the bank and wore expensive jewellery.

Ronald True (1892–1951) (pictured) was a good-looking thirty-year-old man-about-town – tall, dark and handsome with large eyes and a moustache and more dash than cash. He was a jocular, charming man with a ready smile and a fund of stories about his Flying Corps days and his wealth. The reality was sad and desperate. He was a morphine addict with violent mood swings who had been invalided out of the Flying Corps following a very

bad knock on the head. He was married and had a young son. He was perpetually broke despite being given a generous allowance by his stepfather, but regularly left his family for forays into London's demi-monde, signing dud cheques, stealing and leaving hotels without paying. He also invented an alter ego, another Ronald True, who was responsible for all his failings. In short he was mad.

Olive and the Major met for the first time on 18 February 1922. She took him back to her basement flat. He stayed the night and stole £5 from her purse on his departure. She resolved never to see him again. Olive managed to elude him despite his continuous calling for the next two weeks. True finally caught up with her just before midnight on Sunday 5 March. Despite her

misgivings she let him in and they spent the night together. In the morning he made her a cup of tea and as she sat up in bed to drink it he struck her with a rolling-pin, rammed a towel down her throat and strangled her with a dressing-gown cord, stole her cash and jewellery and left her naked in her bathroom.

Miss Young's daily, Miss Emily Steel, arrived at about 9.15 a.m., made herself some breakfast and started tidying the sitting room. True appeared, smiling, and said that her mistress was fast asleep. She was not to be woken up and he would have her collected at about midday. She helped him on with his coat as he was leaving and he gave her half-a-crown. At about 10 a.m. the maid knocked on the bedroom door, opened it and found blood all over the place and her mistress's body in the bathroom. She called the police.

True continued the day as if nothing had happened, ending up at the Hammersmith Palace of Varieties in the evening, where he dismissed his driver, Mazzola. This man had been driving him for several weeks, and the police were awaiting him at his garage. Ronald True was arrested at the Hammersmith Palace of Varieties, and charged with wilful murder. His trial started on Monday 1 May 1922.

He was sentenced to death despite his counsel's plea of insanity. He was reprieved after a panel of medical experts adjudged him insane. He spent the rest of his life as a popular inmate of Broadmoor Hospital. True was not a bad man. He was ill. It was, however, his stepfather's cash that rescued him. Had there been no money in the family his fate would have been that of the common criminal, and he would have been hanged. The press and the Commons protested vehemently against his eventual conviction.

Two's Company

VERA BRITTAIN AND WINIFRED HOLTBY'S PATHS TO FAME

Vera Brittain (1893–1970), the writer and politician, is chiefly remembered for her haunting autobiography *Testament of Youth*, first published in 1933. This book is a description of the experiences of a young woman up to the First World War and until her marriage to George Catlin (father of John and the politician

Shirley Williams) in 1925. Its crisp, clear prose and brutal honesty makes it an unsentimental memoir of a generation scarred by war – a twentieth-century classic. This survivor was to use her agile mind to combat war until her death. Her four year stay, with her great friend Winifred Holtby (1898-1935), in Maida Vale, proved the launch pad for her varied and high profile career.

Vera Brittain (pictured) and Winifred Holtby came from comfortable backgrounds. The former came from a long line of Staffordshire businessmen and the latter from an equally long line of Yorkshire farmers. Vera first learned of the ideas of Dorothea Beale and Emily Davies, two frontrunners in women's education, at boarding school. Whereas it took the paternalistic Brittain household some time to understand Vera's need to go to Somerville College, Oxford, Winifred's mother actively encouraged her daughter to apply to Somerville. The farming community, it seemed, was a more matriarchal one!

Both girls were strong and independent, Winifred the more outgoing. On the outbreak of the First World War, Vera felt that she was needed in the war effort, broke off her studies at Oxford and joined the Voluntary Aid Detachment in 1915, serving as a nurse in England and France. Her boyfriend's and her brother's deaths in the war and her experiences in France profoundly affected her, as it did most of the youth of that time. It was her job, she decided, to read history, to find out all about war and to 'try to prevent, in so far as one person can, it happening to other people in the days to come'.

Winifred, some five years younger, joined the Women's Army Artillery Corps (WAAC) in 1918. Her reasons for joining this corps were 'the desire to suffer and to die – especially when suffering is associated with glory, and a fear of immunity from danger when our friends are suffering'. Her experience was gleaned in part from her boyfriend's experiences as a soldier in the war.

The Michaelmas term of 1919 saw both return to their interrupted studies at Oxford. Up to this time they were totally unaware of each other's existence. It was only in 1920 that the emotionally scarred and bitter Vera noticed Winifred, that tall, almost statuesque, blonde, vivacious, popular, self-assured and charismatic personality. Winifred seemed to be the instigator of various jibes aimed at Vera, or so she thought. Her barely concealed hostility showed the depths of her illness, belatedly recognised as post-traumatic stress disorder. Yet it was the combined strengths and weaknesses of the two that created their deep friendship. 'We go on long walks together and get lost wonderfully.'

They graduated in 1921, travelled on the continent and both agreed that they would share a flat in London where their combined limited incomes, a stipend from their families, teaching and lecturing, might give them a decent flat. They first lived in Doughty Street, WC1, for a year, in 'a partitioned studio with cold skylights and miniature penny-in-the-slot gas fires; egg and cheese suppers cooked on a gas ring'.

In 1923 their landlady mistook their long hours away from the flat as a sign that they were on the game and gave them their notice. They had been thinking of moving to a cheaper area, and they found a large three-bedroomed flat in a mansion block in Maida Vale. Their background was suited to Liberal politics, but their ideals suited the emerging Labour Party – they changed accordingly to Labour where their nascent pacifism could be nurtured. Winifred embarked on a successful career in journalism, which was cut short by her early death in 1935 from cirrhosis of the liver. Her memory lived on in her friend's *Testament of Friendship*, and in her own novels. Vera's pacifism was treated with caution by the British government, especially when she opposed saturation bombing. Yet these beliefs, it was discovered, would have warranted her execution by the Germans.

No Sex Please, We're British
THE GROUND-BREAKING WORK OF HENRY HAVELOCK ELLIS

If you had mentioned Henry Havelock Ellis in the late Victorian era the responses would have been immediate and vitriolic. His books were variously described as 'like breathing a bag of soot' and 'cesspools liable to turn the uncontaminated nine-tenths of humanity into the same depraved state'. This gentleman, a medical doctor, dared to publish books on sex at a time when the relationship between the sexes was governed by puritanical codes, when no one publicly mentioned sex and yet these were the most prurient of times.

Henry Havelock Ellis (1859–1939) was a product of his age. He was the only son and eldest child, by four years, of a sea captain. He was a painfully shy child, highly intelligent and precocious, cosseted by a mother who only saw her husband on his returns from his long journeys. Sigmund Freud, Havelock Ellis's contemporary, put it succinctly: 'A man who has been the undisputed favourite of his mother keeps for life the feeling of a conqueror, that confidence of success that induces real success.'

His schooling in his birthplace, Croydon (he was to spend half his life in South London), brought out his natural talents. By the age of fifteen he spoke French, Italian and German fluently and read avidly. In 1874 he went to Australia to teach – a somewhat unsuccessful venture but one that served as a catalyst for his *raison d'être*: to make his life's work the exposure, explanation and understanding of sex in all its manifestations, a subject he was painfully unsure of.

On his return to England in 1879 he trained to be a doctor at St Thomas's Hospital – a long, hard and impoverished seven-year stint. This gangly, shy, bearded and introverted youth met his first love, Olive Schreiner, a feminist and successful writer, in 1884. She was his first case study. Theirs was an unusual affair inasmuch as it was a sexual misfit. He was painfully aware that he had problems – the ghosts he would try to understand throughout his long life. Although the affair finished in 1889, they remained friends.

During this period he started writing. His first book, *The New Spirit*, was published in 1890 and his marriage to the lesbian Edith Lees followed soon after. They both agreed that they would retain economic independence, recognise complete mutual frankness and not live permanently under the same roof. The marriage lasted twenty-five bizarre years which were interlaced with many extramarital affairs. He proposed the establishment of a Health Service in his 1892 book *The Nationalisation of Health*. The book that created the biggest stink, however, was the first volume of his *Studies in the Psychology of Sex* in 1897, his study

of 'inversion'. He tried to dispel the myths and prejudices about homosexuality, stating that it was neither a disease nor a crime, an opinion he never renounced. This epic study was a groundbreaking encyclopaedia of human sexual biology, and yet it was considered scandalous and obscene.

Henry Havelock Ellis (pictured) moved to a flat at 14 Carlyle Mansions, Brixton, and lived there from 1909 to 1926. It was dirty and dingy with broken and worn furniture. Here he saw some of his 'patients', all women, who were all bowled over by his gentleness and sensitivity and became his friends. He met the younger Françoise Delisle in 1917. She was struck by this tall, grave, shy, astonishingly handsome man and his epicurean cooking. Theirs was a rewarding relationship. He was just starting to reap the harvest of his life's work and in 1927 they moved to a house, 24 Holmdene Avenue in Herne Hill, with her two young sons, and to a semblance of a normal life.

Havelock Ellis was an ardent feminist, believing that women should receive pregnancy or childbirth support from the state or their employers and four or five days off for menstruation. He also argued that women should not be concerned with equality with men but with social recognition of the needs dictated by a woman's physical and psychological constitution. His work was an invaluable study that forms the template for the modern study of sex. At his death in 1939 George Bernard Shaw said: 'We mustn't grudge him his rest. The new generation must carry on.'

Where the Heart is . . .

BRIXTON HEROINE, VIOLETTE SZABO

The execution of three young Englishwomen was carried out one bleak 1945 January evening in Ravensbruck women's prison cemetery. One of these was the 23-year-old Violette Szabo (pictured), the 'Corinne' of the French Maquis, whose almost enchanted youth never intimated her abrupt death.

Violette Szabo, née Bushell, was born in the British Hospital in Paris on 26 June 1921. Her father, Charles Bushell, had met and married his pretty French wife Reine Leroy in Pont Rémy, near Abbeville. But times were hard in France and the Bushell family returned to the paternal home in Hampstead Norris, Berkshire, returning to France in 1926. Work was scarce, so the Bushell family, now with four children (one of whom stayed in France), moved back to England in 1930, moving into a flat at 12 Stockwell Park Walk, Brixton, in 1932.

Violette and her siblings went to the local school, an enormous LCC school in Stockwell Road. She was a totally unaffected and outgoing child, with a definite naughty streak. Her large violet eyes with a dash of green and her long black silken lashes framed by a tumble of dark hair entranced all who met her. She vibrated with personality and was a natural sportswoman.

The six-strong Bushell clan (Noël, the boy who had stayed in France, was now with them) moved to a house, 18 Burnley Road, just round the corner, in 1935. This year was also the year Violette left school and worked first with a French corsetière in South Kensington and then at the Bon Marché on Brixton High Street. Her new-found freedom enabled her to join a cycling club. She cycled to her aunt and uncle in Wormelow in Herefordshire, took up darts and shot with great accuracy at one of the many shooting galleries in the West End.

By the outbreak of war in 1939 Violette had turned into an astonishingly pretty woman, resourceful, totally fearless and with a positive attitude to life. Her tenet was: 'You've got to take a chance in life. All life is chance really.' She met Etienne Szabo, a thirty-year-old officer of the French Foreign Legion in Hyde Park. Theirs was a whirlwind romance and shortly after the wedding Etienne was called back to active service. Violette decided to do her bit for the war effort and joined the ATS. Etienne's brief homecomings became even briefer and his death at the battle of El Alamein was a bitter blow to the young bride, particularly because he never saw their daughter Tanya. The romantic girl now had to grow up, and it came as a relief when she was accepted to work for Captain Buckmaster in the Special Operations Executive. She looked older than her twenty-two years and took to the regime like a duck to water. She relished the intense physical training and was particularly good at weapons training and parachute jumping.

'Corinne Reine Leroy' was ready for her first mission and landed in the Chartres area in April 1944. She was arrested twice but persuaded the Gestapo to let her go.

Her second mission was to the Limoges area, the heart of the Maquis, in June 1944. The purpose of this mission was to cause as much havoc as possible to confuse the Germans in the wake of the Normandy landings. The local Maquis chief 'Anastasie' and 'Corinne' left on 10 June, only to be ambushed by the elite Das Reich SS Panzer division at Salon-la-Tour. 'Corinne' was captured but not without causing considerable damage. She was eventually taken to Fresnes prison outside Paris. She was tortured, and eventually sent to Ravensbruck in August.

Violette Szabo was the first woman to be awarded the George Cross, albeit posthumously. Recent War Office information seems to suggest that her French was heavily accented, she was emotionally and academically unsuited for her war work, her capture more prosaic than had been believed and her death a very good PR job which the British public needed.

The War of Words

H.G. WELLS'S LAST YEARS IN NW1

On taking over the lease of 13 Hanover Terrace, NW1, in 1936, H.G. Wells (pictured) told the previous owner, Alfred Noyes, that he was 'looking for a house to die in': stark words for a man who had written so many readable science fiction classics such as *The Time Machine*, *The Invisible Man* and *The Island of Dr Moreau*.

Yet by 1936 Wells was in his seventieth year. His impoverished youth was far behind him and so were his first tentative steps into the world of writing. Now he was a much-respected author, political commentator and social theorist. He was also waiting for the inevitable Second World War, which he had been predicting for so long. Such was his influence over his readers that it was said that when Ford Madox Ford found himself at the front during the First World War, 'He noted that he had been so conditioned to modern warfare by reading the novels of Wells that when he actually experienced it he felt apathetic and resigned'.

Wells was convinced that the next confrontation of world powers would be an even bloodier conflict with even more terrifying consequences for the human race. It was after the First World War that Wells started his onslaught on education, whose failures and shortcomings he blamed for the ignorance of humanity, and the inevitability of war. His interests led him to join the Fabian Society.

Beatrice Webb painted a portrait of the man: 'He is an interesting though somewhat unattractive personality except for his agreeable disposition and intellectual vivacity. . . . His career has given him a great knowledge of the lower middle class and an immense respect for science and its methods. But he is totally ignorant of the manual worker on the one hand, and of the big administrator and aristocrat on the other. He does not appreciate the need for a wide experience of men and affairs in administration. A world run by the physical-science-man straight from the laboratory is his ideal. But he is extraordinary quick and a good instrument for popularising ideas. He forecasts the segregation of like to like, until the community will become extraordinarily variegated and diverse in its component parts. This seems to us a brilliant and true conception.'

Certainly Wells had his critics. George Bernard Shaw was one who castigated his efforts of diplomacy in Russia, where Wells met and talked with Stalin. Stalin, so Shaw opined, gave Wells a lesson in the political science of Marx, but Wells only heard his own voice. Stalin, said Shaw, 'was a magnificent listener, never in a hurry to talk. Wells, on the other hand, was a very good talker, but the worst listener in the world. His vision was so wide and assured that the slightest contradiction threw him into a frenzy of contemptuous and eloquently vituperative impatience.'

It was with a helpless horror that Wells saw the approach of 1939. His bouts of gloom and despondency deepened as he realised that, try as he might, humanity was intent on destroying itself 'like monsters of the deep'. The human race had been granted the divine power of shaping its own destiny and yet chose to ignore it. As the bombings began the inhabitants of Hanover Terrace left. Wells stayed, with a handful of others. Several times blasts blew in the front door and a bomb fell almost opposite the house. Yet he clung on, perhaps trying to shape his own destiny. He found war fascinating and the way men chose to fight unendingly stupefying. He revelled in the cacophony created by the whistling bombs, the flashing response of the guns lit up in the night sky. The excitement of war and its total abandon on a scale unmatched in history sometimes took him over the edge of the subjective into a total detachment, almost from the inner depths of space, where he saw one species after another rising and returning to the mud.

He wrote his own obituary: 'Died at the age of 97. . . . His keenest feeling seems to have been a cold anger at intellectual and moral pretentiousness.' But he actually died in 1946 aged eighty.

Starman

THE WRITER ALGERNON BLACKWOOD IN NORTH-WEST LONDON

H.P. Lovecraft, that master of horror, described this tall, permanently sun-tanned, almost gaunt individual as the 'one absolute and unquestioned master of weird atmosphere'. He was describing Algernon Henry Blackwood (1869–1951), one of the most mystical authors of twentieth-century Britain. Algernon Blackwood is associated with tales of horror and the supernatural, yet this was only a fraction of his prodigious output. It was his early life that seemed to influence his peculiar writing style, not his later years spent flitting from Hampstead to Highgate during the Second World War.

Algernon Blackwood was the product of an age of piety mixed with looser mores, two extremes that created one of the most fertile minds. Born in Kent, he was a son of Sir Stevenson Blackwood (incidentally born at Rosslyn Lodge, Hampstead) and the Dowager Duchess of Manchester. Blackwood was brought up in an almost Calvinistic discipline by his parents. It was at school in his teens that he first became interested in therapeutic hypnotism. A year's study in a strict Moravian Brotherhood school in Germany introduced him to the Hindu religion and its writings, *The Bhagavad-Gita*, *The Vedanta*, *The Yoga of Patanjali* and theosophy. He rounded his education at Wellington College and at Edinburgh University studying medicine, a course he never finished.

His year off before university had been spent in Canada. He returned there in 1890 after his abortive studies at Edinburgh, in a very conscious rebellion against the parental yoke combined with a very real desire to 'find himself', a rite of passage. His ten years on the American continent was a great influence on his future writings. His autobiography *Episodes before Thirty* shows that change was his mistress and chance his counsellor, and also conveys that Canada agreed with him. His later story *The Wendigo*, shows this. This tall gangling naïve youth first started a dairy farm with an acquaintance. Brief success turned into failure so he invested the little money he had been given by his father into an hotel. This proved more successful but again failed. An offer of a break on an island in the wilds of Canada proved too tempting and he disappeared for some months, finding the great outdoors and the wild untamed land a great solace and a wondrous tonic for his soul.

Algernon Blackwood.

His impulsive move to New York proved to be soul-searching. He was penniless, resorting to selling his personal effects including his overcoat to feed himself. He became an artist's model to make ends meet but fell foul of corrupt policemen. He became a reporter for the *New York Evening Sun* in 1892 but fell foul of cynical reporters. Malnutrition and cold nearly killed him – it was only his iron constitution and the ministrations of a diminutive elderly drug-addicted German doctor that cured him. To cap it all, his roommate Boyde, a charmer, proved to be a swindler and fraudster. Blackwood's hunt for him in the 'New York Hell', aided by his gnome-like doctor, ended with Boyde's arrest and international press coverage.

In April 1894 he left once more for the great outdoors, his backwoods heaven, and tried his luck in the goldfields. Luckless in this latest venture, but exhilarated, he returned to New York to work as a reporter, this time for the *New York Times* later in the year, and finally left for England in 1897.

His adventures had taught him that 'no man is a failure who has an objective and works for it, even though he never gets within miles of accomplishment'. Its very starkness may not have given him a purpose but what it did was hone his burgeoning writer's talent by drawing on the extremes of emotion he had felt during his almost ten-year exodus. He travelled to Europe and this reawakened his interest in the paranormal and spiritual interests of his childhood. In 1906 he published his first stories *The Empty House and Other Ghost Stories* followed by his John Silence detective novels. These were a success.

During the First World War he became a secret agent. He continued to write stories including what is considered his finest, 'The Centaur'. He was invited to read ghost stories on BBC radio in 1934. At the onset of the Second World War Algernon moved in with his nephew Patrick Blackwood, at 3 Lawn Road, Hampstead. It was here on 13 October 1940 that London suffered its worst air raid yet and their house suffered a direct hit, destroying, in the process, most of his personal papers. He maintained that a sausage had saved his life. He and his nephew were cooking sausages in the Andersen shelter when a bomb hit one of the nearby houses. They ran out to see what had happened when his nephew remembered the burning sausages, so they rushed back – at the very moment when the house was hit!

In August 1942 he moved to rented rooms at 3 North Drive in Highgate, near his good friends the Henry Ainleys. He was a great success with the Ainleys' children, and seemed to find an affinity with children throughout his long life. He was prepared to talk to them as equals, unlike most other adults. He was to stay there until after the war, but not without danger. In September 1944 a bomb caused ceiling damage. He had to sleep in a friend's cellar for the rest of the war.

Like his father before him Algernon enjoyed the expanse of Hampstead Heath and the country walks around Highgate. Nevertheless he left north London for good in June 1945, for Kensington, where a pleasant stroll through Kensington Gardens and Hyde Park took him to his work at Broadcasting House.

Algernon Blackwood was an intensely private man with a deep affinity and love for nature. Although associated with horror and the supernatural, a very marketable subject area, he resented this and claimed quite rightly that he was concerned with 'questions of extended or expanded consciousness'. The variety of his writings show this, particularly *The Starlight Express*, a nonsensical piece of escapism where a family of children trapped in the world of adults form a secret society whose members collect stardust and live in starcaves. Elgar was to dub him the 'Starlight Man' as he liked nothing better than looking towards the stars in the wilds of Canada or upon Hampstead Heath.

Vive De Gaulle!

CHARLES DE GAULLE'S STAY IN HAMPSTEAD

Mme De Gaulle rented Frognal House, Frognal Rise, Hampstead, from September 1942. The De Gaulle family had previously rented a house in Petts Wood, but the bombing came perilously close. They had then moved to a house in Ellesmere, not far from Acton Burnell, where Elisabeth De Gaulle pursued her studies. But this proved too far from London. However General De Gaulle, ensconced in the Connaught Hotel during the week, found the precious time he shared with his family at weekends cut short, so Hampstead seemed a suitable compromise.

There, Yvonne De Gaulle, her mentally handicapped daughter Anne and her carer settled to be near central London and close to Oxford where her daughter Elisabeth was to study. Philippe, the son, was in the Navy and her husband, Brigadier General Charles André Joseph Marie De Gaulle (1890–1970), was actively leading the Free French forces from his headquarters in Carlton Gardens.

This imposingly tall career officer, described by Churchill as 'looking like a female llama surprised in her bath', was no stranger to controversy. Indeed, he revelled in it. His climb up the military ladder had been painfully slow, not because of lack of ability, but rather because of his open criticisms of the organisation of the French army and its outdated methods of warfare. His ideas about a mobile and professional force were met with derision. Even his mentor and old commander, Marshal Pétain, urged caution. But De Gaulle's attitude to current policies was openly defiant. He was considered wild and unreliable – brilliant, but dangerous in his ideas. His short career in active service at the start of the Second World War provided the French with their only victory at Laon in May 1940.

By June the newly appointed brigadier general realised that France would capitulate to the invading German forces and left for London while Pétain pleaded for an armistice. De Gaulle made no secret of what he thought of Pétain's actions: Pétain, he said, was a fine man; he had died in 1925!

How does one treat a man who seems to have an unshakeable belief in himself and his destiny? How do you speak to a man who will brook no opposition, who is the incarnation of everything that the English mistrust about the French, and who treats his country with a reverence, love and loyalty that seems beyond comprehension? Very carefully!

His 'Call to Arms' transmitted by the BBC on 18 June 1940 brought many French to London. One notable exception was Antoine de Saint Exupéry. Despite being outwardly friendly with Churchill, De Gaulle mistrusted him. This was reciprocated. His fight for acceptance and cooperation was painful. He found the people of Hampstead and the man in the street 'kindly and reserved   each one respects the liberty of the other', but he told his secretary, Elizabeth de Miribel, that 'les Anglais sont des alliés vaillants et solides, mais bien fatiguants' (the English are brave and strong allies but quite tiring).

De Gaulle's attitude towards the United States was coloured not by the inherent French distrust of Americans but by their machinations to discredit members of his staff, notably

Admiral Muselier, a loose cannon, against whom a fabricated charge of treason was brought, engineered, it seems, by the US government. The outcome proved De Gaulle right and he even far-sightedly predicted that America would be of no help to France.

Frognal House proved a quiet haven for the family. He was entranced by its huge walled garden and manicured lawns, its mock-Tudor windows and its corner tower, which became his study. Here he entertained Henri Frenay and d'Astier de la Vigerie, the founders of the *Combat* and *Liberation* newspapers, and members of his close entourage such as Gaston Billotte, his Chief of Staff, General Delestraint (shot at Dachau) and André Philip as well as Jean Moulin, a Resistance leader who died at the hands of the Germans.

Proximity to London also meant a family home to which De Gaulle could return more often. Here he also worshipped in the neighbouring church of St Mary, praying for his family, strength, peace and France.

Generating the Computer
ALAN TURING OF MAIDA VALE AND HIS CLANDESTINE LIFE

Alan Turing's reputation rests on his pioneering work in mathematics and the deciphering of the German Enigma Code, which led to the Allied victory in the Battle of the Atlantic. He is also recognised as the father of modern computer science. This mathematician, scion of a family that had served the Empire since its creation, was also to suffer an ignominious trial and a tragic early death.

Alan was the second son of a colonial administrator and was born in a nursing home called Warrington Lodge, now called Colonnade Town House, in Maida Vale in 1912. He spent his very early years in London. His parents and most of his immediate forebears were Londoners. He was educated at Sherborne School where they noted but did not encourage his early predilection for maths. While he was there he formed a great romantic attachment to another pupil, Christopher Motcomb. This proved a deciding influence on his sex life and a possible factor in his tragic death.

Alan was sheltered from harsh reality and the politics of academia at King's College, Cambridge, where his sexual preferences were tolerated. His stint at Princeton University from 1936 to 1938 was, however, an unwelcome revelation. Princeton was in its way a microcosm of American society, pushy and intolerant of 'sexual aberrations'.

Turing never really belonged to the halls of academe, nor did he fit into the upper middle-class society of which he was a part. He rejected the outward pretensions of his set yet his thinking and his beliefs were very much in the mould of a 'son of the Empire'. This apparent lack of an easily identifiable identity was mirrored in his attitude to women – as a general rule he toed the male line, and women were regarded as objects, housekeepers, organisers. Yet his deep friendship with Joan Clarke, a colleague at Bletchley during the war, contradicted all these set rules. Their friendship became an engagement, a 'marriage' of equals which never materialised as he realised he was a too committed homosexual.

His lack of respect for everything except his own perception of truth was totally uncompromising when it came to beliefs, and this was to land him in deep trouble. In 1948 Turing's abilities and his reputation enabled him to join the team building the prototype computer at Manchester University. While there he wrote a philosophical paper on machine intelligence and purchased his only house in 1950, in Wilmslow, 10 miles from Manchester. By 1951 he had been elected a Fellow of the Royal Society, a crowning achievement. At last, it seemed Turing was free.

During his time at Manchester Alan had met a younger, impecunious man, Arnold Murray. Arnold welcomed a little affluence in his life, and even stayed at Wilmslow several times before Alan suspected that Arnold was filching money from his wallet and confronted him. They argued and Arnold walked out.

On 23 January 1952 Alan's house was broken into. He immediately reported it to the police and detectives came to take fingerprints. Turing, suspecting Arnold, wrote to him. It transpired that Arnold probably did know the perpetrator and Alan duly informed the police. The prints were identical to those of a man in custody on another charge. The moment he mentioned Arnold having 'business' with Alan, the police realised there was indeed a crime here – 'gross indecency'. Alan was quite candid about his homosexuality and the trial was set for 31 March 1952.

Homosexuality was still illegal then, and people of Alan's ilk were expected to do the honourable thing and shoot themselves – curious because female homosexuality was tolerated. America had tried hormone treatment for sex offenders and the results had been mixed but encouraging. Back in Britain the Criminal Justice Act of 1948 had emphasised the duty of the community to provide treatment for the habitual sex offender. So in view of Alan's undoubted assets he was offered prison or organo-therapic treatment for a year. He chose the latter.

Alan lost his security clearance, but retained his OBE and started growing breasts. He seemed, however, to sail relatively unscathed through his treatment – until Tuesday 8 June 1954 when he was found dead in his bed. It was suicide. A cyanide-laced half-eaten apple was found by his bedside. There was no tangible reason for his suicide. Perhaps it was just society.

Bibliography

Ash, Russell, *James Tissot*, 1983

Ashley, Robert, *Wilkie Collins*, Arthur Barker, 1952

Baker, Howard, *Charles Dickens London Guide*, 1972

Kensington and Chelsea, B.T. Batsford, 1961

Bedford, Sybille, *Aldous Huxley, A Biography*, Alfred A. Knopf, 1974

Brumwell, Stephen and Speck, W.A., *Eighteenth Century Britain*, 2001

Burns, Michael, *Dreyfus – A Family Affair*, Chatto and Windus, 1992

Cadeac, Dr M., *Le Chevalier d'Eon*, Librairie Maloine, 1966

Cameron, David K., *London's Pleasures*, Sutton Publishing, 2001

Cathcart-Borer, Mary, *Hampstead and Highgate, A Story of Two Villages*, W.H. Allen, 1976

Clapham Society, *The Buildings of Clapham*, Battley Bros, 2000

Clark, Ronald W., *The Huxleys*, William Heinemann Ltd, 1968

Cobban, Alfred, *Ambassadors and Secret Agents*, Jonathan Cape, 1954

Coward, Noël, *Future Indefinite*, Doubleday, 1954

——, *Present Indicative*, Doubleday, 1954

Decker, Michel de, *Le Chevalier d'Eon*, France-Empire, 1998

Dossiers Bleus, Bibliothèque Nationale de France

Duckworth, Colin, *The d'Antraigues Phenomenon*, Avero Ltd, 1986

Ebel, Suzanne and Impey, Doreen, *London's Riverside*, William Luscombe, 1975

Emerson, Giles, *Sin City*, André Deutsch, 2002

Fido, Martin, *Bodysnatchers*, Weidenfeld and Nicolson, 1988

Fletcher, Geoffrey S., *London Nobody Knows*, Hutchison, 1962

Fox, Celina, *Londoners*, Thames and Hudson, 1987

Freeman, Sarah, *Isabella and Sam, the Story of Mrs Beeton*, Victor Gollancz, 1977

Gaunt, William, *Kensington and Chelsea*, B.T. Batsford Ltd, 1975

Hawkey, Arthur, *The Amazing Hiram Maxim*, Spellmount, 2001

Hibbert, Christopher, *Captain Gronow*, Kyle Cathie, 1991

——, *London – The Biography of a City*, Allen Lane, 1969

——, *London Encyclopaedia*, Macmillan, 1997

——, *Wellington – A Personal History*, HarperCollins, 1997

Hodges, Andrew, *Alan Turing – The Enigma*, Burnett Books, 1983

Honeycombe, Gordon, *Murders of the Black Museum*, Hutchinson, 1982

Hudson, Roger (compiler), *London – Portrait of a City*, Folio Society, 1998

Huguenot Society Proceedings

Jerrold, Walter, *Beautiful London*, Blackie and Son, 1935

Kamm, Josephine, *How Different from Us, Miss Beale and Miss Buss*, Bodley Head, 1958

Langford, Paul, *Englishness Identified – Manners and Character 1650–1850*, Oxford University Press, 2000

Laver, James, *Vulgar Society*

Le Vay, Benedict, *Eccentric London*, Bradt Travel Guides, 2002

Macintyre, Ben, *The Napoleon of Crime*, HarperCollins, 1997

Marshall, Francis, *London West*, Studio, 1944

Martin Bailey, *Young Vincent – the Story of Van Gogh's Early Years in England*, 1990

Massingham, Hugh and Massingham, Pauline, *London Anthology*, Spring Books,

Newton Dunn, Bill, *The Man who was John Bull*, Allendale, 1996

Norrie, Mavis and Norrie, Ian (eds), *The Book of Hampstead*, High Hill Books, 1960

Okokon, Susan, *Black Londoners, 1880–1990*, Sutton Publishing, 1998

Pevsner, Nikolaus, *The Buildings of England: London, North, South, North West*

Pickvance, Ronald, *English Influences on Van Gogh*, 1974

Piper, David, *Companion Guide to London*

Pryce-Myers, Sam, *London South of the River*, Paul Elek, 1949

Richardson, Joanna (ed.), *Letters from Lambeth*, Boydell, 1981

Richardson, Ruth, *Death, Dissection and the Destitute*, Phoenix, 1988

Rowse, A.L., *The Tower of London*, Cardinal, 1974

Shaw, E.A., *A Second Companion to Murder*

Shute, Nerina, *More London Villages*, Robert Hale, 1981

Smith, Eric F., *Clapham*, LB Lambeth, 1976

Throne, James, *A Handbook to the Environs of London*, Godfrey Caves, 1983

Treasure Press, *Crimes of Passion*, 1983

Tumin, Stephen, *Great Legal Fiascos*, Arthur Barker, 1975

Van Gogh, *Complete Letters*, Vol. II, 1958

Visram Rozina, *Ayahs, Lascars and Princes*, Pluto, 1986

Warwick, Alan R., *The Phoenix Suburb*, The Norwood Society, 1991

Wentworth, Michael, *James Tissot*, 1978

William, Guy R., *London in the Country*, Western Printing Services, 1975

Williams, Harry, *South London*, Robert Hale, 1949

Wilson, A.N., *The Norton Book of London*, W.W. Norton, 1995

Zwart, Pieter, *Islington, a History and Guide*, Sidgwick and Jackson, 1973

Index